'Jim was a happy man to live with. My best mate.'

Irene Greaves (wife)

'I had the most amazing relationship with him. He was like my rock. Dad had a really, really close relationship with the grandchildren.'

Lynn Greaves (daughter)

'Dad was very kind, very generous and very supporting.'

Danny Greaves (son)

'The true spirit of the man, the great family man, the great footballer, who transcended the rivalries of clubs, never changed.'

Des Benning (cousin)

'We were best men for each other because we had grown up together. We were mates.'

Dave Emerick (best man)

'Jim proved himself to be the greatest goalscorer there has ever been.'

Cliff Jones (teammate)

'As Jimmy reached me he ruffled my hair [after 17-year-old Perryman made a Greaves goal]. That moment will live with me forever.'

Steve Perryman (teammate)

The Authorised
Celebration of a
National Treasure

THE **JIMMY
GREAVES**
WE KNEW

MIKE DONOVAN

pitch

First published by Pitch Publishing, 2022

(pitch)

Pitch Publishing
9 Donnington Park,
85 Birdham Road,
Chichester,
West Sussex,
PO20 7AJ
www.pitchpublishing.co.uk
info@pitchpublishing.co.uk

A CIP catalogue record is available for this book
from the British Library.

ISBN 978 1 80150 374 7

Typesetting and origination by Pitch Publishing
Printed and bound in Great Britain by TJ Books, Padstow

Contents

PART THREE: THE PEOPLE *Treasuring Their Treasure*

Dedications

James Peter Greaves (20 February 1940–19 September 2021), my football hero.

The Greaves family, friends and fans.

Rosemary, Matthew and Benny.

Dave, Kev, Mac, Mark, Nick, Ray and Tony, thanks for six decades of friendship.

Christine Patricia Ellen and Sean James.

Rod Goodway, rest in peace.

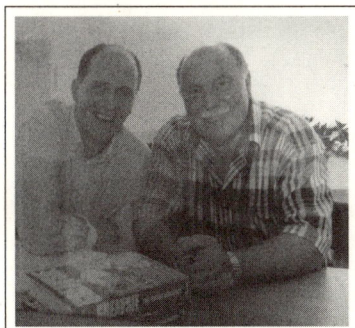

Mike Donovan with Jimmy Greaves

The author with his magnificent seven mates (from the left) Ray Flores, Nick Saloman, Dave Harley, Kevin Rogers, Tony Harris, Mike McNamara and Mark Friedlander, plus a Spurs cockerel!

Also by the author

National Treasure

n. An artefact, institution, or public figure regarded as being emblematic of a nation's cultural heritage or identity.

— Concise Oxford English Dictionary

* * *

Part of the royalties for this book will go to the Jimmy Greaves Foundation, which supports Alcoholics Anonymous, Stroke Association and Dogs Trust.

Foreword

THE IDEA for *The Jimmy Greaves We Knew* came to me at my great friend's funeral when I could see how much people loved him. I wished for a heartfelt tribute to the one and only Jimmy Greaves, someone I believe remains England's greatest goalscorer and someone I loved very much, and for as many people as possible – family, friends, team-mates and in-the-game admirers – to simply recount their memories of the 'Jimmy Greaves they knew'.

In addition – through running Jimmy's Facebook and Twitter pages – I asked for fans to tell us what he meant to them.

I requested Mike Donovan to put the whole thing together because he has written fantastic books on other Tottenham Hotspur legends, including Dave Mackay, Terry Dyson and Alan Gilzean, although Jimmy will always be his number one Lilywhite hero.

I felt I knew Jimmy before I met him. He was my favourite player from when I was eight years old. My hero. And in 1995 I met him. By the following year, we were firm friends and I was his agent. We were such friends that when he received his 1966 World Cup winners' medal in 2009 he took me with him to 10 Downing Street to be presented with it by the prime minister, Gordon Brown. It was a monumental honour to be with him on such a great occasion.

Incidentally, Jimmy was a staunch Tory but the two times he went to Downing Street there were Labour prime ministers in office. Harold Wilson was the other one. He hated their politics. There wasn't a single policy they had which he remotely agreed with but he found both of them very personable.

After Jimmy received his medal, we rushed off, along with the other ten players who had also belatedly received their medals, to Wembley. Those players were Peter Bonetti, Ron Springett, Jimmy Armfield, Gerry Byrne, Ron Flowers, Norman Hunter, Terry Paine, Ian Callaghan, John Connelly and George Eastham. Jimmy and the others were presented on the pitch before England beat Andorra 6-0 in a World Cup qualifier. What a great day that was. As all the others had taken their wives with them, I was dubbed 'Mrs Greaves' for the day by them because they found it funny.

I have been privileged to have lived the life countless football fans would love to have lived, having my greatest heroes become my friends after working with them. None more so than Jimmy Greaves, who I think was Tottenham Hotspur's greatest ever player.

He was a schoolboy and youth phenomenon with Chelsea to start with. Better than anyone then as a young footballer, breaking through as a 17-year-old into the Chelsea team. He is the best youth product the club have ever had – to this day. Irritatingly so for lots of players, I should imagine, as all of Jim's ability came second nature. He showed what a natural he was throughout his career with all his clubs – which also include AC Milan, Spurs and West Ham United – and England.

I *think* he was England's greatest ever goalscorer. I *know* he was one of the nicest people I've ever met in my life and I will always miss him so much.

It was an honour to have worked with him for 25 years. He said to me on many occasions that he had the longest working relationship of his life with me, and I love that as I loved him.

He was a great speaker just as he was a great television presenter and a great, great footballer. And within that he became my great, great friend.

We spent hundreds of hours in theatre dressing rooms up and down the country talking football and nonsense, having serious conversations, but most of all laughing and laughing and telling each other stories about our lives. His was monumental, mine relatively normal, but it was so wonderful for me to get to spend so much time with this great man.

Jimmy told me stuff over the years that has never been published. I used to say to him that when he retired we should write a book entitled *Jimmy Greaves: The Truth*. But he always said if he published it no one would ever speak to him again. I used to say to him, 'It doesn't really matter because you don't speak to anybody from the past anyway.' That's because on 28 February 1978 he made the decision to stop drinking. A large part of that process involved giving up on his past friends and colleagues from a social perspective. And he succeeded in his mission. It was typical of the man that once he made his mind up properly he could achieve almost anything.

There will be other parts of this book with statistics. I know them off by heart but I don't need them here to tell you that Jimmy Greaves was my friend and, like he was to so many people around the country and further afield, my footballing hero. My hero as a person. It was one of the honours of my life not just to have worked for Jimmy for 25 years but also, of course, to have known him as a friend all that time.

I hope you find this book the ultimate tribute to the most beautiful soul I have known in my life.

Terry Baker

Terry Baker
Christchurch,
Dorset,
June 2022

Prologue

I WALKED from Seven Sisters station down Tottenham High Road, or rather – for me – Memory Lane, recalling the nine and a bit years Jimmy Greaves spent at Tottenham Hotspur in my mind's eye, while en route to watch Antonio Conte's Spurs face Jürgen Klopp's Liverpool at the Tottenham Hotspur Stadium, which was constructed on the site of the hosts' former home, White Hart Lane. A mild for December but cloudy day just before Christmas 2021.

I went past the site of The Swan – a pub turned pizza restaurant – where my dad played darts in the company of Bobby Smith, when the Spurs centre-forward was taking downtime from partnering Greaves.

Past the building converted into flats which once housed the Prince of Wales General Hospital where Dave Mackay and Cliff Jones, two more of Greaves's team-mates, were treated for broken legs.

Tottenham Town Hall, from where Greaves, Mackay, Jones, Smith and co finished their open-top bus parade from Edmonton the morning after Our Jim had scored to help them lift the 1962 FA Cup at Wembley. The shops and flats that had replaced the Tottenham Royal dance hall where Spurs players attempted to 'cut a rug' on a night out.

The junction where Lansdowne Road – which had the Donovan family among its residents – met the High Road, the spot Greaves saw my mum shopping and gave her a huge smile as her jaw dropped.

15

The alleyway down the side of the hostelry then known as the Bell and Hare – now No.8 – where I collected Greaves's autograph when he came out after a post-match get-together with team-mates and fans.

All the while my mind kept wandering back to Saturday, 15 April 1963 when I stood on the Park Lane terrace at White Hart Lane with my dad in the midst of the away supporters and saw Greaves score four goals to help the Bill Nicholson-managed hosts defeat Bill Shankly's Liverpool 7-2 a month to the day before the Lilywhites became the first British club to secure a major European trophy with the help of two goals from Greaves (I was with my dad who hoped I wouldn't get too over-excited as we stood in the midst of the Reds' following).

Spurs' motto is Dare To Do. There's another which states Dare To Dream. Could my favourites produce something similar against Klopp's 2019 Premier League and – at Spurs' expense in the final – Champions League winners this December day? Conte's chaps gave it a go and it ended in a thrilling 2-2 draw. But what would have happened had Greaves been there in his prime?

Sadly, of course, we had all lost him three months earlier. He passed on Sunday, 19 September, when my brother Sean and I joined Spurs and Chelsea players, supporters and neutrals in an emotional minute's applause before the derby between two of Greaves's old clubs at the Tottenham Hotspur Stadium, while a friend, Kevin Rogers, wrote a poem (see appendices) about James Peter Greaves MBE.

Greaves was also in my thoughts for another reason as I joined the throng marching towards the stadium for the meeting with Liverpool, appearing increasingly towering the closer we got.

Going back to the time I got to meet him, one-to-one. I will always remember it as clear as day and treasure it for the rest of my life.

It was a case of right place, right time for me. A message had come through to my office desk – that one Jimmy Greaves was 100 yards away inside a warehouse for a retail chain from which copies of his autobiography were being distributed, and he was visiting to sign a few before they went out. Did I want to go and see him? I could not say 'yes' quick enough. Alongside my loved ones and any surviving Beatle, Jimmy was the person I most wanted to spend time with, however fleeting.

As I caught sight of the distribution building, I spotted him in the shade of an open double doorway on what was a sunny autumn afternoon. He was the picture of health.

My mum and dad had bought me his first book, *A Funny Thing Happened On My Way to Spurs*, for my 11th birthday, and even got it signed.

I had got him to sign my Spurs handbook and other publications in my early teens, the West Stand gates beside the Bell and Hare proving ideal entrapment spots. And I had queued up at a succession of bookstores as he promoted his latest publication so he could sign his moniker and the message 'Be Lucky!'

There was the handwritten 'thank you' letter he sent to me on Greaves Travel-headed notepaper in reply to my supportive missive to him during his struggle to control an addiction to alcohol. I treasured that letter more than any other possession before it inexplicably went missing during a home move. A regret ever since.

But meeting him personally? Me all grown up and a professional? That was a most-favourite dream turned reality.

I was on a natural high and mentally floated the short distance to our rendezvous, buoyed by expectation, excitement.

I knew Jimmy was only flesh and blood like all of us; a down-to-earth, approachable, modest character. Yet, to me, he was – if you will excuse a phrase which sounds like hyperbole from someone perhaps deranged – more than on a mere pedestal. He was almost a God-like figure wafting in the heavens who had come down to Earth to unleash a tsunami of endorphins inside me. He would, I believe, have had the same effect on every Spurs supporter either alongside me on the terraces with my dad and friends or sitting in the stands at White Hart Lane throughout the 1960s.

But his humanity cut through my delusions. Never meet your heroes is the cliché. Why not, if they are like Jimmy Greaves? He cracked wise as we shook hands on my arrival; his famed sense of humour to the fore.

His new satnav installed in his car was the subject. The system had recently developed into the latest rage and 'Gentleman Jim', as gentlemanly Tottenham team-mate Pat Jennings dubbed him, was telling me about the vagaries of adjusting to this new-fangled technology in fun-filled style.

He had been driving around the south coast on a book tour, promoting his autobiography *Greavsie*, produced with writer Les Scott. It was 2003.

The erstwhile footballer turned rally driver turned television personality turned theatre entertainer had arrived at this latest destination punched into the satnav with his publishers' publicity manager Tamsin Barrack in the passenger seat. A large building on an industrial estate on the edge of Brighton and Hove; a warehouse for a chain of book stores.

I struggled to maintain my professional veneer as we talked; my mask slipping. And no wonder. But Greaves could not have been more accommodating, patiently answering all my questions about his careers. Praising Jimmy Hill, a resident close by, for helping players smash the maximum wage barrier; reckoning he should be declared 'the patron saint of footballers'. Fondly recalling former team-mates Alan Mullery, Bobby Smith, Joe Kinnear and Mel Hopkins, who had extended their careers by moving from London N17 to the south coast. Spurs' 'great European nights'. His freakish goals numbers – he scored a staggering 465 for clubs and country ('scoring gave me a big satisfaction'). Missing the 1966 World Cup Final. Being sold by Spurs. His problems with alcohol. The issues of the day (Roman Abramovich taking over Chelsea, David Beckham mania).

He even indulged my own reminiscences about him, posed for a picture with me and signed a copy of the book as I battled to keep my 'mask' on.

Hop in the time machine to 2010 when our paths crossed again at his 70th birthday night at the O2 Arena in London where he displayed his skill as an amusing raconteur in front of a packed, appreciative house with a host of former team-mates in support, thriving in his third career.

And when friend/agent Terry Baker approached me to write this book in the wake of his passing to celebrate a national treasure and raise funds for the Jimmy Greaves Foundation, I was honoured and privileged as Jimmy means so much to me. He was my only real football hero and will always remain so.

I was fixated on, in the main, doing the best possible job in his memory and for the sake of his family, and also for his friends, team-mates and fans. It is why I wanted to go to primary sources as much as possible. I'm delighted Jimmy's widow Irene, children Lynn, Mitzi, Danny and Andy, sister Marion, best man Dave Emerick and close friend Brian Doherty felt able to contribute. Also the host of those he played alongside (Cliff Jones to Sir Geoff Hurst, Terry Dyson to Harry Redknapp), broadcasting colleagues, aficionados such as Glenn Hoddle and supporters. They all told me about the Jimmy Greaves they knew, and wanted to celebrate an individual who is a national treasure. I hope you enjoy a book written from the heart.

Mike Donovan
Sussex, June 2022

PART ONE:
THE PRIVATE LIFE

Nearest and Dearest

1

Irene Greaves
Wife

IRENE GREAVES laughed affectionately and softly as she told a tale which touched her heart and funny bone. It concerned a variety of roses in her Essex garden which reminded her of her late husband.

She said, 'He loved gardening while mucking about with the fish pond every day. All the roses I've got here in the garden, he planted. I do the gardening now. All the shrubs have been lovely this year. I can't lift the pots like I used to which is frustrating but I've got to keep his roses going. They are in all sorts of colours and normally come out June time.'

And, with tongue in cheek and an overload of fondness, she added with a smile, 'What he did, which "annoyed" me, was he took all the labels off! So I don't know the names of the roses!'

The widow of Jimmy was warmly recalling the twinkled-eyed man she knew as a boyfriend, husband, father of five children and best friend for more than 60 years; someone who would have laughed along with her.

She said, when asked to sum up her time with him, 'Jim was a happy man to live with. The most incredible sense of humour. My best mate, without doubt. And he was so generous. Not just with his money, but with his time. We used to confide in each other and I miss that.

'He loved his dogs. Walked them every day. Unfortunately, two years ago we lost a beautiful golden retriever. He was only seven. His back legs went. I still miss him. It's amazing. It's nearly three years. I still miss that dog. His name was Lester.

'Jim's favourite sports person was Lester Piggott [who passed on 29 May 2022]. So he called our dog after him. We used to go racing and actually met Lester the jockey himself, might have been Newmarket. Jim was thrilled to meet him.

'Jimmy and I did a lot of moving. Everybody said that. We were professionals in the end! But I've been in our last home – in Danbury – for a while now, nearly eight years. That's good for me.'

Staying put, of course, kept her late husband and the time they spent together inside that particular structure of bricks and mortar in her mind's eye. A source of comfort. One, of course, much needed. Irene said, 'I'm on my own after 63 years now. It's a huge void. It really is.'

How else did Irene try and keep her spirits up? She said, 'Just think of the good times. Some days it's bad. I don't really like living on my own, to be honest. Even as a kid I slept in the same bed as my sister. So I've never really been on my own. Like most people, you get on with it. There's loads of widows around.'

It was love at first sight with her life partner. Irene said, 'It was. We were married 63 years. It's a long time, isn't it? I can't see the kids doing that today. They get married later and then they grow apart. They don't stick to it, do they?

'We met at a youth club. And then we had a mutual friend who was going into the army. So we went into London, can't remember which station it was, and dropped him off. And I said to Jim, "What are you doing today?" He said, "Well, I'm going training." So I said, "Well, I'll come with you." And I sat up on the stands at Chelsea and watched him train. And that was it.

'First impressions were pretty good. Was it his dark good looks? Probably. It did help. We dated. Probably went to restaurants and parties.'

The couple married at Romford Register Office in Essex, on 26 March 1958, when both were 18. Irene recalled home life with her husband.

She remembered Jimmy as a home bird despite his football career trajectory swiftly moving him into the superstar bracket via Chelsea, AC Milan, Tottenham Hotspur, West Ham United and England.

She said, 'Jim was, strangely enough, quite a private man considering he was so famous. And he preferred to be home than anywhere else, to be honest. No, he wasn't domesticated.'

The couple suffered tragedy when their second child, Jimmy Junior, born in June 1960, died before his first birthday (see Mitzi Robinson and Dave Emerick chapters). Irene said, 'That was a very sad time. But in those days you got on with it. You didn't get counselling. It's a different life completely now; social media and what have you. I'm technophobic by the way. I don't do anything like that.

'I would say the World Cup in 1962 was hard at home because Jim was away for a long time and I had a baby, Mitzi, as well as our first child and daughter Lynn. But on the whole you got used to that sort of thing as he was going away every other week with his club.'

They were a sociable couple. Irene said, 'We used to meet up with team-mates and the partners. There were always parties. Bobby Moore, who Jim played with for England and West Ham, was a mate. An absolutely lovely man. I can still see him sitting there in our living room.

'I don't think the camaraderie now is the same in the dressing rooms as it once was. There are so many players from different nations. You can't have that sense of humour that they used to be able to share during the time Jimmy was playing.

'Also, we used to leave Tottenham after a game and go up to the Bell and Hare pub [on the High Road]. The fans used to come in. You can't catch the players now, can't get near them.'

The couple had two more children, Danny, born in January 1963, and Andy, born in February 1966. Irene said, 'I remember when Danny was born. It was in the middle of a terrible, cold winter. They didn't play football for weeks. What did Jimmy do with himself? Not a lot. Planning our next house move? Could have been!

'Andy was born in the year England won the World Cup, with Jimmy missing the final, although nowadays they have subs and he might have got 20 minutes!

'Jim was a very good dad. He played with the kids. Used to take them to places, including the football. He was very, very generous. The children loved him. That shows what he was like.'

Irene remembered when she first started watching Jimmy play. She said, 'When I first went to go and see Jim play at Chelsea I'd go into the stands with the fans. I was just a young girl. I wasn't really a football fan, although I amaze myself by watching it now. I quite like sport, and played netball.

'Jimmy's career just grew and grew. We went off to Italy [when Greaves joined AC Milan in 1961]. He just really couldn't get on there with [coach Nereo] Rocco. We lived in Milan. We just had the two girls, Lynn and Mitzi, of course. Then we came back and went to Tottenham. Probably the best times because it was a great club. It was super. We had a lovely time. A good time in our lives.

'All the wives were lovely. We just got on, unlike today when they are going round suing each other [in reference to the 'Wagatha Christie' court case between Coleen Rooney, married to former England and Manchester United striker Wayne, and Rebekah Vardy, wife of England and Leicester City striker Jamie, over social media posts].

'We had what they called a tea room we went into at White Hart Lane. I used to enjoy going with my brother Tom regularly to the matches. He was in business with Jimmy. He's passed away now, bless 'im. I've lost all my siblings this year.'

Irene revealed how bemused her husband was at his exit from Spurs to West Ham United in March 1970. It seemed one bad performance – an FA Cup defeat against Crystal Palace – led to manager Bill Nicholson deciding to let him leave White Hart Lane after close to a decade of service as a makeweight in the deal which brought World Cup-winner Martin Peters from London E13 to N17. And it shook Spurs' players and fans, who didn't understand the decision. Irene said, 'Neither did Jim.'

Irene accepted she had had to 'share' her husband with the public due to the attention he received with being rated the game's greatest ever goalscorer. She said, 'You had to share him, in a way. You got used to it in general, to be honest. Sometimes it was irritating, but on the whole you just got used to it.

'Jim was always good with people. He was quite private, as I said, but connected with the public. The general public liked him. He just had this way with him. I think he was a people's person really. Approachable. He'd let people come up and interrupt him but he never, ever got cross. He was always civil and what have you.

'He was a national treasure. Absolutely. The adulation when he died was amazing. It was just incredible. It was an outpouring. And it wasn't just football fans but whole households.

'The carers that used to come in. To them he was just "Jim". After he died, they suddenly realised just how famous he was. They knew he was famous but they didn't know how famous.'

That relationship with the public was reflected when Jimmy went into television after his full-time professional football career came to a close with West Ham, followed by spells at non-league Brentwood Town (see Dave Emerick chapter), Chelmsford City, Barnet (see Barry Fry chapter) and Woodford Town.

Irene giggled when reminded how Jimmy got into TV following a 'prompt' from her after he had turned down an initial offer; an action which might get her described these days as an 'influencer'. And she remained proud of what her husband achieved on the small screen.

Irene said, 'How good was Jim there?! So good. Especially when he did *Saint and Greavsie*. If I had £1 for everyone who said to me how good he was! Even the players who were going out to play on the day it went out would watch it. It was so funny. It might be considered non-PC in places now. They wouldn't cope with those bits! He was off-the-cuff, just like he was in life. He went straight into it. He'd just have a quip. Just so funny. It was just him.'

There were bumps in the road over the years that Irene shared with the love of her life. She said, 'It was interesting being with Jim! Well, it's ups and downs in life, isn't it? That happens to all people. When people say, "We've never had an argument," I don't believe it. It's impossible to live with someone all that time and not fall out. It's life. In the end you can always apologise, and say, "I don't know what I'm apologising for, but I'm apologising."'

The biggest bump, perhaps, was when Greaves revealed he was an alcoholic in the wake of retiring from the professional game at the age of 31 in 1971. It led to a brief separation and divorce proceedings for the couple before reconciliation.

And Irene was full of praise for her husband getting his condition under control and abstaining for the rest of his life. Irene said, 'As a character, he was a nice bloke. As I've told you he was funny and generous, but Jim also had strength of character which he especially showed when he gave up the booze. It was a tough time. Not an easy thing. It was like talking to someone who was under anaesthetic all the time. It's just they are not listening.

'He did give it up a couple of times previously, but on one particular night he said "no more" and that was it! Amazing. It's like people giving up smoking. It was difficult, because it is such a social thing.'

Did Jimmy become sober because of his love for Irene and the family? She said, 'No. I don't think that happens with alcoholics. Think they have to make up their minds themselves. Jim woke up that one day and said, "I'm not going to drink." And that was in 1978. And he never did. Even though wherever he went after that, people were drinking. He did well. Really well.'

The couple were able to enjoy more good times together once more. Jimmy enjoyed his television career and developed as an after-dinner speaker and theatre entertainer in public. The couple also revelled in a settled home life, but it all changed when he suffered a major stroke on Sunday, 3 May 2015.

Irene said, 'It was absolutely awful. Life completely changed overnight. Bless him, it was the start of six years he didn't want to be here. It was hard work. Carers were coming in four times a day. A terrible situation, just awful. Absolutely awful. It would have been better when he had his stroke that he'd have gone then because the six years that he lived were just not nice. It was hard. The kids were supportive. Lynn helped quite a lot at home. And Danny helped on the football side of it. And I have to say Tottenham were very good.'

She recalled how Jimmy was cheered by former team-mates. Irene said, 'Jonesy [former Spurs winger Cliff Jones] used to ring up Jim a lot. Jim would try and answer him and what have you. I have to say, he was very good, Jonesy.

'Alan Gilzean and Pat Jennings came to see Jim. It was lovely. Lovely men. That was the only times he used to cry when the players went. Alan has gone now. We're all getting to that age, that's the trouble.

'Quite a few players came to the funeral, including Jonesy and Pat. Also, I saw Jonesy's wife Joanie there. Hadn't seen her for years. It was lovely to see her. I like her.'

Irene revealed she kept her husband's ashes in her bedroom. She said, 'I always say "goodnight" to him every night.' Irene planned to scatter Jimmy's ashes in the near future. She said, 'We were lucky because we lived almost in the middle of National Trust woods. No one is going to build on them. As you turn left and go out of the house you go into loads of woods to where our dogs' ashes are. That is where Jim's going. I'm going to take him over there and spread his ashes.'

2

Lynn Greaves

Daughter

IT WAS there. Pictured in the imagination of Lynn Greaves, the eldest child of our subject Jimmy and his wife Irene. A family wedding, which provided a 'really special time' for her dad. Lynn's daughter Victoria was walking up the aisle with her grandfather at the 'most fantastic' chateaux just outside Orange in the south of France on a flaming June day in 2010.

Many years earlier Jimmy had given Lynn away at her own wedding. This day, the sporting and television icon was doing the same for one of his ten grandchildren.

Groom Oliver Berquez, the son of a French father, was expectant at the altar.

Lynn said, 'It was lovely. My dad was very much a father figure to Victoria and she always looked up to him, loved and adored him. So it was wonderful he could give her away. We have these amazing photos of that most fantastic chateaux. Unforgettable memories.

'That was a special time in all of our lives. I remember Dad saying that was a really special time for him.

'Victoria would come over and spend a lot of time with her grandparents. She absolutely loved and adored her grandparents in turn. She was very, very close to them.

'She was devastated when her granddad died. She tried to get back and unfortunately didn't make it, because Dad went so quickly.

'The wedding is all on video but none of us can watch it yet because we don't think we can get through it. I can't watch (the BT Sport film) *Greavsie* either. Every time I try to, I burst into tears and have to turn it off.

'I've got every single newspaper from when he died all wrapped up beautifully under my bed and I haven't read one of them. One time I'll be able to do it but just not yet.

'Dad had a really, really close relationship with the grandchildren. They are, in age order, Gemma, Victoria, who has lived in France for a couple of years, James, Louise, Thomas, Hannah, Sam, Shane, Harry and Madeleine. He really loved and adored them. Probably like all grandparents, he had a bit more time.

'My dad grew a moustache and it really suited him. I remember he shaved it off once and one of the grandchildren burst into tears so he put it back on.

'He also had six great-grandchildren: Cecilia, Rafa, Jack, Rebecca, Annabella and Stanley. They were all born before he died but, unfortunately, three were born after Dad had a major stroke in May 2015. My grandchildren are Cecilia and Rafa. He's a brilliant little footballer, my Rafa. He is already banging in goals at the age of six with his left foot!'

Lynn treasured the relationship she had with her dad. She said, 'I had the most amazing relationship with him. He was like my rock, really. Everybody goes through trials and tribulations. I've been divorced twice. My dad was always very supportive. Even though he probably knew we were making wrong choices, he wasn't an overbearing father saying, "You are not doing this, that and the other." Perhaps he'd try and give us a bit of guidance. Whether we took it or not is another thing. You make your own mistakes, yes, but that's kids for you!

'He always made me laugh. Over the last six years of his life, I'd been his main helper with my mum and though things were very difficult as he was severely disabled with the stroke, we could still communicate with him. And he still had the capacity to make me laugh.

'He was the most loveliest of dads. People used to say, "What's it like to have Jimmy Greaves as a dad?" or, "What's it like to be Jimmy Greaves's daughter?" It's always very difficult when people ask you those things when you've got a famous dad, but for me, he was just my dad. He was amazing. A kind, really loving father. Always, as I said, making us laugh.

'Despite having to travel a lot with playing, he was very much a home bird, loved spending time with his wife and his children. Growing up, he was a really wonderful dad, staying very supportive of everything I wanted to do. Very interested in everything we all did in our lives.'

Lynn's early memories of her dad will always remain strong. She said, 'It was slightly more difficult because we were restricted. We couldn't perhaps do normal things like going to the cinema a lot and stuff like that because he was famous and would just draw too much attention.

'But he did used to take us to places. I did a lot of athletics and he came and watched me. I had ponies. Did the pony club and he used to come and watch me there. He'd play with us in the garden. Just like a regular dad, really. Nothing really out of the ordinary. When we were home he was "Dad". He wasn't "Jimmy Greaves". We also went on lovely holidays to Portugal. He spent lots of time with us in the pool. It was just great. He was, as I've said, always making us laugh. He was just a lovely fun dad.

'Special occasions? When he was playing it was restricting for us because he'd normally have a game. So we'd work round that. Christmases and birthdays, we'd always get lovely presents. At Christmas, Dad and my granddad would wait for us to go to bed and creep up and put all the presents at the bottom of our beds, which I went along with until one day I woke up and said, "I'm sure I saw you put the presents at the bottom of the bed." He'd go, "No, no, it wasn't me, it was Father Christmas." All the usual stuff. We had lots of fun. Lots of lovely laughter.

'I remember he came home just prior to Christmas one time and he had a big gash over his eye, and a black eye. He came through the door and I burst into tears and I said, "Oh, Dad, what's happened? Have you been beaten up or something?" He said, "No, I just had an unfortunate challenge with Pat Jennings at training." To me it was like a terrible head injury. But then we went, "Oh, it's OK." They'd just clashed heads.

'They were very sociable, my parents. They had real big circles of friends. There were always lots of parties.

'I remember Bobby Moore coming to our house. My dad and Bobby were such great pals. Bobby was such a nice man. Dad was terribly upset when he died, very young. I remember that day. Think it was near my dad's birthday, February time. We were going up to London. I said, "Dad, do you still want to go?" He was very, very upset.

'I used to go to Tottenham when Dad was playing there and at some stage, and – I don't know how they allowed us to do this – come up through the [players'] tunnel and go along to seats right at the front. Everybody got to know us. They knew that we were Jimmy's children so made a real fuss of us. That was absolutely lovely.

'I remember one time I took my friend. My dad – I can't remember who Spurs were playing – was trying to defend. Anyway, the ball got knocked off the pitch and nearly hit my friend on the head. I shouted, "Dad, Dad, the ball nearly hit Sally on the head!" He looked at me and gave me this little smile and put his finger to his lips and went, "Shh! Don't shout at me when I'm in the middle of a game." Little things like that were quite funny. That was great fun going to watch him at Tottenham.

'My uncle Tom would normally drive my dad and us to and from games. There would be fans outside the ground. Sometimes there would be a woman who would get to the car and tell him how much she loved him, and all the rest of it. And I'd say to my dad, "What's that lady doing?" There was all this adulation. Banging on the car. They were all excited to see their hero. That was always nice. I think that was because my football memories are largely always from Dad's time at Tottenham. There was never negativity there.

'We didn't really go to away games but I'm sure Dad got abuse when he did, like everybody. I did ask him once, "Did you hear it [the verbal abuse]?" He said, "Sometimes. I used to block it out. The best way is to get back and score some goals."

'He was in an amazing team in amazing times. Dave Mackay was one of Dad's real heroes. Dad loved and adored Dave Mackay. I think Dave took Dad under his wing at Spurs, didn't he? He absolutely loved Dave. Did Dad say he was Spurs' best player? Yes. Danny Blanchflower was another player my dad admired. Pat Jennings, another team-mate and absolutely lovely man, has told the most amazing, positive stories about dad. The team were almost like brothers. A wonderful group of friends.

'I can't remember Chelsea. I was born in 1958 when Dad was at the club and Mum and Dad had a flat in Wimbledon.

'I can't really remember Italy when Dad played for AC Milan either, but I definitely recall his time at Tottenham, of course, and West Ham United.

'I was terribly, terribly upset when Dad didn't make the final of the World Cup for England. I was very distressed over that. I remember that being quite a difficult time. Dad hid it quite well, but I think it hurt him a lot more than he ever let on, really. It was not until the latter days when I think he came to terms with it. But he did get his medal in the end. So that was nice.'

Lynn remembered mates describing her dad as a 'style icon'. She said, 'I remember this chap, who was my age, saying to me once, "Growing up I ran to the shop to get a pair of winkle picker shoes because Jimmy Greaves wore them. All my mates told me,

"Your dad was like a style icon." I said, "Really?!" He said, "Yeah, everything he did we just copied." Do you know Dad was actually voted pipe smoker of the year? He beat Val Doonican or somebody!'

Lynn told of her parents' propensity for moving. She said, 'Oh, God! They moved around all the time. I don't really know what to say on that. I've no words. Let's just say it was ridiculous behaviour! In the end, I said, "Right, if you move one more time, I'm not helping." Dad gave me a very wry look! They moved for fun. It was, as I said, ridiculous. What can you say? Parents, eh?!'

Lynn is proud of the way her dad turned the negative of a drink problem he developed into a positive.

She said, 'It's true. He probably helped thousands of people. I remember talking to a chap that had a severe drink problem and he actually said to himself, "Blimey, if Jimmy Greaves can stop drinking, so can I." And he did.

'It did help people. People didn't think people like my dad had everyday problems, but they did. They [professional footballers] are just human, like everybody else. They just happen to have an amazing talent.

'Me being the oldest of the children, I've probably got the most memories of that really difficult time. Dad was quite a severe alcoholic, and was probably just drinking all the time. I think Mum came to the end of her tether, but they really didn't split up for very long.

'I spent a lot of time trying to help him through that. I remember having to take Dad into Warley Hospital [a psychiatric institution in Brentwood, Essex, near the family home]. I was, as an 18- or 19-year-old, very distraught, as you can imagine. He was very distressed but we had to get him in there to try and dry him out.

'He came to his senses one day when he walked out of the hospital and in to a pub. I think he had a pint of Guinness and a brandy, walked out of the pub and never had another drink. That pub now doesn't exist. I think it is some kind of restaurant. But every time I drive past it, it makes me smile.

'The years after that were a bit up and down because he got involved in AA [Alcoholics Anonymous] for a while and had to change his lifestyle so much. Not going into pubs. Not socialising much. Those sort of things provided temptation.

'In latter life, he was brilliant. We'd all drink. My mum drinks. He'd pour out a drink for us. But there was never any question he would ever drink again.

'When Dad had been dry for a while, he was great. Fantastic. How he did it I don't know. It was the most amazing achievement. Such amazing strength of character. He was one hell of an amazing man.'

Our subject played it all down when your author spoke to him as he promoted his autobiography, *Greavsie*, in 2003.

I suggested strength of character and willpower must have helped him, but he said, 'Am I strong? No, I'm a weak person.'

Lynn said, 'That was Dad. So humble for all his fame. I've seen people drop at Dad's feet showing absolute adulation of him, but Dad was never one of those who would give it the big 'un or say, "I'm the man!" He was, as I said, just so humble. He just had that way about him. He never took anything for granted. He didn't act like the superstar. He was just what he was.

'At the time, when people used to talk about watching the *Saint and Greavsie* programme on the television, I'd say, that is my dad. What you see there is my dad. It's not an act. Not pre-rehearsed. A lot of it is ad-libbed. He's really bright. Extraordinarily bright – something people don't know about him. He was also unbelievably quick-witted and funny. He just winged it. And that really worked with Ian St John, didn't it? It was just brilliant.'

Lynn revealed how her dad was more concerned about the well-being of those close to him after he had his major stroke.

She said, 'The last six years were not great because in a lot of respects we lost a lot of my father at that time because of the severity of the stroke, but, of course, he was still with us. Still a presence. He used to give me a kiss on the hand. He would still, even with the way he was, always be asking me how I was. Always more worried about everybody else than himself. His first thought was my mum's and our welfare right to the day he died.'

Lynn and most of the rest of the family were present when Greaves bade farewell to Tottenham's White Hart Lane ground in April 2017.

She said, 'It was lovely for him. We went down to the Hall of Fame and on to the pitch. There were lots of lovely memories for him, and Tottenham rolled the red carpet out. They treated us really nicely. Of course they would.'

Jimmy also met his latest successor as Spurs' goalscorer-in-chief, Harry Kane, in October 2017. Lynn said, 'He's a very nice man, Harry Kane, isn't he? Always speaks very nicely about dad.'

Lynn recalled her last hours with Jimmy. She said, 'When dad died, it happened, as I've said, very quickly. I had spent the most wonderful afternoon with him. Just him and I. I have that memory in my head. He was suddenly quite lucid. I fed him. I said, "Would you like some ice cream, Daddy?" He said, "Ooh, lovely." I thought, "Amazing", because he'd not really eaten. And I fed him five little spoonfuls of ice cream, which he really enjoyed. That's the last thing he had on this earth.

'I thought, well, I'll see him again after that – and he died that night in the early hours. I was so taken aback. It was a bit of a shock. Happened so quickly. But he died peacefully and at home, which is what he wanted. We always said he'd die at home with the family.'

Lynn, based close to her mum, has struggled since her dad passed. She said, her voice cracking with emotion, 'I've not been great since my dad died. Even to this day. Sorry, I get upset. I cannot believe I'm not going to see my dad again. I genuinely cannot believe it. I was so close to my father. My dad was someone I would always go to. I miss that so much now.

'I am devastated. Spent an awful amount of time helping to care for him in his last six years. It's left a real void in my life. Really, really trying to come to terms with it. Sometimes it is really good to talk about things, isn't it? But it's been hard. Really, really hard.

'Everyone in the family is finding it hard. My mum's never lived on her own. They were together 63 years, my parents. She misses my dad terribly. But it's life. You grow up and you think, "One day my parents are going to die." But actually you never think it is going to happen. Then one day it does, doesn't it? You think you'll move forward, but you don't.

'In my dining room, I've got a photograph of Dad with Denis Law and George Best. Under that I've got another one with him running out with [the banner behind him stating] "Up The Spurs". With Bobby Moore. With Seve Ballesteros. John McEnroe. I've got this wonderful gallery of amazing photographs that remind me of him all the time in a good way.

'There is his image on a Royal Mail stamp [issued as part of a 2013 Football Heroes series to commemorate the 150th anniversary of the establishment of the Rules of Association Football]. Dave Mackay and Bobby Moore are also featured in the series. And I've been looking at them all framed and hanging on my wall. It's nice I've got lots of memorabilia. Lots of stuff, really, but it doesn't bring him back, does it?'

Lynn attended a tribute lunch put on by Chelsea, her dad's first club. She said, 'On my table there was [former manager] Tommy Docherty's widow and daughter, and [former Blues and England goalkeeper] Peter Bonetti's widow and son also attended. They'd obviously lost their fathers and husbands. And Chelsea – through [former player, now broadcaster and author] Pat Nevin – did a lovely tribute. So that was nice.

'Went back to Chelsea for the Peter Bonetti memorial, which was lovely again. Really nicely done. He actually had his ashes put into the ground. Although Dad didn't play for Chelsea for that long, they really still do have him in their hearts.

'They contacted me to tell me they'd done a survey and got this big mural done. Fans had voted for the 20 best players they wanted in it and they'd actually voted for Dad to be included. Bearing in mind he was only there for a couple of seasons, that was amazing.

'Chelsea are a wonderful club. Have always kept in contact. Sent hampers at Christmas when he was poorly. I've got nothing but praise for Chelsea. All this helps with the healing process; so does remembering the good times, of which there are many more than there are bad. I don't talk about the alcohol thing very often to anybody. I don't want to focus on it. That was just a blip in my dad's life. There are so many good things to talk about with my father. I could talk all day about them and him.

'I want it to come across how wonderful my dad was as a father. How proud I was of him. How loved he was.'

3

Mitzi Robinson
Daughter

MITZI ROBINSON (nee Greaves) was wistful, a hint of a smile betraying an inner warmth supplied by the memories of her dad as she revealed the pair of them were 'Trekkies'.

They shared a taste for the science-fiction film and television franchise *Star Trek*. To them, to paraphrase a famous line from it, resistance was futile to the attraction of Captain Kirk and co.

The youngest daughter of Jimmy said, 'I was very much the daughter that would chat to Dad about *Star Trek*. He was very much a Trekkie. His "Trekkiness" came out when he mentioned in his autobiography how he and Mum called their ten grandchildren "Klingons" [a fictional species featured in the franchise].

'We used to watch it together on television all the time. I remember sitting there once and him saying, "I've never seen this one." I'd say, "I don't think I have either." He liked his sci-fi.

'We'd chat about things in general. He was there if I needed to bend his ear about something. He would always listen. And if he could help me in any way he would. We also had general chit-chats. I miss those conversations.

'Sometimes I'd go with him if he was taking the dogs for a walk, which he did every day. Morning and afternoon. I just used to enjoy his company.

'After he had his stroke I used to sit with him so Mum could go out. We'd watch the cricket, or the rugby. Very often I'd joke with him when we sometimes sat there and watched [the detective series] *Morse* – which he really loved – and *Miss Marple*. Things like that. And I used to say, "I think we'll be appearing in it in a minute. Here we come!" We'd watched them so many times! We'd just laugh. I was very much that sort of daughter.

'I used to giggle with him at other times. After his stroke, his memory wasn't great at times. And if he didn't know people he used to call them all Harry, for some reason!

'I can remember him sitting in the garden and Mum saying, "Just had a visitor. I don't know who she was." And I said, "What was her name? She's probably called Harry." And he just pointed at me and laughed. Like he knew I was taking the p***. He still had a twinkle in his eye. You could still have a giggle with him even then.

'I used to sit with him on a Wednesday afternoon and read a newspaper. And we'd kind of have a kind of discussion about stuff in it. You had to wait for him to gather what he wanted to say to you and then say it. Having worked in that kind of environment [the care industry], you know to give people time. Often people don't. I still enjoyed his company even though it wasn't the same as before he had his stroke.

'Right to the end he knew who we were and what we were saying. Oh, God, yeah! I used to walk in and go, "Hello you!" He knew who all of us were. It was difficult for him to hold long conversations. But he was still Dad. A different version, but still Dad.

'As a father he was kind, loving, tactile, funny. He always used to make us laugh. Give us cuddles. I miss everything about him, including those cuddles. I know my daughters miss those cuddles too, very, very much.'

Mitzi insisted the relationship between them had little to do with Jimmy's public life. She said, 'I didn't get that much involved in his fame. Sometimes I say to myself, "I don't think I knew that part of him much at all." We didn't have that sort of relationship. To me he was just my dad and that was it really.'

Mitzi was born on Friday, 4 August 1961. Mitzi Gaynor was in the hugely popular romantic musical film *South Pacific*, enjoying a continuous four-and-a-half-year run at the Dominion Theatre in London's West End. And Jimmy's second daughter felt the Christian name of the actress and singer might have influenced her dad's decision to pick the name.

She said, 'I was born about 7.30 at night and going to be called Sharon. But the next day, Dad came in and said, "I'm going to call her Mitzi." I don't know why but Mitzi Gaynor was very much a star at the time as she was in *South Pacific*. Maybe he heard it and thought, "I prefer it to Sharon."'

The arrival of Mitzi – who Jimmy described as 'a beautiful girl' – came at a time of upheaval for the family. Jimmy had joined AC Milan in Italy from Chelsea and was due to report to his new club for the 1960/61 season on 17 July. But he delayed flying out as Mitzi was delaying her own big entrance, having been due on 15 July. Jimmy said in *Greavsie*, 'Babies arrive when it suits them and this one definitely had a mind of its own. The 15 July came and went.'

In his autobiography, Jimmy revealed he informed *I Rossoneri*, '[I] would be staying with Irene until she gave birth and would return two days thereafter.'

Mitzi felt Jimmy was adamant about staying by Irene's side because her parents had suffered a tragedy the year before which 'devastated' the couple.

Irene had given birth to Jimmy Junior on Wednesday, 8 June 1960, but the infant, Greaves disclosed in his autobiography, died after contracting 'pneumonia when four months old'.

Mitzi said, 'I assume Dad didn't want to leave my mum because my brother Jimmy Junior had passed. I can imagine it was a difficult time for my parents. That they were very young and probably couldn't understand what had gone wrong. I've always been grateful for the fact that I was a girl because I think that would have been more difficult in some ways for them had I been a boy with what happened with Jimmy Junior.'

The family moved back after a few months in Milan when Jimmy joined Tottenham Hotspur. And Mitzi, with her parents and sister Lynn, with a Hornchurch home having been sold prior to heading to Italy, lived in a 'cramped' two-bedroom Dagenham council house with Irene's parents and sister for four months before a new home was found.

Mitzi had begun a cherished upbringing. She said, 'Dad used to be away a lot when we were kids. I do remember him not being around for long periods at a time, which, when you are young, you don't particularly know why. But when he was about, he used to try and spend as much time with us as he could.

'We used to go to the Algarve in Portugal on holiday. It was not very popular then. So you could go and have a holiday and not have to worry about the fame side of things too much.

'I remember walking along the road with him once and people would stop and talk to him. It used to take us ages to get anywhere. He was very good. He used to stop and chat to people. When I was at school and West Ham, the biggest team in our area, got to the [FA] Cup [Final] people would say to me, "Get your dad to get us tickets," something he could never do. We got a lot of that.

'I was one of those kids who was always out doing something. I wasn't always at home. I used to trampoline at school and I know Dad came to watch me. I often went away with the trampolining for weekends. I bounced for Great Britain as a kid. It used to make Mum and Dad laugh that I could do tricks on the trampoline because I was, apparently, a clumsy child, although I don't remember that! I did it up until I was about 15 soon to be 16 and left school. Being an August baby, I was a late child in school years. I gave it up then.

'It all started because our PE teacher at school was a British trampolining coach and part of a club. I suppose I must have shown a bit of ability and the coach encouraged me to join the club so I did, otherwise I would have never gone on to do it. If he'd have been a hockey coach it would have passed me by. Luck, I suppose.'

Mitzi recalled her dad's reaction when she began to bring boyfriends home. She said, 'He was all right. Dad used to joke with them. I always remember the first boy I brought home he'd say, "You going to marry my daughter?!" That was embarrassing. He was like most parents.

'I've been married and divorced. I guess it is like anything else, you can't tell your kids, can you? I've got my own and you just let them get on with it when they get to a certain age and pick up the pieces if necessary. Got to let your kids make their own mistakes. It's not easy. No one ever tells you that bit, do they? You are parents forever! It never stops.

'I've got five. Two girls and three boys. The eldest is Gemma. Then there's James, Louise, Thomas and Shane. And four grandchildren: Jack, Rebecca, Annabella and Stanley, Mum and Dad's great-grandchildren.

'Dad always used to like to get home whenever he could. He was happiest at home; more comfortable at home.

'He used to like to cook. Pancake Day, he used to make us pancakes. And that carried on once he had grandchildren.

'He used to kick a ball around in the garden with my brothers – and if I wanted to I could go out there and do the same. He'd include me. Was I a tomboy? I probably was back then. I didn't want to be the quiet one in the corner. You never know what opportunities we might have had had women's football been the big thing it is now back then. I remember Dad took us to the training ground a lot when he played for Spurs when we were young.'

Mitzi kept in regular touch with her parents when she had her own family. She said, 'We used to go and visit them and obviously take the kids to see them. We'd spend Christmas with them or something, and try and see them once a week. We took the kids round when they were little. Then when they got older they'd go themselves. All of them. Dad would always take an interest in everything that we all did.'

Mitzi admired her dad for his ability to 'hold an audience'. She said, 'I never saw any of the after-dinners he did. But I have been to see someone that's done two and a half hours just chatting on the stage, though, and admired his ability to be able to do that. And I admired Dad because he could do that too. Anyone who can hold an audience by just chatting must have a real skill.'

Mitzi felt Jimmy's television career gave us a portal into what he was really like. She said, 'I went with him to TV-am when he was on it a few times [as a television critic; see the Nick Owen chapter]. That was always interesting. It was when they used to record a Christmas morning programme.

'On *Saint and Greavsie*, he was very much himself. He was always himself. I don't think he could be anything other than himself. What you saw is what you got at home. I don't think there was ever a persona with him, if that's the right word. Probably why people liked him so much, I should imagine. People could identify with him.

'I was married by the time I was 19. So I didn't live at home with them for some time but when I was round journalists from newspapers and magazines would ring him up and he'd just chat away. I don't think he knew anything about the subject the guys were going to ask him about. He did stuff for *Shoot!* I remember Mum made me laugh when she told me a story about *Shoot!* Mum and Dad had gone on holiday to Kenya once and Mum said, "We were in this village in the middle of nowhere and suddenly this guy is shouting at us." His family used to send him *Shoot!* over all the time from here so he recognised Dad. We couldn't go anywhere and avoid that. Not even in a tiny little village in Kenya.'

Mitzi appreciated how much Jimmy 'adored' Irene. She said, 'They moved a lot, although that was more Mum than Dad. But

Dad would go if Mum wanted to live in a tent in the middle of the Sahara Desert. He absolutely adored my mother.

'When my dad passed away they had been together over 60 years. A long time to be with someone and having a life. They were lucky in many ways.

'Mum's OK. It's tough as she'd been with someone for 63 years. I saw her last week and she said, "I've never been on my own."'

The family went through a testing time, though, when Jimmy fought to control his addiction to alcohol in the 1970s. And Mitzi revealed her respect for her dad being able to win the battle.

She said, 'That's one of the things where I'm immensely proud of him for. He gave up drinking and lived a very long time without drinking. He was a real example to people that you can turn your life around, and you can go on and be successful in something else, which he was when he did *Saint and Greavsie*.

'It must have taken quite a bit of willpower in the beginning. I imagine after a while, like anything, it becomes part and parcel of life. You go out and you don't drink and that's it. I've always admired him greatly for all that because that couldn't have been easy at the time. And to do it and turn your life around like that was a real achievement.

'I was about 15 when he stopped drinking. I'd have been aware of it when I was 12ish. It may have gone on a bit before that, but, as you get older, you become a bit more aware of what's going on. Yet I think generally we were protected from it quite a lot by Mum when she could protect us from it.

'I wasn't around a great deal, anyway. I was just either away with my sport or out with my friends. Out of the way of it. Not out of choice; it was just how I lived. How I was. The boys [Danny and Andy] were too young to know too much. I should imagine my sister took the brunt of it being older than us. Dad got his act together and for the majority of my life with him he was sober.'

Mitzi, a former carer, therapy assistant and activity co-ordinator, had kept busy since her dad died; working in the Post Office close to her Essex home three days a week, looking after her grandchildren and visiting Irene, all the while processing the death of her dad.

She said, 'I still feel it. If you ask my partner Ken he would say I haven't dealt with it. You kind of lost the dad you knew when he had his stroke. You had a new version of him, but had kind of mourned him already.

'I miss him dearly. Every day. All the time. Like, as I said, with the chats we used to have, even though in the end – once he'd had his stroke – they were kind of one-sided anyway. My youngest daughter Louise always says, "I miss Granddad's hugs." The kids do feel it. But it is part and parcel of life, sadly. You lose your parents. If you don't lose your parents then you've gone yourself. They've lost you. That's probably worse in some ways, I would have thought.

'It wasn't the end to his life that any of us would have wanted for him, but you deal with life as it deals with you. You don't get a choice. That's the way it was.

'In some ways, his passing was a relief for him because he is at peace and hopefully happy if you believe in all that stuff. He's no longer stuck in this body he didn't like. He had been in a life he wasn't happy with. That's a kind of a comfort.

'None of us are immortal, but I guess in some respects Dad will always live on. Not just with us but with people like you [your author]. He seemed to be universally loved. That is another comfort.

'We were lucky to have had Dad for as long as we did. Lots of people don't have their parents as long.'

How would Mitzi like Jimmy to be remembered? 'I'd like it known most that he was just a loving man. Popular. And he was what you saw. Kind of sad in some ways, he never got the recognition he deserved football-wise and for the length of his sobriety. My eldest Gemma is 41 and he was sober her entire life. He was sober 43 years and that's a long time.

'I also want it emphasised that he was a good man. A good bloke. There's not loads of them around, in many ways, I suppose.'

As for the future, Jimmy would have wanted Mitzi and the rest of his nearest and dearest to 'live long and prosper', to use the *Star Trek* quote he borrowed for his autobiography.

Mitzi swapped sci-fi for terra firma when she considered her outlook on life without him and said, 'You get on with it.'

Then she gave an example of how by adding with a smile, 'I've got my house cleaning to do now!'

4

Danny Greaves

Son

THE LOVE, respect and pride was palpable in every word when Danny Greaves spoke about the father he knew. There was no doubt every utterance from the son of Jimmy was from the heart.

He had been busy continuing to help build the legacy of his late father, pushing through the development of the Jimmy Greaves Academy, which states, 'It was Jimmy's dream to launch an academy where he could teach young footballers to get the most out of the beautiful Game without breaking the bank or bankrupting their parents.'

Danny was also running the Jimmy Greaves Foundation, supporting 'causes chosen by Dad': Alcoholics Anonymous, Stroke Association and Dogs Trust. A Midlands golf day needed to be sorted in liaison with Our Jim's old TV colleague Gary Newbon, along with raffles and auctions, to boost the charities' funds, while he backed this very project that will see royalties go to the foundation, which insists, 'Our simple aim is to keep alive the Greavsie spirit.'

There were also coaching commitments to add to the hectic schedule for former Southend United striker Danny, who has experienced schools, youth, academy and adult football and assisted former Shrimpers boss Steve Tilson at Basildon Ladies.

But in his head, in this moment, were memories and thoughts of an individual who will always be a football superstar in the eyes of his fans but to Danny was just plain 'Dad'. These memories and thoughts poured out as he made an emotional contribution to this book.

Daniel Thomas Greaves was born on Thursday, 31 January 1963 and named after the Tottenham Hotspur captain who led the club to an historic continental triumph in which his dad got two goals in the decider.

Danny Blanchflower was the skipper, and the dad involved was, of course, Jimmy Greaves, who admired the leader of his team. The occasion was the European Cup Winners' Cup Final in Rotterdam in May 1963 when Spurs defeated Atlético Madrid 5-1 to become the first British side to win a major European club trophy (see the Terry Dyson chapter). It was just four months after Danny was born.

Danny said, 'Danny Blanchflower was my godfather. I suppose Dad got on very well with him and that's why Mum and Dad decided to call me Danny.'

His father was always his main man. Danny, who was a Spurs youth player, said, 'The dad I knew was probably like everyone else's dad. Very kind, very generous and very supporting. Just a very, very nice father. A very gentle man. He would try and help you as much as he could, and be involved with you as much as he could.'

Did Jimmy encourage Danny to play football? Danny said, 'No. Not at all. He was more than happy if we wanted to play football or if we wanted to do other sports, like cricket. It was entirely up to you. He was just supportive. He never said you had to play sport. He just kind of left you to your own devices. He wasn't a forceful parent like that.

'He was someone in your corner. He would come and watch me play football, like he did my brother Andy. But he would never step in and say to us, "You should be doing this, you should be doing that," or say something to the manager or schoolteacher. But if you asked him what he thought, he would let you know and try and help you.'

Danny's first memories of Jimmy were devoid of anything other than that he was his father. He said, 'I don't think you were aware that Dad was anything different to any other dad when you are six, seven, eight, nine years of age or whatever. You probably wouldn't know your dad was probably the greatest goalscorer the country has ever produced, and a very famous person. It wouldn't have been until you were 13, 14 that you then suddenly started to get more interested in professional football.

'Although you went to watch Dad as a kid – I saw him a couple of times for Spurs and a few times for West Ham – you were very young. People think, "It must be great watching your dad play." Well, no, because Dad left Tottenham when I was about seven. As I said, it was only as you got older you realise your father was different from other people's fathers, just because he was famous, recognisable. People wanted to talk to him. You start asking, "Hang on a minute, why are people coming up in the street and asking my dad for his autograph?"

'Then you start to talk to Dad about his career, but he never really opened up. He would never say to you, "I did this, I did that." And he would never tell you whether he thought he was a good player or wasn't. It wouldn't have occurred. It just wasn't Dad to do that.'

Danny recalled how he spent his time with his father. He said, 'We were fortunate to have a tennis court where we lived and played on it. Football and other sports like cricket, rarely tennis.

'Dad would go with Mum to meet friends on a Sunday. And I remember as a kid, Dad coming back with some famous footballers, like Brian Dear, from West Ham, and a couple of others, and playing football with us on the tennis court. But again it was more in the latter part of life when you were past your teens when you start playing a bit of golf with Dad. That was more what you did. Publicly it was limited because Dad was too recognisable and people wouldn't leave him alone.

'When he interacted with his kids, it was about them, not about him. He wanted to spend time with you. You might play cricket or have a kick-about on the tennis court with him, but he wouldn't talk about anything that was going on in his personal life at all because he thought when he was with his kids the time he was spending doing that was for us.'

Danny remembered the Christmas and sunshine holidays. He said, 'Christmas Day was always at home, but Dad would often have to go off and play football the next day. He would train Christmas morning. We would have Christmas lunch, but it wouldn't be until the afternoon when Dad came home from training. People forget that.

'And when he was not playing and working on television – doing *Saint and Greavsie* – he would have to work over Christmas and New Year's Eve. I remember getting up one morning and taking my kids – his grandchildren – to where he was working during this time. It was a similar situation when he worked for *The Sun* and doing after-dinner speaking.

'Even when he was a footballer generally he was doing bits and pieces, running a packing business with my uncle Tom. It was just the nature of his careers. So Dad's time was always limited.

'We would spend more time with Dad going away on holiday than we would over Christmas. We used to go to Portugal as a family for a couple of weeks.'

Danny described Jimmy as a 'family man'. He said, 'When he had time at home he would make time for his kids, spend it with us. But bear in mind there were four of us; two daughters and two sons. It wasn't like he could go and watch me play football every week, because he had my younger brother Andy to see too. And he also had my two sisters, Lynn and Mitzi. And he was fond of all of us. He was very, very good as a father to all of us. So he split his time equally between us.

'Family life was nice. The early part of family life was different in the fact that we didn't see a lot of Dad, because he was a very successful footballer. When he stopped playing and when us kids were growing, family life was good. We lived in a nice house, had plenty of home comforts. Dad always supported you. Everyone knows he had a wicked sense of humour. People have only got to watch his television programmes.'

Danny spoke of how his own mates got on well with Jimmy because of the unaffected way he treated them. He said, 'I've got three or four, maybe five, close friends from school that I still see now. Three of them attended my dad's funeral because they'd known him. If you spoke to these boys they would tell you he was no different from any other dad. As I said, he didn't talk about himself. When he walked through the front door and saw them he would just say, "You all right?" Could have been anyone. That was Dad. He was just kind, warm-hearted. He was happy to engage with my mates but engage with them in what they were doing rather than what he was doing or had done. That was nice.'

Danny recalled fondly the time spent with relatives. He said, 'My uncle Tom and aunt Nancy were very close. They lived across the road from us. We used to spend a lot of time with them. We would go out and eat and drink at the local golf club, and other bits and pieces. We lived in Upminster and saw our grandparents. My mum's mum used to babysit for us. I also remember my uncle Ricky.

'But as for Dad's team-mates, the only real footballer I remember as a kid coming over really was [West Ham goalkeeper] Bobby Ferguson who lived at the bottom of the road.

'Dad, like any work person, didn't really socialise with his work colleagues, which were his team-mates, other than when he was at the club.

'When I was older I met the likes of Cliffy Jones, Pat Jennings and Stevie Perryman. I've been fortunate to meet loads and loads of celebrities. But that, as I say, was when I was older and just in Dad's company. Growing up as a kid it was completely different. It was pretty much my uncle Tom and my aunt Nancy we saw in the main.'

Danny told how the avuncular, friendly, humorous and entertaining character portrayed by Jimmy when he cemented the hearts of the nation on television was no act. He said, 'One of the reasons why Dad was so successful was because he was what he was, with no show. No airs and graces. Dad was like he was on TV at home.

'When my brother Andy and I had left home and you went round to see Mum and Dad – or whether you went to play golf with him – Dad would always embrace you with a big, warm cuddle. A big pat on the back. "How are you, really happy to see you," which was lovely. But at the same time, he'd also embrace the lads at the golf club the same. He just loved people. He was just a very, very friendly guy that loved being around people.

'Dad was more than happy to sit at home and watch the cricket on the telly. If somebody said to Dad, "We'll stay at home and watch the cricket on the telly," he'd say, "Fine." If [agent] Terry [Baker] rang him and said, "We've got a job. We need to do this," he would say, "All right, I've got to earn money so I need to go and do this." Contrary to most people's belief, he was quite shy, if that's the right word, but once he got with people, he was just Dad. Just himself. A genuinely nice guy who got on with people. That's just how he was.'

How much did Jimmy shape Danny's character? Danny said, 'I don't know if I could answer that one. I think it is very difficult unless you are the son or a daughter of someone who says to you, for argument's sake, "You are going to play tennis. You are going to hit 2,000 tennis balls a day. And you are going to do that every day until you become Wimbledon champion," like Serena Williams's father did. Most don't create you, they guide you. And I think that's what we found as kids. We found our own way in life with the help of Mum and Dad there to support us, especially Dad. If you weren't sure about something, as I've said, you could go to him and he would give you his opinion and his advice. I wouldn't say he shaped you at all. Again, he wouldn't say you've got to do that and you've got to do this. It just wasn't him.

'I haven't got a clue about what people think of me. I wouldn't know. But you would hope people, when they meet you, would walk away and say, "He was a bit of a chip off the old block. He was warm and friendly, good company to be in." If that's what people think, well, then that'd be great because that's what Dad was. People always enjoyed being in his company.'

In 1981, Danny followed in his Tottenham Hotspur superstar dad's footsteps to White Hart Lane where he had a spell in the club's youth set-up. A tough call considering the success and adulation his father had experienced during his decade in N17?

He said, 'It was always going to be tough wherever you went. Some people have followed fathers extremely well. Clive Allen [son of Jimmy's team-mate Les], for instance. Clive did fantastically well [for Spurs, West Ham, QPR, a host of other clubs and England]. Also [former AC Milan, Monaco, Rangers and England striker] Mark Hateley, who followed his dad [Tony, the Chelsea and Liverpool centre-forward]. But others have not been as fortunate. I eventually managed to play professional football, which was my dream, at Southend.

'Now I had a famous father to a high degree who had not only been an extremely good player but – unlike a lot of other contemporaries – had not drifted out of the limelight. Mine was, they said, doing the best sports show they'd ever seen in *Saint and Greavsie*. So whether all that helped or hindered, who knows? I wouldn't change it because I wouldn't swap my dad.'

Jimmy supported Danny through his time in the Football League at Southend, where he played for three years – with a respectable one-in-three goal average – before moving on to Cambridge United and non-league Chelmsford City.

Danny returned to Roots Hall to become youth coach. And his dad was even moved to contact the then Southend manager Barry

Fry at the end of the 1992/93 season (see the Barry Fry chapter). Fry, who only came in late in the campaign from Barnet, had kept Shrimpers in the second tier after a relegation fight but reckoned Danny was the true saviour by recommending players on the staff who could do the job.

Danny said, 'I have great respect for Barry. And it was lovely of Barry, not only to say what he said, but put it in his book. I'll never forget my time with Barry. It was wonderful. Great fun. If I could have time again with him I would. A lovely man. He was different class. An absolute entertainer, not dissimilar to Dad in a lot of ways. Barry loved people. Loved being with people. He wanted to help. They were slightly different characters but at the end of the day were both genuine, honest guys who wanted for other people to succeed.

'And again, Barry's probably one of those slightly misunderstood. I don't quite know why. Football can be funny. But you know, he knows his stuff, Barry, because you don't survive in our game without knowing it. I don't think Barry gets as good a credit as he should for being as good a manager and as good a coach as he has been. He managed my dad when they were together at Barnet.'

Danny managed Essex non-league club Witham Town for three years from 2008, with Jimmy a low-key supporter. He said, 'We had two or three great seasons there. Dad used to come pretty much every home game. He would come in the dressing room after the game – and sometimes at half-time. People used to say, "What was it like, your dad coming in? Did it put pressure on you?" No, because the only reason he was coming in was because he wanted a cuppa. That was about it. He used to say, "I'm coming in to get a cup of tea." I said, "OK Dad, no worries." He used to just stand there and when I'd finished he'd then go around and talk to the boys about whatever THEY wanted to talk about. Again, typical Dad.

'If one of them wanted to ask him something, he'd reply, but he would never push himself forward or say anything otherwise. He did have one occasion where he maybe mentioned in one game that one of the lads might be doing something better. And as I said to Dad, "If he could do that, Dad, he wouldn't be playing for Witham." We both chuckled and he said, "Yeah, you're right."'

Danny admitted he had no problem being one of Jimmy's offspring. He said, 'I have never been and never will be Danny Greaves. I am and will always be the son of Jimmy Greaves. I either had to embrace that or leave it. Now, the fact I chose to play football and go into football, it was far easier to embrace it. I'm not trying to make it sound like it was a hindrance. It wasn't. It has been an absolute honour. But you were never going to be yourself. You are always going to be the son of Jimmy Greaves. And that was just how it was.

'Some people might get the hump, disappointed that they are not being recognised for their own achievements or whatever you want to say. For me, as I said, I was always going to be and probably will still always be the son of Jimmy Greaves. I don't have an issue with that at all, because not only was he an absolute legend, he was a wonderful father as well.'

Danny took pride in Jimmy's time working in newspapers. He said, 'Dad did very well with the newspapers. His article in *The Sun* was one of the biggest read articles in a British newspaper; it probably helped that you could read it in *The Sun*, because most people who were into sport at the time would read the paper. But, on a serious note, his columns were followed. If you spoke to *The Sun* at the time you would find a lot of the mail every week from readers was about Dad's column.'

Danny believed the fact that Jimmy expressed his thoughts in plain English and didn't blind the reader with science was an integral part of its appeal.

He said, 'His way was to try and explain the game to everybody, whether you understood the game or whether you were a complete novice and had only just started watching it. Because ultimately, to Dad, it was a game. Now, unfortunately, it is a business, whereas even in the latter years for Dad it was still a game. He was very fortunate that he earned a living from it, whether it be from playing or being a journalist. But it still was a game to him. He had that wonderful level of keeping it that way. Making the column light-hearted, even if it was a situation that might be serious at the time. Still bringing it down to, "Actually, it is just a game.'"

Danny was 'too young' to appreciate the time Jimmy struggled to control alcohol. He said, 'My brother too was too young. It kind of went over me and my brother's heads. You know what it's like, when you are ten, 11, 12 years of age, it's what you're doing, not what's going on in your parents' lives. I was aware that there was a problem, but I couldn't say too much about it because I didn't really know much about it.

'His drink problem was a part of his life, but again, typical Dad, he came out the other side of it. He fought the demons and turned it into a positive because he helped thousands and thousands of people to give up alcohol as well.

'The biggest thing was it was a test of Dad's character. A group of my friends and my brother's friends, my dad's friend Brian Doherty and my dad – about 14 or 16 of us – used to go on those golf weekends. And he was in the bar with us as comfortable as anything, drinking his Coke, while we were all getting half p***ed. He would never touch a drop, having the discipline and willpower to just drink that Coke. Wouldn't avoid sitting in the bar with you or buying a drink for anyone. He would only go to bed when he was ready. Amazing.'

Danny believed Jimmy should have received a higher award than the MBE he was given in the 2021 New Year's Honours list. He said, 'He's my dad and I'm obviously going to be biased, but for the life of me, it is beyond me why somebody overlooked until they are in their 80s is then only offered an MBE after all he did was entertain people from 14 years of age until 75 years of age when he fell ill.

'At 14, 15, Dad was already attracting 1,000 to watch him play football at two o'clock on a Sunday afternoon. And he carried on entertaining through football, journalism, television, after-dinner speaking and books.

'To me, he was the Bruce Forsyth of the footballing, of the sporting world. Bruce Forsyth [who was knighted] was a teenage entertainer who ended up doing *Strictly Come Dancing* in his 80s, and various things along the path to entertain people.

'Also, in one of my dad's books, *This One's On Me*, he came out and said, "My name is Jimmy Greaves. I am a professional footballer. And I am an alcoholic." That helped him help those thousands and thousands of people to stop drinking.

'If you can't make this guy a "Sir", who are you going to make one? I'm sorry for anyone who gets anything now because it has made the honours pretty worthless. Whoever does the honours really should look at themselves.'

Danny viewed it 'an honour' to help look after his dad when Jimmy was struck down by a major stroke in May 2015.

He said, 'It was an absolute tragedy, but it was an honour for me to look after him. It was never, ever a hindrance, an issue. I repeat, it was an honour to look after him as he'd given so much to all us children. I don't think I'm speaking out of turn, but every child would be the same.'

The stroke imposed physical limitations, Danny said, but communication was a bigger problem, 'He knew exactly what was going on, just couldn't communicate to say what he wanted. And for somebody who was such a good communicator that was very frustrating.

'We did a couple of golf days for the [Jimmy Greaves] Foundation and Dad came along to one because we did it at Upminster Golf Club, which is where we'd lived and grew up. It was nice for Dad to go back, to see and remember where we lived, see some of the old boys again. It got him out and about.'

Jimmy was known for the expression 'It's a funny old game'. And Danny was intent on ensuring the fun – and the legacy – endured at the Jimmy Greaves Football Academy in Essex where development plans were 'getting there slowly but surely'.

As the academy website put it, 'He [Jimmy] became a national treasure and it is our privilege to be able to use his name. Join us and catch the Greavsie knack of playing with a smile on your face.'

5

Andy Greaves

Son

ANDY GREAVES knew his dad loved music. Jimmy named each chapter of his autobiography after a popular song to reflect it. He had seen Ella Fitzgerald, the American legend, live at a small club in New York (see the Bobby Moore chapter).

But his eclectic tastes in what the Oxford dictionary defines as 'vocal or instrumental sound (or both) combined in such a way as to produce beauty of form, harmony and expression of emotion' also stretched to opera, so youngest child Andy sorted tickets for the Three Tenors at the original Wembley Stadium, under its iconic twin towers, on Sunday, 7 July 1996.

It was, of course, a venue familiar to his football goalscoring legend of a dad. It was where Jimmy netted three for England against Scotland and four versus Northern Ireland – two of an England record six hat-tricks – besides a winner against the Rest of the World. And he also helped Tottenham Hotspur win two FA Cup finals there, hitting the target on his first one against Burnley.

But listening to Luciano Pavarotti, Plácido Domingo and José Carreras must have transported Jimmy into a world away from the game. One suspects there wasn't a dry eye in the house as our subject, Andy, the rest of his family present and 55,000 others were enraptured as Pavarotti performed his signature aria 'Nessun Dorma', from the last act of the Giacomo Puccini opera *Turandot*, and hit the high B of the famous last line, 'Vincero,' translated as 'I will win'.

Andy said, 'Dad liked his music. I recall clearly taking my mother and father to the Three Tenors at Wembley Stadium. And that was a very memorable evening for me to be able to take them to see it. Dad absolutely loved Luciano Pavarotti, Plácido Domingo and José Carreras. We had a great night. I think it was the only concert I took him to.

'Gardening was a big passion for him too. He always had a fish pond in the garden; loved that. And having dogs. Sometimes he'd have two of them. He enjoyed being at home with Mum, pottering around the garden and walking the dogs. And if the cricket was on the TV it would be happy days for him. His ideal day. He was keen on a lot of things outside football.'

Forget the late boxing legend Muhammad Ali; Andy reckoned Jimmy was 'The Greatest'. He said, 'I think he was the greatest father anybody could ever have, not only a great person for the public. A great man. Supportive. He was always there for me in anything I did, and also supported my two children, Harry and Madeleine. He was a great father and grandfather. I miss him every day. I wish I could have one more round of golf with him; sit with him over dinner with my two children. I'd do anything to bring him back if I could.

'Out of the children, I would be the one who didn't have the best memory of my dad playing football, really, because I was only born in 1966.

'I remember I watched him play football for Brentwood and Barnet. That was about it. Dave Emerick [see chapter on him] was manager at Brentwood at the time. Dave was Dad's oldest friend and best man when he married Mum. Dave used to go on the underground with Dad when Dad played for Chelsea.

'I was lucky enough that I was of an age when he was at home a lot. I spent a lot of time with him, although he'd work on Saturday with *Saint and Greavsie*.

'I remember when he first worked in TV with Gary Newbon, he took me up to the Midlands, where he worked, a couple of times with him. I had a very gifted childhood in that both my mother and father were at home.'

Speaking of what they would do together, Andy said, 'Every now and then we'd have a kick-about with a football in the garden. I don't suppose he really ever wanted to do it much because he'd done enough of it.

'I played more cricket, really. I remember once, myself and my brother [Danny] were playing cricket with him and I bowled one up to him and he smashed the ball straight off his legs through the greenhouse window. We were going on holiday the next day and I remember him uttering the words, "For f***'s sake, don't tell your mother, she'll go mad."

'We'd also play a bit of tennis. Table tennis as well. We had some wonderful times playing table tennis and cricket at my house in France with him and my two kids, Harry and Madeleine.

'A sport we did love to do together was golf. I used to go away with my dad for golf weekends to Le Touquet, Cromer, Sheringham, Hunstanton and occasionally Woburn and places like that. They were fantastic.

'I always admired him because there would be about a dozen of us and he'd be the first to put the money in the "whip" even though he would only have a diet Coke.

'They were special times and I only wish my son Harry could have had those times with him as well, but sadly not. Special memories. He also loved his horse racing and rugby as well as his cricket. I went to Newbury, Newmarket and Cheltenham with him horse racing, and did quite a few meets with him and Mum. He loved a day at the races.

'He had a picture in his office of Lester Piggott. He always said to me that he was always one of his heroes. Fortunately, we got to meet the man at Newmarket once.

'When we were at home we'd try and watch the Six Nations rugby together on the television. In later life, he loved the IPL [Indian Premier League] cricket. That was one of his favourite things. He was watching cricket during his last days, not sure what it was. Dad genuinely loved his sport. It wasn't all about football.'

Andy hoped to follow Jimmy into professional football. He said, 'I went down the route of playing for a local team in Upminster, then got picked for the district. Then, as a young boy, I tried out at Tottenham. It didn't work out.

'I was taken to Southend United and signed as an apprentice professional footballer at the age of 16 for them. I had two years there; never made the first team. I only played in their youth team or reserves. Patsy Holland took me to Leyton Orient. I played for their youth team and reserves. I used to play left-back or they played me in midfield. Danny was a natural striker but I liked to tackle compared to him. I didn't mind getting stuck in.

'People say I was a bit unlucky but I don't think I was good enough. Simple as that, really. I knew I had to get another job, put my career on another path.

'I tried, but the gene doesn't always follow. I had a famous father who was a great player. One of the greatest players who ever lived as a goalscorer. But it just wasn't in me, unfortunately. Don't get me wrong, I enjoyed playing. I played at a very good standard non-league after I went and got a job. I used to love it. I played Sunday mornings with my mates, loved that.

'Went to a lot of Essex teams. I was at Witham Town and Maldon. Won the Essex League. I also played for Bowers and Pitsea. I never really ventured out of Essex.

'I got asked to go to a couple of bigger clubs in non-league at the time but I was working and training to be a trader in the City. I was working 6.30am to 6.30pm. I couldn't really afford at the weekends to be going to be playing for Wokingham who had Torquay away on a Saturday. It wouldn't have been for me. So, as I said, I was quite happy to play in the standard I did.

'I stopped playing football at 26 and played rugby for Harpenden. As I said, I liked a tackle!

'Dad used to come and watch us play football and rugby when he could. A lot of the time I'd be playing Saturday, Dad would be doing *Saint and Greavsie*. He couldn't come as much as he'd have liked to. But would come when he could.

'He took great pleasure in watching my son Harry playing rugby and my daughter Madeleine play hockey.

'He'd always put family first. Dad's priorities were his kids and his wife. I think that is why they were married for 63 years. In modern terms, that's incredible. They were very young when they got together and lucky to have found each other in love.

'I don't remember much about Dad's problem with the drink. I was young. It showed incredible strength to kick the booze, beat the habit and being one of the first to come out and admit it so publicly like he did. He was an inspiration to a lot of people. It was fantastic for him to turn round to them and say, "If I can do it, you can too."

'He deserves more credit for doing that as much as anything else. I did have people, when I was with him sometimes, who came up and thanked him, saying, "Reading your book [*This One's On Me*] and seeing what you did inspired me to give up my addiction." They could be talking alcohol, sometimes gambling, drugs. That was special in my heart as much as anything else. I've always been incredibly proud of him and I was then.'

A campaign called 'Jimmy Greaves Should Be Awarded A Knighthood' on Facebook – one run by a public group from before he died – remained active at the time of writing. The *Daily Mail* had also carried a campaign while Jimmy was alive.

Andy said, 'To be honest, personally, I don't see the point in Dad having a knighthood now that he's not here. But that's just me. By all means, if people want to run a campaign that's up to them.'

Talking about how Jimmy might stand up against modern football's strikers, Andy said, 'I don't think you can compare when it comes to young and old football, looking at the pitches my dad played on, the way he was tackled in his day. There are also pictures of Dad and others smoking cigarettes at half-time and full time. The whole game was different then.

'But I always asked him whether he would have swapped playing when he did and he always said, "No." He loved that generation that he played in.

'He used to play against Arsenal, West Ham, Manchester United or whoever at White Hart Lane in front of, maybe 50,000 or whatever, with everybody crushed in standing, and go to the pub after the game and meet my granddad and have half a beer and be standing there with the supporters. They'd all mix in. The supporters weren't aggressive towards them. They were respectful. What a lovely way that must have been.

'Now the players walk off the pitch holding their hands over their mouths so no one can tell what they are saying to each other. All a bit ridiculous at times.

'Financially, I'm sure he'd have liked to have earned the money they earn now. Even though my granddad on my mum's side, Horace, was a lorry driver and my other granddad, Jimmy Senior, was an underground driver, my old man wasn't earning loads more money.

'When you look back, all the players who are on what they are on now should really take a look back in history and thank the likes of Jimmy Hill, my dad and other players who were threatening to strike virtually if they didn't get their own way.

'One of the reasons Dad went to Italy was because there was a wage cap in this country. That's why people like Denis Law and John Charles started going to Italy.

'I don't feel sorry for any footballer now from the point of view of what they are earning. Bloody good luck to them. In any sport or any walk of life, if someone is willing to pay you something to do it, happy days.

'But they can't go anywhere now without being filmed, pictures being taken. God knows what else. In Dad's era, at least they were lucky enough to walk across to the pub and meet fans and family.'

What would Jimmy be worth in today's transfer market? Andy said, 'I couldn't answer that. There is a picture on my dad's desk of him in the middle and either side of him is Denis Law and Georgie Best. You can ask anyone in your book, "How much would those three as a front line be worth?!"

'The game now? Well you haven't necessarily got to be the best player in the world to be a multimillionaire.

'It's probably now more, sadly, a business than a game. Someone recently came up to me and said that my dad predicted the game would become a business at a dinner he was at about 30 or 40 years ago.

'One of the saddest things about football to me at the moment is that you or I could list the top six for next season. I know we had the blip one year with Leicester [beating 5,000/1 odds to win the Premier League title in 2016]. But if you had to put your mortgage on it you could probably name the top six.'

Greaves, of course, made an indelible mark in the game at Chelsea, AC Milan, West Ham United and England, scoring goals by the shedload. The biggest mark was made at Spurs where he became the club's record goalscorer over a decade in which he thrilled supporters to almost single-handedly create an electric atmosphere at White Hart Lane, in domestic and continental competition.

And, having had a major stroke two years earlier, Greaves returned to the fabled ground with his family in March 2017 to say his own fond farewell to the scene where he conjured magic moments which will forever remain in the mind's eye of those fortunate enough to witness them.

Andy's brother Danny publicly thanked Tracey Levy, the wife of Tottenham chairman Daniel, for being 'different class' as she helped get the club to invite their patriarch to the stadium and the training ground when they were empty to 'stimulate memories' and provide financial support for his medical bills.

Andy clearly concurred. He said, 'Tottenham were kind enough to ask us to go down. We went to say goodbye to the old stadium. They'd started doing some work on the new stadium. We took Dad out on the pitch. He did say he wanted a kick-about! It was nice for his four children and grandchildren to be there for that occasion.'

Andy noted the 'honour' he felt when representing Jimmy when our subject was inducted into the Football Walk of Fame at the National Football Museum in Manchester in June 2017.

Andy said, 'The museum in Manchester very kindly asked me to lay a plaque of my father to join other ones of players on the walk. It was a lovely honour to do it, especially as Denis Law was also inducted that day. And Denis, who was being recognised with a plaque, said to me, "Your father was the best." Eusébio, Alfredo Di Stéfano and Paolo Maldini also had plaques put down. The mayor of Greater Manchester, Andy Burnham, was there and he was very nice. They made a bit of a fuss of Denis and I which was nice. There was a piece about Dad in the museum.'

Andy revealed how Alan Gilzean, one half of Spurs' fabled G-Men strike partnership with Jimmy, confirmed, not that it was needed, why Greavsie was considered alongside the world's elite past and present. He said, 'I had the pleasure of sitting next to Alan Gilzean at a dinner once. And he told me, in a deep Dundee accent, "You see that Messi?" I said, "Do you mean Lionel Messi?" He went, "Yeah. That was your dad. I used to go up in the air, flick the ball on and by the time I was landing the crowd were cheering. I knew the wee man had done it again." I thought that was an unbelievable compliment. He added, "Your father used to go round players just like that, with a big leather ball, on any pitches. He'd have scored double the goals he scored if he could have played on the pitches today." These are Alan Gilzean's words not mine.'

Andy considered what life had been like since the passing of his famous father. He reflected on the circle of life which has been defined as a 'symbolic term for the series of events that unfolds on earth, bringing us from cradle to grave, through ups and downs, love and misfortune, and so on'.

Jimmy's youngest child remembered how his dad sat down Andy's own children to watch the animated Disney film *The Lion King*, which featured Elton John's song 'Circle of Life', underlining the symbolism and, in turn, the theme of the film.

He said, 'There's not a day I don't think of him. Not a day I don't miss him. My dad always watched – and made his grandchildren watch – *The Lion King*. And he always used to say to Harry and Madeleine, it is all about the circle of life. That's what it is, really. We are only here for a short time. Not a long time. And part of the circle of life, sadly, was losing my dad. I can only try and make him proud of me in all the decisions that I've made. I'm sure he's looking down at me now and hopefully still very proud of me. Proud of his grandchildren Harry and Madeleine.

'Getting over the loss of a father or a mother is a very tough thing for anybody to do. Mum's struggled with having to come to terms a bit with the loss of Dad, missing her best friend and the man she loved for 63 years. But they had a good life. They lived into their 80s and had all that time together, which is not bad. Mum always says that she wakes up and thinks about him first thing and falls asleep thinking about him.'

6

Marion Prescott
Sister

MARION STOPPED in full flow as she warmly reminisced about her 'extremely bright' brother from when they first shared a home with their parents. Marion had been asked what she would most like known about her much-loved sibling.

Marion, born five years after Jimmy, took a few seconds to consider and said, 'That very fast brain he had. It allowed him to adapt, be witty, be quick, be clever and make people laugh. People think of him as a footballer who was good with his feet. And he was. Brilliant. But it was that brain that was impressive.

'He looked at our younger brother Paul and myself and thought, "Oh, they are the clever ones. They went to university." But it was silly, really. Given another five years and the opportunities Paul and I had in education which he didn't have, he could have gone. Mind you, he probably wouldn't have chosen to because he would have chosen football. Anyway, he was a very intelligent guy. Very quick. Very witty. Very funny.'

Sister and brother came into each other's lives at the end of the Second World War. Marion revealed how she was told a supersonic V-2 ballistic missile designed to travel in silence impacted close to the Greaveses' East Dagenham Heathway home in Ivyhouse Road as its matriarch Mary gave birth to a girl who was to be their only daughter. She laughed, 'I did land with a bit of a bang! According to my mother the house shook!'

The family had been bombed out of their home in Manor Park seven miles west when their eldest Jimmy was six weeks old at the start of the war. Jimmy and his mum evacuated to Suffolk while his dad Jim stayed to drive District line trains on the London Underground. When the bombs and missiles stopped, the country got used to peace breaking out and got back to the everyday. Jim continued to work the green line as depicted on the tube map, while Jimmy attended Southwood Lane Junior School and his wife tended to baby Marion.

They eventually moved to a newly built council estate on Huntsman Road in Hainault five miles north of Dagenham. Marion said, 'My mum and Jimmy got evacuated away from London because of the bombing. She did come back at some point before the war ended. But Jimmy wouldn't have been much aware of it all at that age, though, particularly when they were living out in Suffolk. Dad was driving his train through the bombing, of course. Although he was in the Home Guard, he was protected. He didn't have to go and fight.

'As we were growing up, we were very much aware of the shortages. The rationing, the coupons, all that sort of stuff. If you had a school party you had to take your coupons in so that they could get the food for the school party. Of course, it has affected my generation. We are incredibly careful with money. We don't throw stuff away, we are not obsessed with dates on food, and we recycle. You don't have to tell us that sort of stuff as we've been doing it since we were children.

'When I was quite small, and Jimmy was at junior school, we moved to Hainault. And Dad moved to the Central line with Hainault towards the eastern end of it. Mum and Dad stayed in Hainault for the rest of their lives. Even when they were both old, they moved out to a flat in the area.

'It was very nice where we were. Very green. Fields at the back of us, school fields in front of us. It was a very pleasant place to grow up. It was completely different to how you might think a council estate might be. It was very decent, civilised.

'I don't think Jimmy – who was always called "Jimmy" around the house because our dad's name was Jim – had any problems with his upbringing.'

Marion described the relationship she had with her big brother. She said with wry affection, 'We got on well enough. When I was about six or so he shortened my first name Marion to Mau. Everyone knew me as Mau. And at that time, the Mau Mau were the terrorists in Kenya [the Mau Mau uprising or rebellion took place from 1952 to 1960]. That might give you a clue that he thought I was a bit of a nuisance! But the name stuck right through to my teenage years.

'We weren't great friends at that time but when you get older you become more friendly. You are more adult. You talk about things more. As there was five years' difference in our age, he was 11 and going to secondary school by the time I was five or six. I don't have much memory of him before then.

'When we went to live on that big new council estate in Hainault, there were no schools and he had to go by bus to Dagenham. He was very much involved, even early on, in Dagenham schoolboys football [scoring regularly aged ten as he helped Southwood Lane to the Dagenham Junior Schools league and cup double]. Football was his main thing.

'It was clear when he went to his secondary school – Kingswood Secondary Modern in Hainault – that he was extremely bright.

'He had been expected to pass the 11-plus at junior school. There is a rumour, he wasn't too bothered about it because the Catholic boys grammar school my mum would have sent him to – my mum was a Catholic – played rugby. Most grammar schools did in those days. And he wasn't interested in rugby. I doubt he'd have gone to the length of deliberately failing, though.

'In his day there weren't even comprehensive schools and people at secondary modern finished at 15 which was why Jimmy did not get the educational opportunities that Paul and I got later. It was a different age and they didn't do exams or anything. I went to a grammar and Paul went to a very good comprehensive and we were both able to progress. But, as I've already suggested, it probably didn't matter to Jimmy because he was always going to be a footballer. He was popular at Kingswood. Head boy. I remember him in a play playing Captain Hook in *Peter Pan*. He was very much not just the footballer. Very much a definite personality and respected in the school.'

Marion outlined her brothers' relationship. She said, 'Paul didn't really get to know Jimmy because by the time Paul was five or six, Jimmy was 16, 17, and at 17, 18 he was away. So Paul and Jimmy were never close, although they were good enough friends as adults. There was such a big age gap between them.

'Paul and I became closer because we lived at home longer and got to know each other better. He's still around. He was 71 on 6 May in 2022. He trained as a teacher but really didn't like it, so ended up doing accounts and eventually IT. He was an accountant for a housing association. He and his wife are cricket mad and they play a lot of bridge. They live in Worcester. They are very happy; they've been together a long time now.'

Marion reckoned Jimmy displayed characteristics of each of their parents. She said, 'My dad was a very keen sportsman. He'd played hockey and football and tennis in the army. I think hockey was his main sport. He actually played at senior level. And he ran a football club of amateurs in one of the Sunday morning leagues, which was everything from choosing the team to managing to doing the laundry at the local laundrette. I used to go up sometimes and watch them play up at The Lake in Hainault Forest. They were called Lakeside.

'Jimmy didn't play for them. He was well above their level. These were grown-ups. People already at work but wanted to play as amateurs on a Sunday. Jimmy's sporting side definitely came from my dad. My mum was a very strong personality. You didn't argue with her. You did what you were told. I suppose he got a lot of discipline from her, being able to follow rules and hopefully work with others as a result.

'She was very much a power in the family. She wasn't a nice, sweet person who sat at home and knitted. She'd go out and work part-time. She was a cook. Some people would say chef these days. But "chefs" were only men then. Women were "cooks". Mum did for a while hold a pastry cook position in a very upmarket local restaurant. That's what she enjoyed doing, although she didn't do that all the time.

'She only ever worked part-time, having three kids. She definitely contributed to the family. She was very strong, one of five sisters who were very close. We had a lot of lovely cousins – with Jimmy the eldest – and regular family parties. It was a strong family.

'My dad was more gentle and placid. He didn't argue. He was much quieter. But if you pushed him too far he could have quite a strong temper on him too. He wasn't a softy but he was, of the two, more relaxed, kinder and sweeter to the kids than my mum was.

'As a couple, our parents complemented each other. My dad was well paid as an underground train driver. We were never short of money. We never thought we were poor. He was in a strong, unionised, and, as I said, well-paid job. And as my mum contributed to the family as well, we were also able to have holidays and everything we needed.'

Was Jimmy more like his dad or mum? Marion said, 'I wouldn't say he was like either of their extremes. He was somewhere in the middle. He wasn't someone who was very much forceful and strong like my mum but he certainly was no gentle, quiet person in the background. Yet, remember, I only knew him at home until he was around 17. And he was out and about a lot, playing football and so on.'

Marion remembered a temporary rift in the family when Jimmy married Irene in 1958. She said, 'Jimmy got married very young and Mum was very angry and upset by it. She would have liked to have seen him develop other aspects of his life first. But what can I say? These things happen. This was the late 1950s. It was a different world back then

'There was a hiatus for a few years when there wasn't much communication between the families. I was doing my O levels and didn't feel it too intensely. My dad and I did go and watch Jimmy play tennis. He was good at tennis. I don't think relationships broke down completely, but it was definitely my mother who was upset by the fact that Jimmy had made such an early marriage.

'My mum and Jimmy were not happy with each other. There was a gradual re-establishing of contact over three to five years. I would say by the time I got married things were OK again. We had the wedding reception at Jimmy and Irene's home.

'I never felt I'd lost any contact with Jimmy. It was just I wasn't seeing so much of my elder brother because of what happened. When he became more famous, the whole family was delighted and Mum absolutely revelled in being Jimmy Greaves's mother. She was never slow in letting people know the relationship. She could be embarrassing at times, boasting about her son. But you know, sons and mothers, it is a special relationship.'

Marion kept scrapbooks of cuttings about her elder brother as his football career floated into the stratosphere. She said, '[Jimmy's oldest child] Lynn's got them now. I cut out anything from any newspaper and pasted them with flour and water in those days into these big scrapbooks. Yes, I followed his career avidly.

'I still very much follow football, follow Tottenham. Jimmy wasn't happy with the way he left Tottenham but I still went on supporting them. It's very hard to change your loyalty once, let alone twice. It was hard enough to change from Chelsea to Tottenham.'

Marion believed she had seen something of Jimmy in modern-day Spurs player Son Heung-min in his partnership up front with Harry Kane. She said, 'The thing I recognised that my brother had when he played was this intense awareness of what was going on round him. And the ability to know that someone behind was running at such-and-such a speed. You could put the ball exactly in front of him or vice versa. He just had total control. An understanding where everyone was moving, the speed they were moving at. You see it with Son Heung-min with Harry Kane, I'd say it was instinctive but it is a kind of intelligence of speed and movement. That's what made Jimmy so exciting to watch. He got told off once for being greedy. The manager was telling him to pass but Jimmy went on and scored. And he told the manager, "You didn't tell me who to pass to." That just about summed him up.'

Marion felt the television career Jimmy had was successful because it played to his mental strengths. She said, 'It was not surprising he did so well. The success of the *Saint and Greavsie* programme thing was not a shock. He was very intelligent, as I said, a great communicator and a leader. They gave him that second career. And of course he earned more in that second career than he ever earned as a footballer.

'He was on fixed pay until he went off to Italy. Other famous English league players started going abroad so they could earn more money then. Things started to change, though, and the Professional Footballers' Association, with Jimmy Hill its chairman, got the maximum wage prohibited. It has gone to the other extreme now. It is absolutely incredible what they get now. I think the players still play for the love of the game. However much money you earn, you still want to win, and do your best.

'Football was much more of a local thing when Jimmy played. Your fans were local-based. Even when people moved from the north to the south it was a big deal, changing your location like that.

They were completely different days, but the level in football now is utterly amazing. What you see now is very impressive.'

Marion praised Jimmy for winning his battle with alcohol in the 1970s. She said, 'That was the biggest challenge he ever had in his life and the biggest success despite all his footballing trophies and his successful businesses. To actually stop. Not to drink for over 40 years. It was certainly an amazing thing he did. And we know so many other famous people who never did it, who didn't cope with it. He did brilliantly there.

'I think his daughter Lynn was a great support to him at that time. She has to take a lot of credit. She was just about old enough, about 18 or a bit more. She did an awful lot to help him. Help get the family together again [after Jimmy and Irene had temporarily split up].

'Why did he start drinking? Well, I think there was all the thing around the World Cup. It must have been the biggest disappointment in his life. And Jimmy and Irene also lost a baby son [Jimmy Junior]. And there was a drinking culture in football.

'I've got a bit of the gene, myself, of course, but I'm totally under control. When I was younger and drank too much, which I don't do any more, the next day I was ill. Most of us are like that when we drink too much and don't do it again for a few days. Jimmy could drink as much as he liked and never suffered with a hangover. I think that is a very dangerous, physical aspect of alcoholism.'

Marion, who has underlined Jimmy's intelligence and ability to communicate, found it 'hard' when he struggled to speak after suffering his major stroke. She said, 'One of the sad things was the speech impairment he had. He couldn't be quick and witty like he used to. It was so hard to see him struggle with his words. You could have a conversation but it was tough. He really wasn't enjoying his life after the stroke. He'd had enough.'

Marion read a poem called 'The Dash' at Jimmy's funeral at the Chelmsford Crematorium on 22 October 2021. She said, 'It was a very nice poem about the written dash between birth and death dates representing a life and philosophising about it. I enjoyed doing that. It was nice to contribute.'

And the occasion also raised a smile when her 'extremely bright' brother's wit extended to requesting Lonnie Donegan's 'Have a Drink on Me' be played. She laughed, 'He would only have had a cup of tea himself!'

7

Des Benning

Cousin

DES BENNING has revealed how he felt the 'true spirit' of Jimmy never left him. Des attended Jimmy's funeral in October 2021, paid tribute to him at a Mass and uttered prayers on what would have been our subject's 82nd birthday on 20 February 2022.

And he said of the football superstar, family man and household favourite, 'It's quite remarkable, that over 50 years after Jimmy finished playing, he is still so remembered and loved. I believe fans everywhere saw him as one of them. Jimmy transcended the rivalry of all football supporters everywhere. A life lived that gave so much to so many.'

Football fan Des saw Greaves play at the start of his professional career. He said, 'My first recollections of Jimmy were back in 1957 when he made a first-team debut for Chelsea. Coincidentally, all my family were Chelsea supporters. Jimmy would leave tickets for us in the cottage outside Stamford Bridge, sometimes being there to meet us for a chat before or otherwise after a game. On one occasion, he took my elder brother into the dressing room to meet players before the game.

'It was sad for us all when Jimmy went to AC Milan in 1961, but the culture of the Italian clubs in the 60s didn't suit Jim, so he returned home to Blighty to join the Spurs double team.

'We always joked that Jimmy split the family, for my father and brothers remained Chelsea fans, but I followed Jimmy to Spurs. And so for the next decade, I watched Jimmy score most of his home goals, plus some away, including a European tie in Split, in the then Yugoslavia in 1968.

'I felt proud on many occasions going into the players' car park at White Hart Lane on matchdays. As everyone arrived, including the away team coach, players would drift across the car park for a pre-game chat with Jimmy, one I was part of. Looking back, it was quite a surreal situation for a teenager, who would shortly be hearing 50,000 fans chanting "Jimmy, Jimmy".'

Des told how his cousin connected with the fans. He said, 'Jimmy was always accommodating to fans, giving autographs, having a few words. At his house, he showed his medals to a friend of mine who had asked to see them.'

Des played against Jimmy. He said, 'In the mid-60s, the local club I played for, Wickford Town FC, had a Sunday afternoon friendly against Jimmy's tennis club team at Abridge. Jimmy played in goal, wearing [Spurs goalkeeper] Bill Brown's Scottish international jersey. He couldn't play other than keeper because Spurs would have been annoyed, risking injury, invalidating insurances.

'The 70s were worrying times as I was aware of Jimmy's drinking problems. I had a friend working in Warley Hospital, where Jimmy would be "drying out", as it was described. Fortunately, Jimmy overcame the problem and went on to TV, in programmes such as the *Saint and Greavsie*, punditry and stage shows to great success.

'I saw various shows Jimmy did, mostly in theatres, like the Mercury in Colchester, where we met backstage for some banter. The fans loved every show I saw. The big one was Jimmy's 70th birthday at the O2. Many former players were there that evening. Great fun.'

Des remembered the day he took Jimmy by surprise. He said, 'Jimmy wrote a few books. On one occasion, I walked into a Waterstones in Basildon, where he was doing a signing. I thought

I'd surprise him and joined the queue. As I reached the desk where he was sat, Jimmy looked up, jumped up and we embraced.'

Benning recalled how Greaves spoke at 'family funerals'. He said, 'Jimmy would also bring some humour or stories to the family funerals. His mother Mary was one of five Mansbridge sisters. After the last one, Kath, died in 2011, Jimmy remarked, "I must be careful now we've lost Kath because I'm next in line!" Jimmy remarked on an aunt Maria, a kind matriarch, at another.'

Jimmy stayed the same character throughout his years, according to Des, 'For myself, Jimmy never, ever changed. In looks and health-wise he did, but the true spirit of the man, the great family man, the great footballer, who transcended the rivalries of clubs, never did. All the fans loved Jimmy.

'Quite remarkable, that over 50 years after Jimmy finished playing, he is still so remembered and loved. Jimmy wrote for me in one of his books, "To Des, Thanks for the Memories, Jimmy". As I touched his coffin in a final farewell in Chelmsford, I whispered the words, "God bless, Jimmy. I love you."'

Benning recalled speaking at Mass for his cousin. He said, 'A Roman Catholic friend of mine advised me about a month after Jimmy passed that a priest, Father Jeff Woolnough, of St Peter's Church, Eastwood, Essex, had planned to offer the Holy Sacrifice of the Mass for the "repose of Jimmy's soul", a practice done in the church in Rome. The priest was born in the East End, a fanatical West Ham supporter and Jimmy was his hero.

'I decided I would attend. Knowing me to be Jimmy's cousin, Father Jeff asked if I would like to talk to the congregation about Jimmy's life, during the Mass. I humbly accepted. I was privileged to do so for 15 minutes. Afterwards, I was humbled that virtually all the congregation came up to thank me and ask questions. A case indeed where Jim transcended the rivalry of all football supporters everywhere; Father Jeff being an example. I'm not so sure a modern-day player would hold that affection across the divides.'

Des told of how he remembered Jimmy on a particularly poignant date, 'My thoughts turned to Jimmy when we approached the date that would have been his 82nd birthday. It was tinged with sadness with Jimmy for me, naturally, but that was so far outweighed by a life lived that gave so much to so many. I said prayers and raised a glass to the great man on the 20th.'

Jimmy came into Des's mind during the 2021/22 FA Cup. Des said, 'I thought of Jimmy when it was third-round FA Cup weekend in January 2022. It went back to a personal time in 1968. Spurs had been drawn away to Manchester United at Old Trafford [in the third round of the 1967/68 competition]. I travelled with a couple of friends from Wickford up to Manchester by train.

'Just after half-time, the Tannoy announced that if there was a Desmond Benning in the crowd he should please contact the police. Checking with a nearby officer, I was allowed to phone the hospital in Yorkshire, where my father had been ill for many months.

'Sadly, I was advised on the phone call that he had died. My mother and younger brother were with him at the time. His passing had been expected imminently. Each weekend, the family had travelled to Yorkshire for the weekend on a rota basis, so as someone could be there with him. I had seen him the previous weekend and the family knew I would be at Manchester on 27 January if I needed to be contacted.

'I remember at the time I felt very alone. If Jimmy had been there, I could at least be with him after the game. As it transpired, he didn't play that game because he was injured. He probably would have got me back on the team bus with him, but he wasn't there as the moment came. I often think back when we approach the third-round FA Cup time, remembering the game I most wished Jimmy had played.'

8

Dave Emerick

Best man

AN UNBREAKABLE bond for life is more than implied if you perform best-man duties at each other's weddings. It becomes a confirmed reality when you are informed by your friend's widow at his funeral that you had known her husband for a greater length of time – outside blood relatives – than anyone there.

Dave Emerick met Jimmy when they were both seven years old, just after hostilities ended in the Second World War. The friends were 18 when Dave assisted Jimmy for his wedding to Irene Barden in 1958, and he revealed that Jimmy was happy to return the favour when he got married.

The pals had mostly lived just a handful of miles apart in rural Essex villages and were still in touch when Jimmy passed.

Dave said, 'We were best men for each other because we had grown up together. We were mates. Irene said to me at the funeral as we looked around, "Do you know among all these invited people, you are the one that knew him the longest?"

'I met Jimmy on the street playing football when we were seven, four years before secondary school. Everybody played on the streets. There was no television in those days. It was on the brand-new Hainault Estate built by the London County Council in 1947.'

LCC had been allowed to build outside its territory after the Blitz destroyed urban areas in the capital and, with evacuees returning to it and a 'rapid' population growth, there were housing shortages. The Greaves and Emerick families were among those who moved from affected areas to the estate by Hainault Forest.

Dave said, 'I was from Walthamstow and Jimmy was from Dagenham after being born in Manor Park. Walthamstow, I've been told, now has properties worth £1m to £2m and in Walthamstow Village they go up to £3m. It was a slum when I left there. I used to play Cowboys and Indians on a bombsite – a flattened dairy – after coming out of the cinema watching a western, slapping my backside as if I was a horse! We got bombed out, or rather bomb damaged. That's how we got a council house in Hainault.'

The Greaves brood moved in at Huntsman Road after similar experiences. Dave said, 'If we hadn't moved next road to each other my life wouldn't be what it is. Funny how it pans out.'

The pals' friendship swiftly developed. Dave added, 'We lived over the fields playing football. That was it. Children now, or so I hear, are not allowed out because of the way the world is, but we used to play until it got dark.

'There were hockey as well as football pitches there. They used to take the posts down on the football pitches, like they did at Hackney Marshes. But they used to keep the nets up for the hockey pitches. That was magic for schoolchildren like us. A hockey goal is smaller than a football goal so, naturally, we used it. There were three of us who used to go about together – Jimmy, me and a local lad called Micky Locker, who was a year older than us, and was a goalkeeper. He went in goal and we just fired shots until the light went. We used to get shouted at by the groundsman, who said, "Get off the pitch!" Lovely days.

'Micky, by the way, went on to play in goal for QPR and Barnet and was good and moved to New Zealand and sadly died not long ago. I visited him over three years ago. He was in a social home in Gisborne [on the north island] and I thought, "This is the last time I'm going to see Micky."

'Jimmy and I didn't go out other than football, really. We might go to the cinema every now and then. We didn't do a lot of socialising. Just round each other's houses. He was a home bird. So was I; still am.'

Dave and Jimmy travelled together by bus to attend primary school in Dagenham as there were no primaries at Hainault. He said, 'Jimmy went to a school called Southwood Lane and I went to another one, called Charlecote. We went on the bus to them from the ages of seven to 11. I don't know how we got split up to go to different ones.'

But they both attended senior school at Kingswood Secondary Modern in Hainault. Dave said, 'It was literally a five-minute walk from where we lived, but it used to take us an hour to get there because we were playing one-touch off the kerb. One against one. If there was a little group of you it'd be two against two.'

Dave told how the pair were inseparable in school. He said, 'It was a lovely school. Brand, spanking new. When we went there, we were among the first pupils in, Jimmy and I. When you are 11 you don't know what's happening. We were strangers in a new school. Virtually held each other's hands. We sat on the same desk in the same class and were in the same "house". We were together all the way through.'

Dave recalled how the pair were involved in sport for their 'house', Lambourne, named after nearby parish Lambourne End. He said, 'Our house colour was yellow. I always remember we were both good at gymnastics. Jimmy was very good at boxing. That's how he got a "boxer's nose", really. He boxed for Dagenham Schoolboys. I used to go and watch him fight. Boxing wasn't for me, though. I had a little few fights but didn't like getting punched on the nose. Jimmy was multitalented. He played for Essex Juniors at cricket, played tennis for them too.

'We played in the same school side at football. Both played for Dagenham Schoolboys, with our school supplying about eight of the

Dagenham team and the girls doing the same for the Dagenham netball team.

'Jimmy was inside-left and I was at right-half for our teams. He went on to play for London Schoolboys and Essex. I don't think he played for England Schoolboys.

'I was with another schoolmate of ours the other day, Jeff Haywood, a neighbour. Jeff was a left-winger who played with Jimmy and I in the school team. We were saying we used to play against terrific school sides. Jimmy used to get three, four, five [goals]. You knew you wouldn't lose. I remember one day, we were in a cup final and Jimmy had to play for London Boys. So he didn't play for us – and we lost 1-0 to a school from Woodford! It sticks in my gullet!'

Dave reminisced about how just playing in playground matches with Jimmy gave clues as to why his friend became a football superstar. He said, 'I always remember as a kid playing football with Jimmy in the playground. The ball was tied to his left foot. You could never get at him, not that I was playing against him much. He was always that bit ahead. Luckily, I was supplying him with all the goals! All the ammunition!

'We used to do sprints and drills in the gym for, say, ten metres. And in that first metre he'd get a couple of feet on you. You can then get hold of him but the damage, in football, is done by then. He was that quick. And he carried on doing that right into his 30s.'

The trio of Dave, Jimmy and Micky Locker continued to keep in touch before the latter was called up for National Service.

Dave said, 'Jimmy and I missed National Service. They stopped it before we were called up. We used to say before they did, "I'm going to be a PTI [physical training instructor] and I'll love it. Looking forward to going in." I'm glad I didn't at the end of the day!'

In the meantime, Irene came on the scene. Dave said, 'Jimmy and Irene met when they were about 15 or 16. She went to a different school to us. I met Irene a bit later. And, of course, I was best man when they married.

'We hardly lived far apart as Essex people. but they moved a lot. The furthest Jimmy went, apart from when he went to Italy, made me laugh. It was to Cornwall. He liked Cornwall, bought a place down there. But within six weeks he was back in Essex again. He said to me, "I was filling up with petrol in Chelmsford to go down there," and said to Irene that he thought they'd made a mistake. When he got down there, he put the house on the market.

'I said to him, "You can't be making money on property now, you must be losing it." Whether it was Irene or him I don't know, but they kept moving. I kept a record. So I know I'm telling the truth about the amount of times they did!

'The first one was in Plough Lane in Wimbledon when he was at Chelsea. They lived in a flat from Wimbledon Football Club. Then he bought a place in Hornchurch. That's when they went to Italy and came back to Tottenham to another place. And he went from there.

'Jimmy used to throw some good parties, like at New Year's Eve, at home in the old days at Chelsea. There were a lot of East End boys at the club then and they used to come to them. Terry Venables, the Harris brothers Allan and Ron, Ken Shellito and all that crowd.

'We used to play tennis for the Co-op over at Abridge. It was a Co-op then. It is now a country club. We played doubles on a Sunday. The families used to go over there.

'Jimmy had a great bearing on my life. Life is like a kaleidoscope. You can shake it and you get a picture, and you shake it again and you get a different picture. I look how he's affected my life and the people I've been in contact with.

'My eldest son, Neil, was leaving school. We were writing to all the banks, which was the industry he wanted to go into. We weren't even getting any replies. My wife said to me, "You've got to get involved." I said, "What's the matter?" She said, "Well, we're not even getting replies. He's a clever little lad." So I said, "Well, I'll ask Jimmy because Jimmy's [youngest son] Andy works in the City."

'It's who you know in this world. So I said to Jimmy, "Can you have a word with Andy for me, please?" My son got three interviews, three job offers. And I said to Neil, "Well, it's up to you now. You've got to do it yourself." Now that son lives in Cape Town in South Africa and works for himself. He's doing very, very well in the tourist industry.

'It is the same with my youngest son, Peter. He is the head of football for Puma, covering the Premier League and other top European leagues like Spain's La Liga and Italy's Serie A. He's done very, very well. And it was only through a contact through Jimmy he got that job.

'I was delighted for Jimmy and Irene as they had children: Lynn, their eldest who is my god-daughter, Mitzi, and the two boys Danny and Andy who gave professional football a go like me.

'Tragically, they lost one, Jimmy Junior. Chelsea had played on the Wednesday night and it was Thursday. Jimmy and Irene were living in that Hornchurch home. It was in Great Nelmes Place. And I went round there about one o'clock in the afternoon. And Irene answered the door and she's crying. I said, "What's the matter?" And she told me, "The baby's died." That was before I'd spoken to Jimmy. The baby was only a few months old.

'They used to go down to the cemetery at Upminster to put posies on [the grave] there. The family still talk about it. It's not an easy thing to dismiss. You can't dismiss it. It scarred me as well. When I had my two I woke them up many, many times because I thought they weren't breathing.'

Both mates pursued a professional football career. Dave joined Leyton Orient before moving into non-league as a player, manager and coach, but it was Jimmy who hit the heights – immediately.

He signed for Chelsea and banged in goals for fun in the youth team. Dave said, 'Jimmy got an illuminated address from Chelsea which is lit up on the wall in their home for scoring a record number of goals (114 in the 1956/57 campaign) in one season.

'We were in Portugal the other week, my wife Naomi and I, and met up with an old mate, Dave Moorkite. It turned out that him and I played against each other in a youth match. I was with Leyton Orient and he was with West Ham. He told me how he had had to mark Jimmy once. I asked him how he got on and he told me, "Terribly. He scored five!" Anyway, I had a barbecue at our house. It was about ten years ago. And Dave and Jimmy were there. So Dave talks to Jimmy and said, "You don't remember me, Jimmy, do you?" And Jimmy said, "Sorry, I don't." And Dave said, "I played against you and actually marked you when you beat us and you got five against me. And I wasn't a bad midfield player." Jimmy said, "Sorry, I don't remember that." Well, he wouldn't, would he? That's Dave Moorkite's claim to fame – he let five in against Jimmy!'

Dave believed Jimmy had innate abilities which elevated him to become a world-class player. He said, 'As a coach, and we still talk about it now, he was a one-off. You don't realise but as a coach the one thing you've got to look for is balance. It is God's gift to you. You can't manufacture that. And that was the gift that Jimmy had. As well as speed.

'I'm surprised. His dad was a good amateur footballer but not excellent. No better than you or I. His mum wasn't an athlete. His sister and brother, whom I saw at his funeral, haven't been. None of them have gone down that road. As I said, he was just a one-off. Like Bestie [George Best], if you like.

'I know it was the old First Division, which was probably not the same standard as they have in Premier League, but I'm convinced Jimmy would have held his own. You don't get many players who can dribble in tight areas. He used to score goals by just putting it in the net. He didn't have to slam it. That's another gift he had.'

While Jimmy carved an indelible mark into football folklore, Dave made a fist of the talent he had. He said, 'I went to Tonbridge from Orient. Malcolm Macdonald was there, the old Newcastle, Arsenal and England centre-forward. He was a right-back in those days. Harry Haslam, who went to Luton and Sheffield United, was manager.

'After about a year, Gordon Jago, the former Charlton defender who was to manage QPR and did well in America, rang me out of the blue. He was at Eastbourne United and asked me if I wanted to play for him. I was still in Hainault and working in the docks at Canning Town. He said, "I know you've got a job to do. Why don't you train at West Ham?" So I used to get away Tuesday and Thursday morning to train with West Ham. And through schools football, I knew Johnny Lyall [future West Ham manager] who was running the reserves.

'I trained with Bobby Moore and Martin Peters, who helped England to the World Cup, of course. I knew them all. Even knew Peters's dad, who worked at the docks. Gordon made me skipper and I played for him for six years.'

Jimmy quit full-time professional football while playing in the top tier at West Ham at the end of the 1970/71 season, aged 31. Dave gave him a route back to football in the mid-1970s having taken over as manager of non-league Brentwood Town. He asked his pal to play for him. Jimmy signed on 21 December 1975, according to Brentwood's official website, which highlighted a 2-0 defeat against Witham Town on his debut six days later.

Dave said, 'I casually said to Jimmy, as a joke really, "You don't want to come and play for me, Jim?" We were in the Essex Senior League. He said, "I'll tell you what, I wouldn't mind."

'I said, "Really?! I can only give you £3 a game top whack." And he did play for me. Never, ever let me down. I thanked him for that. I said to him, "You were good for me." He was renowned for not being a good trainer. We used to hire a floodlit ground up at Warley and he used to be the first up there hanging around waiting to start training. So when the other players came up they couldn't say, "He's only playing because he's Dave's mate."'

But Dave added, tongue in cheek, 'He did let me down on his debut! Whenever he had a debut for everybody, that was Chelsea youth, England youth, England under-21s, AC Milan, wherever else, he always scored in his first game. Always. I know that for a fact. So we're playing Witham Town in the first game he's playing for me. I thought, "We're on a winner here!" He hit the bar, hit the post and the goalkeeper had a screamer. I said to him with a smile, "You owe me one [goal], Jimmy." He made up for it, though!

'I got the sack out of the blue around Easter [1976]. We were getting a good side together and I'd asked for more money for the players for the following season.

'Jimmy saw the season out. He went on to Chelmsford City – I saw him a couple of times for them – and then Barnet, where [former Liverpool and QPR goalkeeper] Dave Underwood was chairman. And I went on to coach Billericay to three FA Vase finals and run Bobby Robson's Ipswich academy in Essex for seven years.

'Jimmy said to me – and Irene has also said – that I helped save him when he played for me at Brentwood. He was in the drink mode very badly then. Playing helped to get him out of it. I can understand that a bit.

'I remember once at Brentwood he arrived and was absolutely green. He said, "I've had a basinful." I said, "Jimmy, you can't play. I'll tell the press you've got a bad back." He got away with it a couple of times.

'It was the best thing that *The People* published it [that Jimmy had become an alcoholic]. It became public, common knowledge. Otherwise, I thought it was underhand all the time.

'He went into Warley – a Priory [private mental health hospital] if you like – to get him out of alcohol.

'When he went to Chelmsford and Barnet, I think he'd virtually stopped. And he eventually stopped altogether, of course.

'Jimmy once told me, "The difference between a prolific drinker and an alcoholic is very, very small. It's a fine line. One minute you are OK and then you've gone over the top." Having not been there you don't know – I don't drink – but you can imagine it, can't you?'

The Greaves and Emerick families continued to enjoy their close, loving relationship as Jimmy controlled his addiction for decades, but life threw a traumatic and ultimately tragic obstacle into the path when he suffered his major stroke in May 2015.

Dave said, 'The thing with Jimmy when he had that stroke was that it wasn't only him who was impacted, but Irene lost six years of her life. It wasn't a minor one. He was paralysed. Just in a wheelchair. For six years Irene and their children lost their lives. They all had to play their part, pay their dues.

'I said to Irene after the funeral, "Maybe you'll get your life back." She has. She's free every day. She hasn't got to think, "Oh, I can't do this, I can't do that, because the carers are coming in."

'She's getting out and about. My wife Naomi and I take her out and she comes over to us for meals. Like Jimmy, she's a mate. I'll never lose contact with Irene. I speak to her nearly every week. We talk about Jimmy in the present tense. We keep in close touch.'

Dave revealed how he and Naomi maintain a six-day-a-week training regime of running, walking, cycling, swimming and gym work. The veteran of 50 marathon runs at 82, Dave remains an avid football fan, having just attended a Billericay match at Braintree and watched Spurs play on the television when we spoke. But he missed his old pal.

He said, 'I've got the card of the funeral service with his picture on it on my desk now as I'm talking to you. I've gone through all the peaks and troughs that life throws at you; seen the highs and the lows of the Greavsie family. I still can't believe he's not with us.'

9

Brian Doherty

Close friend

BRIAN DOHERTY considered Jimmy his 'older brother and best friend', and added, 'If you've got five hours to spare, I can spend five hours talking about the man.' Brian, born in Glasgow and known to the Greaves family as Doc, since he came into their orbit in the 1980s, said, 'When I grew up in the street or in the parks in Clydebank, somebody had to be Denis Law or Billy McNeill of Celtic or John Greig of Rangers. But there was always somebody who would be Jimmy Greaves.

'So actually playing football you pretended you were one of the famous footballers of the 60s. I never thought for a minute I'd end up Jim being my closest friend and consider him my older brother.

'I had the great privilege of being allowed to do a eulogy at his funeral. The gist of it was, "This man was my older brother. The man I knew was funny but so down to earth. So sensible."

'Not only was Jim the older brother I never had, he gave me so much confidence and belief. He was just in my life. He helped me so much, through all sorts of personal financial issues. He was always there as a guiding hand to point me in the right direction. More importantly, the advice he gave me was always usually correct.

'I've now just sold my business, a firm specialising as professional trustees for pension schemes. It's the second of the businesses I've set up, the first a pension consultancy specialising in pensions. All of it is mainly down to sitting with somebody people see as a football icon but who was an entrepreneurial businessman and saying, "You've done business before, Jim. What do you think?" And him saying, "Yeah, you can do it on your own, son." Then after the first business was bought – I worked for that company for a long time – I said to him, "I'm thinking about setting up again." He said, "You'll be even better this time round." If I thought I could do it and he said, "Yeah, you can do it," that was it.

'There were a few other projects I thought of. He'd just look and say, "Do you really think you are that good?" I'd say, "You don't agree with me?" He'd say, "I'm not telling you not to, but I wouldn't invest."

'There was the time I was asked by a relatively famous footballer to invest in a pub with him. I asked Jim. He owned a pub in Collier Row years before and didn't say "don't do it" but left me with enough information which made me think, "I don't think it is a good idea." In hindsight, what he was saying was, "Doc, you can't do it. You're not able to run a pub. One, you like a drink. Two, you are not close enough to it." Anyway, I didn't do it and probably within a year the pub went bust. Unfortunately the footballer went bankrupt as a result, but I am pleased to say he has been a huge success since. So Jim stopped me going bankrupt.'

Brian will always treasure the friendship he had with Jimmy. He said, 'Jim had a lot of acquaintances, people he called friends, but he only had a few close friends and I was privileged to be one of them. Andy, one of Jim's two sons, always introduced me by saying, "This is Dad's best friend." Jim never called me his best friend. He just called me his closest friend because we would spend a lot of time together. We went to Tottenham's training ground and met the likes of Harry Kane, Mauricio Pochettino and Daniel Levy and you are thinking, "How did I come from being some sort of spotty face Jock to this?" But I didn't adulate the guy. I just knew Jimmy Greaves my friend. I didn't know Jimmy Greaves the footballer. I think had

I known him as a footballer I might have treated him differently.

'I only ever saw him play once. I think that was in 1968 when I was in my teens. I came down from Scotland and watched Manchester United play Spurs in a midweek game. It was a bit like Celtic and Rangers – a derby meeting I'd seen a lot – in that the atmosphere was quite toxic.

'So I think I was lucky not to have known him in his football career and know him as somebody who was living a life where he had to earn money. He worked hard. If you were doing this book and he was helping you, he would be at every Waterstones and WHSmith outlet to sign copies. He really would. He never undercharged people and he never overcharged them either. He'd give them value for money.'

Brian believed Jimmy always put his family's happiness at the top of his priority list. He said, 'As I've said, Jim was a very entrepreneurial businessman, which not a lot of people would appreciate. He ran that pub [The Ship] until he and Irene clued up to the fact it was such hard work.

'He also ran a travel agents, a sports shop, a packaging company, an insurance brokers. All sorts of things. He had lots of business ventures. He bought and reinvented the old Bukta brand, which sold football kits, and sold it for a few bob. He had an eye for a deal.

'He also earned a good living on the basis he was Jimmy Greaves, like with after-dinner speaking, right up until he had his massive stroke.

'The only reason he didn't have pots of money was that him and Irene, in the years I knew them, must have lived in about 15 different houses. Estate agents and lawyers must have loved them. "Oh, hello, Mr Greaves, coming to buy a house? Nice to see you, again." I could give you so many different addresses.

'It's frightening. Jim and Irene would buy an OK house, spend fortunes on it to turn it into a show house and then be bored. "What do we do now?" "Shall we move again?" "Yeah, let's move again and

Irene and Jimmy Greaves get married (Alamy)

Jimmy and Irene Greaves with granddaughters Victoria and Gemma (Greaves Family Collection)

Lynn Greaves with mum and dad (GFC)

Eldest child Lynn with beaming dad (GFC)

Lynn and proud dad (GFC)

Greaves' daughter Mitzi with dad smelling a rose named after Jimmy (Getty Images)

Danny Greaves with dad (The Terry Baker Collection)

Andy Greaves (centre) with Denis Law and Andy Burnham (The Sun)

Des Benning with Jimmy Greaves (The Des Benning Collection)

Marion Prescott with pet cat Elvis (GFC)

Marion Prescott's drawings of Jimmy's family homes growing up top left and bottom left (GFC)

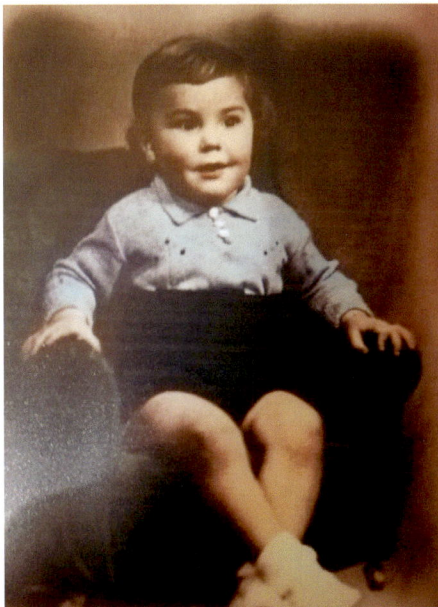
Jimmy Greaves as a toddler (DBC)

Greaves' dad Jim (DBC)

Greaves at Chelsea cutting (The Des
Benning Collection)

Programme for Spurs v Chelsea in which Jimmy
Greaves scored on his league debut (DBC)

Greaves scores the winner for England against the Rest of the World at Wembley in 1963 (A)

Sunday
Tuesday
October 17 1972
No. 28,213 3p

Evening News

Testimonial to one of soccer's greatest strikers

A SALUTE TO THE GENIUS OF GREAVES

by JIM GAUGHAN

JIMMY GREAVES scored 491 goals during a first-class career which spanned 14 years and ended in May, 1971, when he was 31.

His 357 League goals were all scored in the First Division. And for 11 years his England scoring total was 44.

JIMMY GREAVES — as most of his many fans will always remember him...

Glory! Glory!

TONIGHT sees two of the classiest teams in European football, Spurs and Feyenoord, set to provide a display of soccer at its creative best in the JIMMY GREAVES testimonial match.

Spurs, present holders of the UEFA Cup, became the first British club to win a European trophy when they defeated Atletico Madrid 5—1 in the final of the European Cup Winners' Cup on Feyenoord's Rotterdam ground in 1963.

Feyenoord, the crack Dutch team, past one of the most powerful sides on the Continent, won the European Champions Cup when they defeated Celtic 2—1 in Milan in 1970.

EVERYONE knows the fantastic record of Jimmy Greaves scoring in all at his debut games. Pictured (above) is his very first debut League and winning goal for Chelsea at White Hart Lane of all places, against Spurs in 1957...

Among those great debut goals

...and Jimmy does it again for his last club, scoring against Manchester City when he made his debut for West Ham in March 1970.

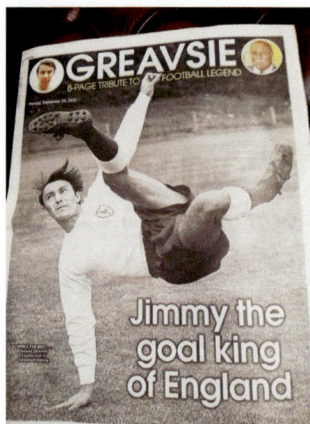
Newspaper pays tribute

Dave Emerick next to Greaves (far left in front row) at Kingswood School (The Dave Emerick Collection)

Dave and Naomi Emerick on their wedding day with Greaves (DEC)

Emerick and Greaves (DEC)

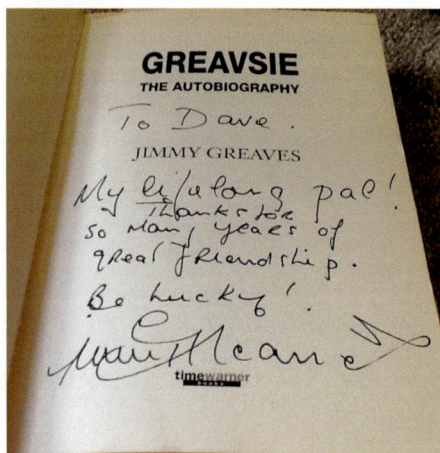
A personal message to Emerick from Greaves (DEC)

Brian Doherty marries Alison with best man Greaves (The Brian Doherty Collection)

Brian Doherty golfing with Jimmy Greaves (BDC)

Freda and Terry Baker with Greaves (TBC)

Campaigning journalist Matt Barlow (The Matt Barlow Collection)

Matt Barlow on Greaves campaign trail (Associated News)

Phil Beal
(Tottenham Hotspur/Gl))

Greaves family with patriarch say goodbye to White Hart Lane (Gl)

do it all again." I said to him, "You are not making money. You are the only person I know who is not making money on house moves." There was one time they moved and within two months – I was sitting in the garden – Irene said, "I can't live here." I said, "Why not?" She said, "Can you not hear the traffic in the distance?" I said, "Yeah." She said, "Well they are going to build a new road between us and that traffic. That would drive me mad."

'They moved to Harpenden to be near son Andy and his children when he was newly married and then Andy announced he was going to Sheffield. They stayed on for a week or two until he moved up to Sheffield and then moved back to Essex from Harpenden. Jim made some strange decisions but that meant he had to keep earning money. Also, he was so generous. He got 57 England caps and I asked him once, "Where are they?" He said, "People would ask me to donate to a charity or a local school doing a raffle." He gave most of them away. I think there may be three or four left in the family.

'Dave Mackay, his Spurs team-mate, I heard, used to give away the jacket he was wearing to somebody who said they liked it. That was Jim too. His value was always his family. That was the only value he had. He loved his family massively.

'To him, belongings are just possessions you can't take with you, whereas your family you keep with you all the way through. His wife, four kids and his grandchildren were his pride and joy.

'Every now and then he'd listen to someone talking about his great achievements. I'd look and he'd say, "Don't f***ing start. Do you know what my greatest achievement was? Marrying Irene and having the children."'

Brian, now settled in Essex, will forever be grateful to Jimmy for being his best man as he married his second wife Alison at Leez Priory in Essex on 14 April 1998, agreeing, in his fun-filled way, to fulfil the role if allowed to wear a kilt presented to him by Scottish club Hamilton Academical.

He said, 'Choosing the best man? I was very close to Danny, Andy and also Jim. I said to Alison, "What if I asked Danny? It would p*** off Andy. If I picked Andy it would p*** off Danny." It was Alison who said, "Why not Jim. You're even closer to Jim." I said, "Don't be stupid. I'm hardly going to ask Jimmy Greaves if he would be best man at my wedding." She said, "You never know." So I went to see him when him and Irene were sitting at home one day and told them, "We're getting married." He was going, "I'll get you a beer and congratulate you." And I said, "I've got something to ask you, Jim. Would you be our best man?" And he just got up and walked out of the room. I looked at Irene and said, "What's up?" She said, "No idea." I thought he'd got the hump. And he came walking back in with a kilt. He said, "I'm the honorary president of Hamilton Academical. I've never had a chance to wear this kilt. I'll be your best man if I can wear it."

'What he didn't know was that I'd always be wearing a kilt. So the one and only time he wore a kilt was at my wedding. I've had a few people who said when Jim was alive, "You know Jimmy Greaves? Have you got his autograph?" I said to them, "I've got it on one bit of paper." They'd say, "What bit of paper is that?" I'd say, "It's on my wedding certificate." I've only got one autograph of Jim and that's the one on that.

'As you can imagine – and if you were sitting here now I'd put the wedding video on – when it came to the best man's speeches and organising the whole wedding thing he was a different class. You realised then how naturally talented he was talking to people in an audience. It didn't matter who was there. And Alison's mum, God rest her soul, had had a bit of drink inside her when she was talking. And she started giving a little bit of abuse. But the way he played it was just perfect. Just wonderful. Very witty. Always comfortable in other people's company. But Jim in a kilt was something to behold.

'I'm Scottish and I've still got friends in Scotland who said, "Jimmy f***ing Greaves was your best man!" Being Scottish we don't really like the English – but everybody loved Jimmy Greaves! That is why Hamilton Academical made him honorary president. He used to talk about them on his *Saint and Greavsie* television programme, take the micky out of the Accies, and eventually he went up there when they were going to move grounds and they gave him the kilt. The tartan was Hamilton. So, of course, he had to wear those colours.'

Brian and Jimmy met on the sidelines at non-league Witham Town's Spa Road ground in the late 1980s. Jimmy, who had become a witty television personality after his glittering playing career, had come along to watch his sons Danny and Andy turn out for the Essex Senior League team.

Brian said, 'I didn't know Jim during his football career, as I said. I met Jim at the time he was doing *On the Ball* on the television. It was before *Saint and Greavsie* started. His sons had come to play football on the same team I was in. Jim was about ten to 12 years older and his youngest son Andy was around the same amount younger.

'It was a lovely friendly club where you brought your kids along. So Jim would finish *On the Ball* and shoot off to Witham Town. In those days there was a little dugout and only one sub. And I was sub more than I was on the pitch. He used to come up and say, "Doc, move over a bit," and then he'd ask, "What's the score?" as he wasn't able to get there for kick-off. We'd have a chat.

'Danny would come with his two young kids. His sister Lynn would come with her kid. Mitzi, the younger daughter, came with her kids. I had my kids up there. So I think half the time the manager wasn't picking me because it was a case of, "You say this is a friendly club and bring your family here so you can look after all the kids." I spent more time on the bench looking after Jim's grandchildren than playing! Running the crèche!'

Brian, Jimmy and the two sons enjoyed each other's company, often going away together on golf trips. He said, 'Jimmy, the boys, myself and a few others would go. We left St Andrews golf course once, driving back in a hired car to Edinburgh. And we'd stayed the night before in Dundee before crossing the River Tay. So, as we were leaving St Andrews, I said to Jim, "Best check that I've got my car key for when we land at Stansted." I'd picked him up so I could drive him home. I couldn't find this key anywhere. I convinced myself I must have left it at the hotel in Dundee. So we went back across the River Tay which was the wrong direction to Edinburgh to go to the hotel. We went into the room, moved the furniture, shifted everything. We searched everywhere, but no sign of the key.

'I was convinced we'd lost the key and Jim said, "One more chance, have a look in your case and see if it is there." Blow me down, it was there. It had slipped into the lining. So Jim just looked at me, looked at the time and I said, "We're not going to make that flight." He said, "Jump in the car. I'm driving it now." I forgot he was a rally driver [Jimmy competed in the 1970 World Cup Rally – see Tony Fall chapter]." Do you know how long it takes to get from Dundee to Edinburgh? Well halve that time. That's how quickly Jim did it.

'You realised why rally driving was one of his great talents. The speed and sharpness of somebody's brain to know when to overtake, go round roundabouts and getting by a slower car ahead without cutting them up or causing any problem. We made it in time. And when we got to the airport and I took my breath in, he just went, "What did you say? We wouldn't get this plane?!" And then he just laughed as we walked into the airport. He could have lost his temper with me. He would take control of situations, which was wonderful.

'The four of us – Danny, Andy, Jim and myself – went to northern France to play golf. It was at Le Touquet in France and the hotel we stayed was the Westminster. Jim and Irene used to go there. The French food was magnificent, wonderful. Anyway, we were playing golf on the last day. We came down the 18th. Jim's teed off on it. One of the boys has gone, "Dad, you know you are having the best round of your life?" He said, "I know. I know that if I get five here on the last hole, a par four, I'll have shot 79. I've never broken 80 in my life."

'Jim wasn't a great golfer, but very steady. He had a good second shot, duffed his third and got on to the green, a bit of a long way away from the hole. He three-putted and walked off with a six. I've never seen a man so crestfallen in his life. I said to him, "Jim, you got an 80. That's a brilliant score." He went, "Doc, I've scored goals in front of 100,000 people at Wembley, played in World Cups, I've been on television and millions of people have watched me. Now I'm here with my two sons and my closest friend and I've bottled it. Nerves got to me." One bad shot, three putts instead of two and he was so crestfallen because it meant he didn't get a 79. He was a man who went through life without suffering from a nervous disposition of any sort and there he was with just the four of us playing a round of golf in France and he'd got a six when he should have got a five.'

Brian knew Jimmy as his pal developed into a leading television celebrity. He said, 'I used to laugh when we'd go out somewhere for a bite to eat, Jim would always face the wall. He'd say, "We'll go in that corner." And he'd deliberately face the wall so that people couldn't see his face. Otherwise, he'd always be interrupted. People would go, "Oh, you are Jimmy Greaves. I saw you in this game. You did this and that." He used to say to us, "I was drunk half the time. How would I remember some of these things that people talk about when I was playing!?" But if anybody would come up and say, "You're Jimmy Greaves, the famous footballer." He'd say, "No." They'd go, "Oh, gosh. You look like him." Jim would go, "I'm Jimmy Greaves, the famous TV broadcaster." He would say to people, "I spent more time broadcasting than I ever did playing football, but people still remember the footballer."

'Not being disrespectful to him, but as a TV commentator or doing the *Saint and Greavsie* shows he was very good, as was Ian St John. But as a footballer he was in a very elite stratosphere. At his time, he was probably one of the top three or four in the world, and I'm counting Pelé, George Best, Bobby Charlton and Denis Law. And even over history he is still up there in the top ten. That takes some doing, especially as it is 50 years after he stopped playing and you are still thinking there's somebody who might want to buy a book on him.'

Brian believed Jimmy helped promote more female interest in football through his appearances on the small screen. He said, 'I still think the best thing he ever did for football wasn't scoring all those goals for England and all the club teams he played for, it was when he became a TV broadcaster because I think his style engaged a lot more women. Certainly in my life, when I mentioned Jimmy Greaves to people in the late 80s, early 90s, the women would go, "Oh yes, I watch him with my husband sometimes. He's on television. He's very funny." I think that was the thing. He actually opened the door more, I think, to the female generation. He was just a cheeky chappy.

'There was no acting in Jim. There are clips of him with Muhammad Ali, Mike Tyson, all these celebrities and he had no script. In *Saint and Greavsie*, the Saint was very professional. He knew what was coming on. And Jim would have a few prompts but most of it was just ad-libs. Of course they were hilarious.

'If he came back to this world now and wanted a career, I'd almost say to him he could be like Billy Connolly. Not as a comedian, though. Without being unkind to Billy, I don't think he is a comedian. He just tells you stories about what people do in real life. But the way he tells them is funny. Jim would be the same. He'd just tell you a story about everyday things but tell it in a funny way.'

Doherty, who had had a mild stroke, spoke of the six years after his 'brother and best friend' suffered his major one, 'The cruellest thing to Jimmy Greaves was having the stroke and not dying. He was a man of huge independence, self-pride. And he really did not want people pushing him around in a wheelchair, having to do everything for him. It was so degrading for him.

'I tried to make sure I'd see him at least once a week. At this stage, Jim was in the hospital in Maldon. Mainly it would be Danny and I who would take him out. A friend of mine, Andy Keen, had got a minibus, a proper taxi with wheelchair access. We would take Jim somewhere, like a little eatery in Danbury or Maldon me and Danny had sussed out. Jim liked his food. And for the next six years big Andy, who I knew when he was a Witham goalkeeper before the Greaveses came along to the club, would be around so we could take Jim out on a Friday. So I feel, if he were able to communicate from heaven, Jim would know I didn't desert him.'

Brian reckoned Tracey Levy, the wife of Spurs chairman Daniel, and the club deserve 'all the credit' for enabling the White Hart Lane legend to have treatment at the exclusive Wellington Hospital in north London.

He said, 'Danny has a lovely relationship with Tracey Levy. Spurs had kindly invited Jim to come up to the training ground and Tracey introduced herself to me. I stretched out my right hand to shake hers and she stretched out her left one. She said, "I do it that way because I had a stroke a couple of years ago." I said, "Oh, I didn't know that, Tracey." I really empathised with her because I'd had my stroke some years before. Jim had had his stroke and was in the wheelchair.

'Jim had had treatment for his stroke at the Wellington Hospital near Lord's cricket ground. Family friend Big Andy took him there. I remember saying to Tracey that neither I nor the family could figure out who had paid for Jim to go into the hospital. It's state of the art. There's machines in there to get you to try to walk. Unfortunately, Jim's stroke was so bad it didn't improve one iota.

'I was convinced it must have been Chelsea. I'd heard that Roman Abramovich at that time used to do things very secretly. So I said to Tracey about all the stuff Chelsea had done for Jim.

Spurs held events to raise money, which was great. But I said, "The only thing is, I'm surprised we haven't heard from Chelsea, but I'm quite convinced Mr Abramovich has probably paid for Jim to go to the Wellington." She just laughed and said, "Don't be silly. That was me and Daniel. I had my stroke in California and Daniel flew me back on a private plane to get treatment in the Wellington because it is world-famous. I knew how good they were and this is why I'm in the [healthy] state I am in now." So what Tottenham did for Jim – never mind that he played for a few other clubs – is on a different planet altogether! So if you were ever going to give any credit to the others, don't. Give it all to Tracey Levy and Tottenham Hotspur. They were phenomenally good.

'Anyway, they took us up to the boardroom, put on a lunch. And I'm sitting on a table with Jimmy Greaves at one end, me at the other. Either side of me is Alan Gilzean and Ossie Ardiles the other side. Pat Jennings was sitting halfway down the table. Opposite Pat is Cliffy Jones with his son. And Danny, of course.

'I just looked round and thought, "Look at the collection here. You've got the Irishman [Jennings], the Welshman [Jones], the Scotsman [Gilzean] and the Englishman [Greaves] with the Argentinian [Ardiles]. And collectively how much would they have been worth now at their peak?! Mauricio Pochettino [then Spurs' manager] came in to say hello and was very gracious. Then Harry Kane came up and him and Jim had their picture taken together with Danny. As did Christian Eriksen about ten minutes later. Harry and Christian were both charming.

'The training facility was out of this world. The training complex dressing rooms get bigger and bigger from those for the seven-year-olds up to those for the first team. The changing room for the youngest talent that goes into Tottenham Hotspur is nothing flash so the kids don't get ahead of themselves. A basic square room with just pegs to hang your clothes, no keys to put them away, and a bench. There is a picture of Jim on the wall with all his statistics up with it. When the changing room was designed, they said the first thing they wanted the children at the age of seven to know was that Jim was the greatest goalscorer Tottenham ever had.'

Brian reflected on his friend's long goodbye and the end itself. He said, 'I took off with my family to go to Egypt on the Sunday. And I turned my phone off because you had to to go on the plane. When I landed in Egypt I turned it back on to discover all these text messages. And I thought, "What the hell's happening?" There's messages from the boys saying, "Dad's had a massive stroke." And I phoned them back. I was going to fly back but the first flight back was not until the Tuesday. Danny said to me, "Doc, don't worry. They say he's not going to live 48 hours. Don't break a gut to get back here." Well, that was wrong – to the tune of six years. That's how strong he was. Such a strong human being physically. And such a strong-willed person.

'I saw him the day before he died. I was round there on the Friday and he died late Saturday night [into the morning]. And I still think to this day he mentally must have said, "I've had enough." Mentally closed down. Even after the stroke I think there was a bit of him that whilst he wanted to die and not have the life he had, his body and brain wouldn't allow him to turn himself off. The bottom line was, he loved Irene so much. I think, it broke his heart he was not able to look after her.

'To say I even knew Jim was an absolute joy, let alone the fact he was my closest friend, best man and mentor. The celebration of a national treasure is a wonderful title for the book, but it is just very sad he is no longer with us.'

10

Terry Baker

Friend and agent

TERRY BAKER was unashamedly emotional as he recalled his life and times with Jimmy, as his friend and agent for 25 years. He said, 'I'm crying as Jim was fantastic not just for what he did as a footballer but for what he did after that and for what he was like as a bloke. The Jimmy Greaves I knew was funny, humble, very intelligent, occasionally grumpy but very rarely, generous, someone with extraordinary willpower and an all-round great person.'

Jimmy's humility was striking to Terry. He said, 'In around 1970, a publisher contacted him to write a book. The subject was *How to Score Goals*. Jimmy wouldn't sanction the idea because he said he had no real idea how to score goals. The publisher and the author thought he was joking – as he did it on so many occasions, to become, I feel, England's greatest ever goalscorer – but he wasn't. From the youngest age in his memory he could just do it. It came completely naturally. It was instinctive and almost unexplainable.

'For those reasons – and it was typical of the man I knew – he wouldn't take the public's money under false pretences.'

But Jimmy did pass on a tip or two. Baker said, 'Not long after Jimmy told me about how he struggled to spell out his art of goalscoring, we went to do a speaking engagement venue just outside of Portsmouth. There were some older people, probably in their late 30s, early 40s, playing a five-a-side game. When they saw Jim they asked him to come and watch.

'So he and I went to look at these guys, who were quality players that had played a reasonable level in their younger days, just enjoying a five-a-side tournament. Anyway, the ball spun out to one of the guys in front of the goal with just the keeper to beat and he screwed it wide. Jim turned to me and said, "Look at that, that's not how you do it. As soon as he received the ball he became tense and you don't score goals like that. You relax when you get the ball and stroke it home." I said to Jimmy, "You should've written that book." And we laughed.

'He had a wealth of knowledge but he was so modest he didn't really realise it. But, as a player, a striker, he never felt tense. Not ever. When he received the ball in any position – however marked he was, however tight the space – he relaxed. And, along with his inborn genius, that's how he scored goals. Genius is an overused word for sure, but in the case of my mate, it was – honestly – appropriate.'

Terry believed Jimmy displayed his iron will by winning a fight to control alcoholism. He said, 'Just imagine the willpower when on 28 February 1978 he decided it was time to stop drinking. It has been well documented that he went through a terrible time with alcoholism and always felt remorse for the problems he caused the people close to him. But his willpower was incredible and on the day he came out of Brentwood's Warley Hospital, a psychiatric institution where he was temporarily resident, he had a pint, looked at the people rushing to get last orders and decided to stop.

'This involved pretty well giving up a social life. I was totally honoured for my 50th birthday that he came with his wife Irene to the party. Later he told me that, other than family occasions and work, it was the first social event he had attended in over 25 years. He felt he had to keep away from such temptations to maintain his sobriety. He helped countless others, including his Spurs team-mate

Cliff Jones who movingly recounted how Jimmy helped him in the movie *Greavsie*, which I produced.

'When I first started working with him I didn't drink for the first couple of times and he looked at me and said, "Are you an alcoholic as well? Tell me." I said, "No, I was just being respectful and not drinking in front of you, Jim." And he laughed and said, "Have a glass of wine. It's my problem not yours."'

Terry knew a meticulous, tidy side to Jimmy as his friend and client's post-football, post-television career was taking off on the after-dinner circuit and bound for sell-out theatre tours. He said, 'Jimmy was fastidious. He always hung his coat up. I know you are supposed to but if I take a jacket off I'll put it on the door knob and if it falls on the floor I'll leave it there. Jim wouldn't take a jacket off without hanging it on a hanger.

'I used to laugh at him. He'd turn up in his car, park, get out and if he considered he was parked two inches to the right of where he wanted it to be, he'd get back in the car, reverse it out, and put it back in so it wasn't. He'd ask, "Is that all right now?"

'Another time we were in Torquay, in a hotel room before a dinner. Me and my wife Freda went up to Jim's room and on a table in it was a big bowl of fruit sweets. Jim is coming out of the bathroom. He has just had a shower, getting ready to go down to the dinner. I have had two or three of these boiled sweets and he went mad at me because I'd left the wrappers on the table instead of putting them in the bin. I said, "We are leaving the f***ing room. We are not coming back now." He said, "Yeah, but the wrappers go in the bin."'

Terry also discovered that Jimmy could be 'very particular'. He said, 'Jim had bought a BMW M3. We were doing a job at The Stables in Milton Keynes. He turned up in this car, brand new. A really fast one. It was a really, really stupidly souped-up one, went from 0 to 60 in four and a half seconds or something ridiculous. He thought it was fantastic. Two weeks later he turned up in a different car altogether. I said, "Where's the M3?" He said, "Oh, I didn't like it, sold it." He'd taken it back to the garage after keeping it three weeks, lost about four grand on it rather than keep it. Funny he was. Very particular.'

There was the situation comedy when Jimmy and Terry attended functions. Terry said, 'I've given up wearing glasses now because my eyesight has improved so much I've got perfect vision, long and short sight. But I was having to wear them back when I was with Jim at shows. I was doing an auction with the audience. Anyway, I got up to conduct it and put my hands in my pocket – the glasses weren't there. So there was a mad panic with everyone – about 150 people – looking for them. Jimmy got up and went off to the loo in case I'd dropped them in there. They were found in the end under the foot of a dignitary who had attended!'

And, of course, Jimmy's sense of humour was always to the fore. Terry said, 'We were at a big function with the mayoress of Poole. She was in all her mayoral regalia and introduced Jimmy to speak. I hadn't been working with him for long. He got this standing ovation before he started. The first thing he said was, "F**k." He continued, "A lot of people think that's a bad word. Me, I think 'murder' is a worse word." He turned to the mayoress and said, "You'd rather be f***ed than murdered, wouldn't you your honour?" Unbelievable! Brought the house down. I said to him afterwards, "You must have been concerned about saying that." He said, "Nah, I could tell she wouldn't mind."'

Terry alluded to the 'pioneering' qualities Jimmy possessed. He said, 'When he retired as a player he changed the face of football punditry. And made it fun for as long as he linked up with Ian St John for the *Saint and Greavsie* television show, which wasn't long enough given its popularity.

'So what did Jimmy do? He became that after-dinner speaker, as we know, but not just any after-dinner speaker. He became literally the funniest one of all.

'Jim's timing was immaculate and you won't be surprised to know that it came naturally to him. When I suggested we start doing the show in theatres, he agreed to trust my judgement. And we did them. I think we appeared on over 300 theatre stages – and everybody loved him. He was so funny, and so insightful when the serious parts came around.

'Greaves worked with players contemporary to him on his theatre tours. We did shows with George Best. He and George got on well. Ron Harris [see his chapter] was the one we did the most shows with.'

Terry recalled how amusing anecdotes and jokes flowed from the stage from Jimmy to an ever-receptive audience. He said, 'There seemed to be millions! One example was about an international. England were trailing 1-0 to someone they shouldn't have been at half-time. Alf Ramsey came in. Alan Ball was in the loo listening to the 3.50 from Haydock Park, because he was a gambler. Nobby Stiles was cleaning his contacts or something. Somebody spilt a cup of tea and Jack Charlton fell over on it, banged his head and they were all rushing around to sort it. And the bell went for the second half. Alf Ramsey hadn't said a word yet. Going back up the tunnel, and these are Jimmy's words not mine, "Alf Ramsey said, 'Pull your fingers out, you w**kers.' The second half went well and England came back to win 3-1. Of course, they were saying what a fantastic team talk it must have been at half-time!"

'Another one Jim told was the time when the England players were coming off the pitch at Wembley. The band of the Coldstream Guards were coming up the tunnel as the players were going down it. Jim said, "You couldn't get passed them as they were banging their cymbals. One of them told us, 'Get out the way. You're just footballers. This is my big moment.'"

'Jimmy also mentioned some fun he had with Gordon Banks when the World Cup-winning goalkeeper was to play his 50th game for England. All of the press corps were there and Jim said to Gordon, "Let me take a penalty. You save it and we'll get these great photographs. I'll put it in the corner to your right." They got 20 photographers laid on the ground with the big lenses they had in those days. Jimmy rolls up. Gordon dives to his right and Jimmy puts it in the other side.'

Terry used to find himself on the receiving end of our subject's quick-fire wit. He said, 'When I first started with Jim, I had long hair with big circular earrings and a cross dangling off them. He came out and said, referring to me, "Look at the state of him. Calls himself my agent. Have you seen the f***ing earrings. The only person I know that would wear those would be pirates and I don't see too many galleons in the car park."'

Jimmy knew how to finish a show in the most amusing style, remembered Terry, who said, 'Jim had a number of ways to finish. One was, "I've got to go. I've got a neighbour problem. I don't know if any of you have had a neighbour problem. I've got this f***ing great German shepherd who is climbing over our fence and crapping on the lawn. I can live with that but he's bringing his dog with him now!"'

Terry revealed the fun he had with Jimmy in off-the-cuff moments on their theatre tours together. He said, 'He was the quickest-witted person. When we had our first contract with Pelé we would raffle a Pelé shirt at every theatre show. That involved selling tickets. I'd rush around like a maniac at the interval doing that. I'd always say to the audience, "If you buy a raffle ticket someone will be able to come up on the stage and have the pleasure of having Jimmy present you with the shirt." People thought this was going to be fantastic.

'The very first winner was this young bloke with long blond hair and a massive pair of ripped jeans, a fashion which had come in. Jim says, "Congratulations, mate. Here's a genuine hand-signed shirt by the fantastic Pelé. You can take that home, put it on eBay and sell it and get yourself a decent f***ing pair of trousers!"

'One other time the winner was a bloke who didn't look as though he'd be that physically attractive. Jim said to him, "Put this shirt on when you go to bed tonight. Pelé always scored when he wore one!" Every single day it was a different comment on whoever came up. Funny things always used to come up in the Q and As with the audience. He also had a different "in joke" to amuse me every time too.'

Terry cited what he believed to be unpublished tales on Jimmy, who was involved in several books. He said, 'One involved Jimmy's old trainer at Spurs, Cecil Poynton. These days his equivalent have all this medical paraphernalia. In Jim's days all they had was an ice bucket, a bit of water and a sponge. Jimmy said many a time with a smile, "It didn't matter what part of you was injured, the trainer would come out with an ice-cold sponge and splash it on your b*****ks and you'd be right in no time!"

'A little-known fact is that Jim didn't wear shin pads. He thought they slowed him down. But right up until he had knee operations, the only scar on his body was the one he got on his shin when he was injured against France in the group stages of the 1966 World Cup finals and ended up out of the rest of the tournament.

'He told me, "I never knew why I became an alcoholic, but it definitely wasn't missing a game of football. When you've lost a son at a few months old, missing the World Cup Final is nothing."'

Jimmy also revealed his favourite footballers while he was on stage. Terry said, 'Jim thought Dave Mackay was the greatest Tottenham player of all time, that John Charles was one of the greats too and that Pelé was the greatest of all time.'

Meanwhile, Freda Baker, Terry's wife, said, 'I remember how funny Jim was. We worked together at the shows with my husband Terry for 20-plus years. He was very down to earth and never pretentious. He always had time for everybody and never had a bad word for anyone; always had a smile and a joke and it was obvious how much the public loved and revered him. He loved a piece of cake and a biscuit before a show. He was never late.

'I didn't see him play football and didn't love him before I knew him as Terry did. But he was a lovely man and I loved him along with all of the public that came out to see him. He is missed and will never be forgotten.'

PART TWO:
THE PUBLIC LIFE

It's a Funny Old Game

11

Matt Barlow

Campaigning journalist

MATT BARLOW, a journalist with the *Daily Mail*, got to know Jimmy Greaves through discovering the size of his popularity.

He was at the forefront of a campaign his newspaper undertook in 2020 to try and secure a knighthood for Greaves. Matt wrote, 'Jimmy Greaves was approaching his 80th birthday and an excellent documentary by BT Sport was set for release. All of which got people thinking at the *Daily Mail*. Jimmy was such a much-loved figure, be it as an iconic footballer, a broadcaster and an inspiration for those fighting addictions. Quite how his contributions over the years managed to evade the honours system remained a mystery.

'His name was a glaring omission. He had always been quite anti-establishment and this probably didn't help him in the days when he was a footballer. Then, there was perhaps a time when his alcoholism counted against him. In truth, it ought to have counted in his favour. As a big football star with the courage to go public on his struggles with addiction, he helped countless others to confront similar issues.

'Anyway, at the time, the *Mail* was going through one of its enthusiastic campaigning phases under the editorship of Geordie [George Carron] Greig, and the idea of a "Gong for Greavsie" took hold. We launched it on a Tuesday with the help of his friend and former team-mate Sir Geoff Hurst. The response from the readers was like nothing I'd seen in what was at the time getting on for 14 years at the newspaper.

'Letters and emails poured in from Tottenham supporters but just as many from the fans of rival clubs. Some had seen him play and insisted he was the greatest of all the goalscorers. Others had been reared on stories passed down through families or had, like me, enjoyed watching him on TV with Ian St John in *Saint and Greavsie*. We published a spread, two days later, featuring some of the correspondence.

'What became clear was that Jimmy, as well as being a genius in the art of scoring goals, also had a genuine gift for communication. He spoke to the masses. This he did, first through his football, and then through television. He moved people. They adored him and here he was moving them again with the power of his story, five years after a serious stroke, which almost ended his life and certainly ended the public side of it. Most of these people, like me, never really knew him.

'Harry Kane got behind our campaign on social media. Managers and players were keen to add their voices, and well-known broadcast personalities and journalists. Iain Duncan Smith a former Conservative Party leader and Spurs supporter, promised to take the case to cabinet. One of the Queen's lord-lieutenants reached out to explain the complexities of the honours system in the hope it would help us navigate it. Love for Jimmy shone through.

'The overwhelming feeling was that he deserved a knighthood, but when the MBE arrived in the 2021 New Year's Honours, it felt like a measure of formal recognition, however small, for everything he had achieved in his life and better late than never. Just in time, too, it turned out.'

12

Phil Beal

Team-mate

THERE WAS no artifice with Phil Beal when we spoke. Phil was completely unstarry, although he had every right to be starry having helped Tottenham Hotspur seal three major prizes – missing out on the chance of another through injury – and got within an ace of a fourth.

This impression was underlined by the image your author had in his head of Beal in paint-splattered overalls as he told me about how he remembered his old Spurs team-mate Jimmy Greaves. After all, he had taken a break from brushing the walls with a coat of emulsion at the west country home he shared with wife Val in a previous conversation.

After assurances the decorating had now been completed and he was merely 'relaxing' in civvies, one of Spurs' most decorated players spilled out personal tales, fun-filled to poignant, which reflected the warmth and respect he felt for Jimmy.

Phil, who told how he was an occasional confidant for Jimmy, was the polar opposite to his high-profile colleague in terms of scoring goals. Jimmy couldn't stop finding the target, once joking how he had had a 'goal drought once – worst 15 minutes of my life'.

But Phil was only able to hit the back of the opposition's net once in more than 400 competitive appearances for Spurs while, in the 1970s, helping the club seal two League Cups, a UEFA Cup and a second European final.

And the former defender disclosed it was Jimmy who laid on the opportunity against Queens Park Rangers under the White Hart Lane floodlights on Wednesday, 29 January 1969, much to his surprise.

Phil said, 'Our goalkeeper Pat Jennings threw the ball out to me. I was about ten yards outside our penalty box. I ran with it and no one came near me and they thought, "He's not going to keep going with that, is he?" I never used to go over the halfway line.

'Anyway, I kept going and going and ended up on the edge of their penalty box. And I saw Jimmy Greaves to my left so I thought I'd give it to Jim, and let him carry on from there. So I gave the ball to Jimmy – and he gave it back to me! I was a full-back on the edge of the penalty box and moving inside it. No way would you ever think he would do that. And I thought, "Flipping heck, this doesn't usually happen!" I'll never forget it. Mike Kelly was in goal for QPR and he came out and I just chipped the ball over his head into the goal.

'A couple of days later we're running around the pitch during training at White Hart Lane and I said to Greavsie, "Jimmy, why did you give that ball back to me when I gave it to you just inside the penalty box?" He said to me with a smile, "Bealy, look up there. See that TV gantry?" I said, "Yeah." He said, "Well the night we played QPR there were no cameras there, so I thought I might as well give the ball back to you. If the cameras had been there you wouldn't have got it back." My only goal – and there were no cameras to record it!'

Phil met Jimmy when our subject first turned up at White Hart Lane, amid much hullabaloo in 1961 after a handful of unhappy months at AC Milan, for a record £99,999.

Phil said, 'I was still a 15-, 16-year-old, in the juniors. I think I was the first person to meet him. He'd turned up in his Jag and driven into the car park at the stadium – and I was just walking through the car park. He just stopped and shook my hand. He didn't know me from Adam. He must have thought I was a youth-team player. Funnily enough, I saw a picture recently from around that time. It was with Jimmy, me and two other youth players at some sort of function.'

Phil formed a further early impression when he joined Jimmy as a first-team player, making his debut in a 4-2 league win over Aston Villa at Villa Park on 16 September 1963 when Our Jim was twice on target.

He said, 'Jimmy was established in the first team and I remember neither of us were very good at long-distance running. And he'd have said that. Never liked the long-distance stuff. There were a few of us who weren't very good at long-distance running. Steve Perryman and Martin Chivers weren't very good either. You'd get the good ones, of course, like Cyril Knowles, Joe Kinnear, Mike England and Alan Gilzean.

'But Jimmy was good over the short distances, 50 yards, 20 yards and doing quick turns. And he was good in the gymnasium as well when we used to play five-a-side. You couldn't get the ball off Jimmy because he kept it so close. It was a nightmare.'

There at the beginning, it was ironic that Phil attended Jimmy's final theatre show, three days before our subject suffered his major stroke in May 2015.

Phil said, 'It seemed very, very strange that I was with him on the Thursday before he had the stroke. We were doing a Q&A at Exeter City FC with Steve Perryman [at the time the Grecians' director of football] and Gilly [Alan Gilzean]. I was talking to Jim in the VIP area before we went out – and we were just going through old times. Old players we used to play against, where's so and so, etc. I said to him, "Are you driving back tonight or are you staying the night?" He said, "Oh no. Once the Q&As over I'm driving back." So I said, "Oh, fine." That was it. He looked as right as nine pence. You wouldn't have thought anything like that stroke would have happened to him.'

Phil told of how he shared a private moment with Jimmy, shortly before the national treasure's passing. It was at a charity golf day in Essex. Phil said, 'I asked Jimmy's eldest son Danny, "Is Jimmy coming along?" And he said, "Yes, he is if all goes well. If he doesn't have a relapse and feel weaker." Jim turned up and Danny said to me, "You can go and speak to him now, because he's on his own." So I went over to Jim and I could tell he knew who I was because he tried to break into a faint little smile. His lips just moved to the side. And I was talking to him about one or two things. I said to him, "Do you remember this, Jim? Do you remember that?" I could tell he was concentrating and listening to what I said. Jim was quite bright. His eyes were bright. He could understand what I was saying.

'He put his hand up – he could just about move his arm a fraction – to shake hands with me, which also showed he knew who I was – and that was it. It was just about a week after that he passed away.

'It was sad to see Jimmy like that when you think what he was like. I always think it is sad to see anyone who had that sort of thing happen to them. They can take everything in, I think, what you're saying, and listen. But they just can't move much or talk to express what they want to say.'

Phil cheered when he recalled the fun times he had with Jimmy, whose sense of humour – highlighted by his catchphrase 'it's a funny old game' – was very much prevalent, for instance, when they worked together at theatre shows.

Phil said with a smile, 'Jim had a great sense of humour. At one of the Q&As he picked on me! Gave me so much stick. What was he digging me out about? Everything! He said to me, "I can't believe it, but I've got on my list here that you played over 470 games for Tottenham! Cor, bugger me, the other players must have been really bad!" He always used to give me stick. Of course, he's got the microphone and I can't say anything back to him as I've not got a mic. I'm just sitting, listening to him and watching him. Afterwards he went, "Bealy, I think when I do my Q&As in future, I'll have you sitting in the front row!"

'He was brilliant on *Saint and Greavsie* on the telly as well as being a good stand-up. Such a good talker.

'Jim also used to make me laugh in the dressing room and around the place at Spurs. He put a smile on everyone's face. He had time for everybody – not big-headed at all, good as gold. One of the greatest players ever, but he was a great guy too. Great with the supporters and always signed an autograph. He always had time to speak to people and would not ignore them.'

Phil revealed how Jimmy was considerate of a superstition the defender had. He said, 'He always wanted to come out last, Jimmy. I always wanted to come out last too. He said, "Go Bealy, you go out before me." I'd say, "No, I like to go out last." He said, "Why?" I said, "Just a little superstition I've got." So he then said, "All right then, I'll let you off. I'll go out before you then." So he let me go out last, which was good of him.'

Phil revealed that Jimmy had an aversion to getting his Lilywhite shirt dirty. He said, 'Oh blimey. I remember after one game I said to him, "Jim, it looks like you've just come in from the car park, changed and hadn't played a game." He said, "Yeah, it's nice to look really clean isn't it?" Then he shouted to the trainer, "Cecil [Poynton], you might as well lay my kit out for the next game. It doesn't need washing."

'Jimmy would always arrive at training looking smart, suited and booted,' said Phil. 'Jim was always in a collar and tie and wearing a suit and was away after we'd finished as he was running a business. But he always used to say, "If anyone wants a quick half in the pub across the road I can stay five minutes and I'm off?" So if you were there the same time as Jimmy was getting changed you'd always go off for a drink with him. He'd have a swift half of light ale and off he used to go. That was it. Never classed him as a drinker at Tottenham. Never (in reference to Greaves' battle with alcohol addiction revealed in the 1970s).'

Phil loved playing with Jimmy – and disclosed how the star confided in him about his attitude on the field, explaining, 'He was some player, some goalscorer. Jimmy used to say to me before games, "You won't get me coming back over the halfway line. If anybody wants me to do anything I'll be doing it in the penalty box. It's no good me coming back tackling, what do I know about tackling? I do all my damage up at the front. If I don't do it I get an earful from Bill Nick."

'He made it look so easy. Him and George Best (a Beal team-mate at Los Angeles Aztecs) I'd say looked similar when they played with the things they used to do. Their close control of the ball with either foot, and the way they would glide past people as if they weren't there. They made it look so easy. If Jimmy and even George played on pitches now and not on the mud heaps like we did, goodness knows how many more goals they would have both got.'

Phil also lent an ear when Jimmy confessed to him his belief that his Tottenham career was over. Jimmy, along with Alan Gilzean, Cyril Knowles and Joe Kinnear, were axed after an FA Cup defeat against Crystal Palace in January 1970. Phil said, 'Bill Nick hit the roof after we'd got beat by Palace and I can remember Jimmy coming up to me and saying, "Well, Bealy, looks like I've played my last game for Tottenham." It was – and he knew it was.'

Jimmy left Spurs nearly two months later, after nearly ten years at the club, and signed for West Ham United as a makeweight in a swap deal which saw England World Cup-winner Martin Peters arrive at the Lane.

Phil said, 'I think Jim said, "It was strange leaving. All you do is pick your boots up when you are told to leave. And that's it. No goodbyes or anything like that."'

Internationally, Phil insisted Jim did not feel sorry for himself on returning to the club for the 1966/67 season after missing England's

World Cup Final triumph in the summer. He said, 'I found Jim all right when he came back for pre-season training. No different to before. He wasn't downbeat at all about anything; not sulking. You wouldn't have thought he'd missed out with England. He was fine. Jovial, joking, like a normal player comes back to training.'

Phil was Spurs' Mr Dependable while the bigger names sprinkled the stardust as Bill Nicholson rebuilt the side following the Glory Years of the early 1960s.

He said, 'It was an honour for me to play with players like Jim but I was never in awe of them. They were just my team-mates in a team game. It didn't bother me they got the attention. I was out there to do a job to the best of my ability, to know I'd given it my all, and that we were successful. The other players were brilliant and never looked down on me.'

Phil, who attended Jimmy's funeral and wake, believes his old colleague will always be remembered, 'Jim was one of the best players I've ever seen. He was that good, I was lucky to play with him. To know him.

'I rate Jimmy more than I would rate Lionel Messi. They are a similar pair. The way Messi has kept the ball tight to him with close control and weaved his way through. I suppose I'd be biased because I saw more of Greavsie in his heyday than I saw of Messi in his heyday. Jimmy would always be my favourite. He lit up the place when he played.'

13

Frank Blunstone
Team-mate

FRANK BLUNSTONE played alongside Jimmy when our subject started his career as a professional footballer at Chelsea.

The England winger was six years older than Jimmy and an established first-teamer when the young striker came to his attention.

Jimmy had signed as a junior in 1956 and scored a club-record 114 goals in his first full season after being discovered by scout Jimmy Thompson as Chelsea secured their first top-tier title in the 1954/55 season. Thompson, a 1920s Blues striker, quoted by the club's official webite, said Jimmy was the 'Player of a lifetime. What a dribbler. What an individualist. He plays it as we played it years ago: forward – not across the park.'

But Jimmy was clearly unknown to Frank, who helped Chelsea to that historic championship triumph.

Midfielder Frank, speaking to Chelsea's website in an article published the day Greaves passed, said, 'We used to have first team versus reserves. This particular Tuesday morning we were short of players. So they sent for two players and these two kids turned up – 16, 16 and a half, that particular age group. We didn't know them and they went in the reserves.

'We started the game and after about 20 minutes, this kid picked the ball up, started off on a run. And at that time, Albert

Tennant was the first-team coach and he used to have one of those megaphones on the touchline, shouting instructions, and he's shouted, "Get rid of it!" and this kid went on and beat another one. "For Christ's sake, get rid of it!" And he went on and beat another one, and drew [first-team stopper] Reg Matthews, who was an England goalkeeper, dipped his shoulder, and Reg went that way and he rolled it in the far corner of the net.

'He jogs back to the halfway line and shouts out to Albert Tennant, "Albert, you didn't tell me when." Do you know who that was? Jimmy Greaves, and I'll never forget it. I'll tell you what, we knew him after that.'

Frank was impressed with Jimmy's ability to strike the ball with either foot over the two years they played together.

He said in the same article, 'I still don't know whether he was left- or right-footed.'

14

Barry Davies

Television colleague

BARRY DAVIES affectionately recalled how he made his television football commentary debut working alongside Jimmy Greaves, then a Tottenham and England striker.

Barry believed summariser Jimmy – with experience of playing for both sides involved – was himself making a first appearance in his role. The man with the microphone was grateful that his fellow debutant aided his broadcast with handwritten notes during Chelsea's 2-1 Inter-Cities Fairs Cup victory against AC Milan, achieved through goals from George Graham and Peter Osgood, at Stamford Bridge on 16 February 1966.

Davies became a pre-eminent TV sports broadcaster. He commentated on 12 Olympic Games in all; more, it has been claimed, than any other British broadcaster. He also covered tennis, athletics, cycling, gymnastics, badminton, ice hockey and ice skating from 1993 to 2004.

But he garnered the most affection and respect for his football commentaries. He had a series of one-liners such as, 'Look at his face, just look at his face,' when Francis Lee delightedly celebrated a goal for Derby against former club Manchester City in 1974.

Barry spoke more from the heart than a notebook of stats, capturing the moment with an infectious, immediately lovable effervescence. And the Spurs fan remained the same when talking about the Lane legend Jimmy he knew.

Barry said, 'He was so easy to talk to when we met at the Chelsea – AC Milan game – and, subsequently, always was – and helpful, which was so useful given this was the first match I'd ever done on television and, I think, it was Jimmy's too.

'I found I had Jimmy as what would now be called "another commentator" which I believe is to the detriment of what is a commentator and what was then called a summariser. The job of a summariser was someone who had good ideas on what team B needed to change to turn the match around if team A were beating them. And you can't do that so easily if you are constantly involved with every little bit of action that there is. These days, you can't have a shot on goal without reference from the guy sitting alongside the play-by-play commentator.

'Jimmy might never have done this job before – to the best of my knowledge – but he could not have been more helpful. He made his points. He did not interrupt. He got notes down on a bit of paper to suggest things to me. Things that he could easily have said – and would have. Anybody doing his job now would. The thought of somebody writing a note to the play-by-play commentator these days would be unheard of. I never worked with anybody else who did that. But it was an extremely helpful way of doing a tolerable job.

'Redifusion [one of the first companies to win a terrestrial ITV franchise] had given us the job. The important thing for me was that it was in the run-up to the 1966 World Cup. Two weeks later they got me to commentate on England against West Germany in a friendly match that was won by England. After my first meeting with Jimmy, I did a few commentaries on him when he played. He was always a delight to commentate on because his attitude to playing football was to go forward. His art was seeing the situation in his mind's eye and offering himself; absolutely amazing. His control with the ball was extraordinary. From what I could tell, either foot. He would suddenly go on his own or pass. Tottenham were a good passing team at that time.

'A lot of Jimmy's matches would have been done by Kenneth Wolstenholme or David Coleman. I was the new kid on the block at that time and Motty [John Motson] came a couple of years after that.

'But I happened to do the commentary of Manchester City versus West Ham at Maine Road in March 1970 which was the last time Jimmy scored a debut goal for a league team. He had a knack of scoring in every first match, wherever it was, international or whatever. He did it for Milan, Chelsea, Spurs. Then he did it for West Ham in this match against Manchester City. It was just classic Jimmy taking an opportunity quicker than anybody else. I remember being quite pleased that he did that. And he got a second [in a 5-1 win for Hammers].'

Davies was at Wembley in the ITV commentary box for the 1966 World Cup Final in which England defeated West Germany, with Greaves out of the team having been injured in the final group game against France.

Barry said, 'I was one of the four ITV commentators at the 1966 World Cup. I covered the group which saw Italy beaten by North Korea. I did the quarter-finals, wrote the official report for the third-place match and suggested to [ITV head of sport] John Bromley to keep commentator Hugh Johns and summariser Dave Bowen at Wembley for the closing stages. I was standing behind Hugh for the final.

'Jimmy didn't play in it, of course. It was quite hard work holding back the tears at the end of the final for him as he hadn't played, wasn't it? Jimmy had the chance to help win a World Cup Final if he had played in Mexico 1970. This is something that is not brought forward. England might have been two goals up in the quarter-final against West Germany. If Jimmy Greaves had been playing they'd probably have been three or four up. But his international career finished pretty soon after England won the World Cup.'

Barry, who moved to the BBC from 1969, was flattered to be painted in a favourable light by Jimmy in his 2005 book, *The Heart of the Game*.

Jimmy wrote in the chapter headed 'Televised Football Has Become Chewing Gum For The Eye', 'In 2004, Barry Davies announced his retirement from the BBC. After 35 years with "Auntie", Davies decided to call it a day rather than be moved down the roster of BBC football commentators. I suspect it was not just demotion that prompted Davies to announce his retirement. Perhaps, like many of us, he was not too enamoured with some of the new commentators who now cover the game. Barry Davies, like the rest of his generation of commentator, was always impartial. When covering an England game, you never heard him use the word "us" and "we". Barry Davies always allowed the viewers to think for themselves with just two or three words on his part prompting such thoughts.'

Barry said, 'Jimmy must have followed what happened with me and *Match of the Day* quite closely and almost got it absolutely right when I stood down. It's flattering that Jim thought me a half-decent commentator.'

Barry was full of praise for the way Jimmy's broadcasting career developed, especially in ITV's *Saint and Greavsie*. He said, 'It worked like magic. I was always working on the other side with the BBC then. The BBC had a football programme but *Saint and Greavsie* was remarkably good and I think the BBC suffered.'

Of Jimmy's legacy, Barry said, 'Was it crazy he retired so young at 31? Absolutely. I don't think you can say he under-achieved because he scored goals at will, won trophies and was part of a remarkable time in Spurs' history. But whether he was often enough in a successful side to win trophies is questionable.

'The question of whether he achieved would have been moot if he had come to Tottenham a year earlier. Coming into the side which had just won the double must have pushed Jimmy a little bit.'

Barry believes there 'should' be a place for Greaves in any all-time world XI. Does that mean Jimmy would be beyond Lionel Messi in the modern day in terms of goalscoring when you factor in the pitches he played on and the heavier balls then? Beyond anybody? Barry said, 'I wouldn't give you an argument with that. When he got the ball or made a run, the chance of a goal was pretty high. His whole approach was to be positive, to go forward.

'I think that Jimmy would still have been supreme in today's game. Goalscorers are like gold dust no matter what system you play. It would have been an absolute failure by a coach today if he had Greaves available to him not to use someone who did things better than anybody else in terms of scoring goals. I think that his quickness of mind to see openings would be of most benefit. Jack Grealish has shown that too. Jimmy would be very happy to have a Grealish in his side as his provider.'

How would Greaves fare as a broadcaster today? Barry said, 'He would do perfectly well. Jimmy had his way, which was always chirpy.'

15

Terry Dyson

Team-mate

THERE WERE 39 steps which led up from the platform after getting off my train at Stevenage railway station. At least, it seemed like a reflection of the title of John Buchan's thriller classic novel. And what did I see when I reached the top of the flight of the stone steps? An advertisement for Dyson vacuum cleaners. It seems James Dyson, the inventor of these sucking machines, is the most talked about Dyson of today. But, to my mind, I was en route to another, unrelated individual more worthy of the limelight: one Terry Dyson. And I'm sure his former team-mate and friend Jimmy Greaves would have agreed. He achieved a series of historic football feats with – and without – Jimmy.

Among Terry's multitude of football achievements was a European Cup/Champions League scoring record only broken by Portuguese superstar Cristiano Ronaldo in November 2021.

Terry held the English club record jointly for netting in the opening four games of Spurs' run to the semi-finals of the continent's premier club competition in the 1961/62 season, before Manchester United's Ronaldo went one better.

The former Spurs winger remained at the time of publication the only Lilywhite to score a hat-trick against Arsenal. Added to that, he scored what the official Spurs website has described as arguably the most important goal in the club's history when his header from a Bobby Smith cross sealed the 1961 FA Cup and, with the league already won, the first double completed in England in the 20th century. To top it off, Terry put in a player-of-the-match performance in the 1963 European Cup Winners' Cup Final against Atlético Madrid to ensure Tottenham became the first British club to lift a major European trophy. And he did it in harness with Jimmy as they each netted twice in the 5-1 win. They also linked up the following day on the Heathrow landing strip in front of their plane posing with the glittering prize.

Terry welcomed me into the home he shared with lovely wife Kay, excitedly revealing how much he had enjoyed his first visit to the £1bn Tottenham Hotspur Stadium at the invitation of club chairman Daniel Levy in November 2021, an experience improved by Spurs beating Leeds United on the day.

We adjourned to his conservatory to talk Jimmy Greaves, beginning with the night the Lilywhites crushed Atlético. Next to England lifting the 1966 World Cup, it was the most significant 'first' triumph in British football history and led the way to a series of other home clubs tasting similar success.

Terry said, 'It was quite a night for Jim and myself getting two goals each. It was a big deal. The first time a British side had won something like that, of course, and Jim and I helped to achieve it. Although he got his goals, he just saw scoring as his job. I remember the picture by the plane. He wasn't shy, he just accepted what his role was. That scoring was his thing. There was nothing flash about Jim. A modest, ordinary lad, but funny with it. He was great, Greavsie.

'I heard he thought the Cup Winners' Cup Final was the greatest game he'd ever played in. I'm not surprised. It was one in which I was told I had the game of my life, according to Jim and others. I'm flattered.'

Terry remembered Jimmy's European debut for Spurs in the 1961/62 European Cup, in the campaign which saw the winger create his scoring record. He said, 'It was against Benfica in the first leg of the semi-final over in Portugal. Jim was brilliant. Class. He scored a couple of disallowed goals. It was one-way traffic in the second leg at White Hart Lane but they held out. We were a bit unlucky. We'd have won the cup had we got through. We had a good team and our final opponents would have been Real Madrid who had a great record in the competition but were going off the boil. We would have done them. I hear Jimmy felt the same.'

Terry was a team-mate when Jimmy made his Spurs debut in a reserve match against Plymouth Argyle at Home Park on Saturday, 9 December 1961, as the first team overcame Birmingham City 3-1 with the hosts seeking clearance to play the striker in the league. His new colleague netted – as was his wont on first appearances – twice as the Lilywhites ran out 4-1 winners. Terry remembered the whole experience of the trip, not just what happened on the pitch.

Dyson said, 'Bill [Nicholson] had just gone and got Jim from AC Milan. It was incredible he got him. A big fuss when Jim came to Spurs. They paid big money but Bill didn't care. He wanted him for the club, and decided to put him in straight away for this reserve match. I was playing for the reserves at the time. So was [former first-teamer and Wales international] Mel Hopkins, and we went down to the west country by train.

'We played and came back overnight on the sleeper. You can't imagine that happening today, especially with the top players. Cristiano Ronaldo having to use a bunk bed?! There was a coach waiting for us and we got back seven o'clock in the morning. It took us back to the ground and we got into our cars and went home. Bill gave us the rest of the day off. Good of him, wasn't it?!

'There was a big crowd for the game as Jimmy got his goals. Quite funny, in a way. Teams might normally have been expected to have tried to kick him as a big-name player playing his first game back in England. But Plymouth were quite good. Nobody tried to do that. There was a big crowd, about 13, 14,000 because Jim was

135

playing. There was a speech from the Plymouth chairman Ron Blindell before kick-off welcoming Jim back.

'He made his first-team debut the following week and got a hat-trick against Blackpool at White Hart Lane. Incredible.'

Terry recalled the 'wonderful' team spirit. He said, 'We all got on with each other and we were able to mix with the fans. Jim was great with the supporters. Nothing flash; happy to mix with them in the Bell and Hare pub on Tottenham High Road. He would be sitting with Dave Mackay and got fans to guess who was the tallest. Most thought it was Mackay because of his on-the-field presence, but it was Jimmy.'

Terry had been at Spurs since leaving the army in 1955 and remembered reading about Jimmy's goalscoring exploits during his days at Chelsea. He said, 'I learned he was scoring all the time from the papers but never played against him. When he came, of course, we had just won the double. There could have been a problem, but he was just accepted as he was a lovely bloke. I don't think he said much in the dressing room. Bill used to do all the talking. Then we used to go out and play and Jim used to score. Easy weren't it?!'

'Les Allen generally made way for Jim in the first team, although Les got two when Jim made his debut against Blackpool. Terry Medwin had got my place then, so I watched Jim's first appearance for the first team from the stands.

'Jimmy and I became big friends. I used to room with him when we went away. He was tidy, quiet. On the Friday, if we went away to Manchester or somewhere we used to go to the pictures, come back, and that was it. Go to bed, wake up next morning and get ready for the game.'

Terry underlined the 'knack' Jimmy had for scoring goals. He said, 'It was freakish how good he was in front of goal. He just had this knack. Miles clear of anyone in English football. Very dangerous in the box, nerveless. You couldn't tackle him because he was too quick with his feet and mind. He used to get done for offside because of his pace. He always said you have more time in the box than you thought you had. I knew when he had the ball and was one on one with the keeper he'd score. He was a poacher and also made long runs for goals, like the famous one he got against the Manchester United of George Best, Denis Law and Bobby Charlton. He was just unique. I don't know anyone as good as him. Lionel Messi's a good player who, in recent years, scored good goals as well. But Jim held the European record for scoring top-flight league goals for years for a reason.

'It is all the more remarkable when you compare the pitches we have today. Compared to our day they are like carpets. The pitch we played on at Tottenham could be like a ploughed field when it was raining. And we used to play in snow. There was one FA Cup tie against Burnley in January 1963. The pitch was covered but they cleared the lines and we played – and lost. I played with the number 11 on my shirt and Jim wore ten. It was the first match in defence of the cup against the team we beat in the 1962 final. Also the balls were heavier too back then. Jim would probably have doubled his goal tally today. It's brilliant he remains well known today. A lot of people still remember his goals and if you didn't you can see video recordings to help ensure you will not forget him.

'The crowd used to idolise him. The atmosphere was electric at White Hart Lane when Jim was on the ball. The opposition were frightened to death of him. He was exciting to play with. He took the pressure off us. He appreciated you needed your hard workers in the team like myself who followed what Bill Nick used to drill into us, "When not in possession, get in position." There's nobody like him now. Lots of good goalscorers, but nobody like him. He was definitely a one-off.'

Terry admired Jimmy for launching careers in broadcasting and as a theatre entertainer after being in the grip of alcoholism in the 1970s after retiring from full-time football, 'He was good on the telly, especially with Ian St John. The *Saint and Greavsie* TV show was quite funny, actually. I went to one of those shows. Jim didn't seem to care what he said. He was a one-off at it. It didn't surprise me he was funny. When we were team-mates he would be cracking jokes while chatting. He wasn't bad as a stand-up either, telling stories in that amusing way he had. I remember going along to his 70th birthday event at the O2 in London and he was very funny.

'He certainly got a firm grip on his drink problem and helped other people who had one. He would help anybody, Jim.'

Of where Jimmy would rank among the greatest Spurs players, Terry said, 'Right up there. You'd have him in your side all the time. Flipping heck, he'd walk into any side today.'

16

Mike England

Team-mate

MIKE ENGLAND smiled at the memory. He was alongside Jimmy and manager Bill Nicholson in the White Hart Lane dressing room.

Bill Nick had attempted to admonish Jimmy for his lack of effort in games, his target verbally fighting back in that good-natured way he had while England looked on.

Mike, an FA Cup winner with Jimmy at Tottenham, said, 'They used to say Jim was lazy. I always remember Bill Nick saying, "Jim, you don't work hard enough. If you lose the ball you've got to try and retrieve it." And he said, "No, no, Bill. Bill, I score all the goals and I need energy for scoring goals." Of course, everybody in the dressing room smiled. And Bill Nicholson, bless him, said, "Yes, Jimmy, I suppose you have a point, that's quite true." Bill was laughing and smiling. It was a nice moment.'

Mike believed Jimmy's cool, laid-back temperament reflected how he was pre-match. He said, 'Jim never seemed to have nerves. It was a piece of cake for him. He was always last in the dressing room. We'd go out and warm up, or get our shorts and trainers on and go to the gym. We'd do what they called the "shuffles" down the gym. And Jimmy would be outside talking to people he'd left match tickets for. Then he'd walk into the dressing room with ten minutes to go, take his clothes off and put them up on to the hook, put his kit on, and then walk out with us. He'd never been near the gym or anything! We always thought there was something wrong with him as he didn't do the warm-up in the gym. I really thought it was unusual. It might have been amazing that he would come in with ten minutes to kick-off after we'd been to the gym. But he just said, if I can get the Cockney accident, "Nah, nah, don't want to do all that. I'm not bothered about all that. I'm fine." And he was. When he came out, he did what he had to do.'

Did Bill Nicholson mind? Mike explained, 'Bill used to just go along with it. He didn't want to upset Greavsie. Bill was a strict disciplinarian from Yorkshire. But he used to let Jimmy get away with murder. Most of us would say, "Well you're telling us off, what about Greavsie?!" He just admired Greavsie's ability, his genius. He thought, "If he keeps scoring goals like he does and keeps performing like he does then maybe that's the best way to do it." Old Greavsie was a one-off.'

It was clear that although Jimmy was his own man, he was a popular figure to Mike and the rest of the Spurs staff. Mike said, 'Greavsie was Greavsie, a great guy. He liked to have a laugh, have a lot of fun. So popular. Besides being a super, super footballer, he was a lovely character. That's how he came across when he went on to do television.'

The former centre-half added with a smile, 'A real Cockney-like figure! The sort maybe if he had a watch, say, he'd try and sell you it! Amazing. Like, "I've got a few watches here. Anybody interested in a few watches?" He was brilliant.'

Jimmy's non-conformist approach served him well, particularly in the 1967 FA Cup Final. Mike said, 'Playing in an FA Cup Final is always very special in a footballer's career. Every footballer wants to win a league medal or he wants to win an FA Cup winners' medal. It's very important that you do that. You can look back at your career and can say, "I did that." We were all thrilled to bits to play in one. I walked out thinking, "This is my dream from when I was a little boy." But Greavsie took it all in his stride, that playing in one is something we should be doing, as if saying, "Well, playing in a cup final is what I'm here for. What I always wanted to do." That's how he was. And he had a decent game and we won, beating Chelsea. It was lovely.'

Mike was the last piece of the jigsaw as Nicholson built his second great team after the one which claimed the league and cup double and European Cup Winners' Cup. He joined from Blackburn Rovers for £95,000, a British record fee for a defender, in August 1966.

And he remained grateful to Jimmy and other players already there for helping him make the 'big step'. He said, 'At that time I was going to Manchester United and when that fell through, I went down to join Spurs. And, of course when I got there I met some of the players, like Jim, Dave Mackay, Alan Gilzean and Alan Mullery and thought, "Oh my God, I'm signing for a super club from London." Being from north Wales and Blackburn, it was a big, big step to take.

'Playing with Jim proved just a sheer pleasure. The guy was a genius. He made it look so, so easy. It was incredible when you saw some of the things he did. He went past two or three players and made it look like something you did all the time. A prolific goalscorer. He used to score goals and make it look such a comfortable thing to do. And that is a hallmark of a great player.'

Mike's arrival at the Lane came a month after Jimmy had missed out on England's 1966 World Cup Final triumph.

The Wales international, who later managed his country, said, 'Jimmy was unlucky and got injured. That upset him. He'd scored a few goals in the lead-up and helped England get out of the group in the finals. Overall he should have got more than the 57 caps he got for the player he was. I was very surprised he didn't get more.

'I played against him for Wales. I wasn't actually marking him but I was very pleased I didn't have to. I usually marked the big centre-forward. I felt very lucky that I only had to play against him a few times, and that he was a club team-mate. When I was playing with him he was a handful for any defender. You just had to admire the way he played. His balance and his control, his pace – he was quick, you know! So unpredictable – defenders couldn't guess what he was going to do next, which made him a little bit more special. He loved playing football. And he just took it all for granted. He didn't realise, I don't think, how good he was.'

Mike believed Jimmy was a 'shining light' when controlling his addiction to alcohol, which came to the general public's attention in the early 1970s. He said, 'The fact he took control was a shining light for people with similar problems. A lot of people used to listen to what he had to say because they knew he had had a problem and came through it. They wanted to know how. He did a lot of good work to help them, and tried so hard to help others. A super guy.

'I was delighted, of course, that he went on to have careers in television and theatre shows doing stand-up and Q&As. His super sense of humour came across in *Saint and Greavsie* on ITV. People realised what a gifted and charming fellow he was. He was brilliant.'

Mike recognised 'how difficult the last few years' must have been for Greaves, who was confined to a wheelchair after a major stroke in 2015. He said, 'I suppose looking back he could think that he'd had a super career, and did what he wanted to do. People admired him all over the world with his class and ability. He did what every little boy wanted to do. Jimmy Greaves was a very special person.

'I went to the funeral. I came from north Wales, drove all the way down there. It was a great tribute to him. So many footballers and people in the game went. They travelled distances to be there. I remember meeting so many people at it.'

In terms of remembering Jimmy, Mike said, 'I will always remember him as a really, really great footballer. When you start talking about great forwards he is right up there with them. I will also recall how it was a great privilege to have played with him. I will remember his wonderful sense of humour, his great character.'

Would Jimmy fit into any team today? Mike said, 'Of course he would, because of his sheer ability. Wonderful ball control. It was like the ball was stuck to the end of his foot sometimes. He was a goalscorer who made it look easy. At the end of the day, when you talk about super, super players, they are the ones that make it look easy and make you realise how much ability they have got. Also with Jimmy you could tell he just loved playing.

'The biggest tribute I can pay to him is that I feel he is in the same category as Pelé. World-class.'

17

Tony Fall

Rally co-driver

WHAT'S THE first thing we think of when Panama is mentioned? A hat? A canal? Whatever the mind conjures up it could never match the reality of what happened to Jimmy Greaves and partner Tony Fall in the country where South America meets North America.

Sure, they were in a motor-race event linked to football, but the experience was a universe, let alone a world, away from what football superstar Jimmy knew while forging one of the great careers in the planet's most popular sport.

Jimmy, the navigator that day, was getting some shut-eye as Tony, at the wheel of the pair's Ford Escort, was bombing along a deserted road in the middle of Panama's Nowhere Land at 100mph, keen to improve their top-ten position in the 1970 *Daily Mirror* London to Mexico World Cup Rally.

Out of that nowhere galloped a horse into the path of their vehicle and literally lost its head and life on impact to leave blood on the smashed windscreen and both their overalls.

It was, for Jimmy, the starkest of contrasts to the relatively cosseted existence of the professional footballer, made even starker by the duo wiping the blood of the tragic equine beast from the windscreen and buckled bonnet.

It was a scene graphically described in the *Tottenham Hotspur Opus*, a limited-edition history of the club and its associated individuals such as Jimmy, who had the month before swapped the Lilywhites shirt for the claret and blue of West Ham United.

It was just one moment in a series of character-building moments which helped convince Tony that Jimmy was not just 'a name' but a competitor who 'got used to' an event that turned into one where 'everyone believes it was the best rally ever', in the words of organiser John Sprinzel.

Tony, who passed in 2007, said in the *Opus*, 'Jim hadn't done any racing before this point, so Ford wanted me to get him through the race in one piece. I had to teach him what to do, so in reality I was the brains behind the duo and he was the name.

'Greaves was physically fit, but he found the rally pretty tough. He wasn't used to the conditions and the lack of sleep, but he got used to it after a while.'

Tony was an experienced rally driver who had won the tough 1969 Rally of the Incas in Peru with Sweden's Gunnar Palm.

He said, 'My carrot was a two-week holiday in the Caribbean with my wife [Patricia], courtesy of Ford.'

Jimmy had agreed to take part after an approach from Ford, who were keen to attract an A-list figure to take part. The company's press office revealed how their competitions manager Stuart Turner also wanted to 'test the theory that an expert in one form of sport has the ability, the quick-wittedness, the fast reactions and the nerves to perform just as well – after training – in an entirely different sport'.

The star lived near the car producer's Essex plant and knew people working there, and he wanted to lift his spirits after his football career had lowered them through Spurs axing him in January, while he had also been left out of the England World Cup squad to defend the title in Mexico.

Tony's first impression of Jimmy was a good one – but he wanted to see whether they would get on over the duration of the World Cup Rally. He said, 'They [Ford] introduced us and we got on very well, but before we started planning for the World Cup Rally, we went on a short trip in the car to Yugoslavia to see if we could get on over a long period of time.

'It was here I realised just how famous Jimmy was after we set off for Dover. We got to the docks and the car was mobbed. Even the Customs office emptied.

'We ended up at a hotel and as soon as he walked through the door the receptionist did a double take, rang everybody he knew and the nightclub downstairs emptied as we were mobbed by football fans.'

Jimmy also completed a gruelling training schedule which involved racing over the rough terrain of the British Army's tank-testing course in Bagshot to skid pans in Holland to find out whether he could cope with the demands of a rally which was considered, in 1970, 'the longest test of men and cars yet devised'.

The race, dreamed up by PR executive Wylton Dickinson, who had friends in the FA, saw Tony and Jimmy complete the 16,245 miles of the rally through France, Germany, Austria, Hungary, Yugoslavia, Bulgaria, Italy, Spain, Portugal and into South America via tropical floods, red dust and bumpy roads across Brazil, Uruguay, Argentina, Chile, Bolivia, Peru, Ecuador, Colombia, Panama, Costa Rica, Honduras and finally Mexico. Many of the countries driven through were represented in the 1966 World Cup finals. Tony did most of the driving, with Jimmy taking the wheel on the less hair-raising terrains, it was reported.

Jimmy's pal and new Hammers club-mate Bobby Moore cut pieces of the Wembley turf on which he had skippered England to their triumph four years earlier and put each one into all 96 car boots for the rally, before his national team manager Sir Alf Ramsey flagged the start at the stadium in front of 25,000 on a pleasant and sunny Sunday, 19 April.

And 38 days later Jimmy and Tony crossed the finish line sixth of 23 finishers – in a race which saw the deaths of a driver, an official and a cyclist – in the village of Fortín de las Flores, just outside the host nation's capital, Mexico City, which was to stage the 1970 World Cup Final. They were showered with flower petals. The pair had bloomed as a partnership.

Tony and Jimmy might have only been together for a few months to prepare and race but that limited time provided memories that would last a lifetime for Team Ford.

And, as you have guessed, there was plenty to get 'used to' besides that tragic collision towards the end.

The European section through Austria, Bulgaria, Yugoslavia, Italy and Spain tested what Tony described as Jimmy's struggle with 'lack of sleep'. Some stretches forced the pair to keep going for 55 hours non-stop, travelling up to 100mph on mountain roads 'built with only donkey travel in mind', according to Our Jim. Some roads, due to the speed of putting on the rally, remained open to the public who forced cars to swerve off the road and out of the race. There was even an earthquake in the Serbian stretches.

Tony and Jimmy had to negotiate a herd of wandering cows in the road during speed tests in Italy. But they still managed to finish two minutes quicker than all their rivals.

Tony discovered the size of Jimmy's appeal in the northern part of the country as football fans lined the roads at Camporosso, remembering his brief spell at AC Milan in 1961, although freezing temperatures produced icy surfaces which concentrated the mind.

Punctured tyres began to add to technical troubles the duo were forced to endure but they were closing the gap on the leaders, until near Lisbon and the end of the European section when they ran out of petrol and had to walk to the nearest garage to buy some with a $20 note.

They took a boat from Lisbon to Rio de Janeiro and chilled out on the Brazilian seaside resort's world-famous beaches, where many of the country's fabled footballers got their grounding in the sport.

Reality kicked in once more when the rally resumed as Tony and Jimmy undertook speed tests in the middle of tropical floods, which the footballer reported caused 'treacherous and dangerous' driving conditions on 'miles of flooded, cramped and bumpy roads'. There were also 'clouds of red dust' to see through as the 71 survivors of the European section were reduced to 52.

There was still a way to go and the next stage across the vast grass plains of the Argentinian Pampas to the Andean foothills was reckoned the 'toughest stretch of the race'. It more than maintained the physical and mental demands of the rally thus far. And provided 1,000 miles of 'treacherous paths and tracks', and the thin air at altitude cut the engine capacities by 50 per cent.

Tony said, 'It was difficult to breathe up there.'

Tony and Jimmy, at 15,000 feet in the Andes, lost a rear wheel having already used their spare close towards the end of the stage, so Fall pushed the car over the line with the footballer at the wheel.

The next stage saw them 'literally feet from death', according to Jimmy. Tony swerved by an 'old peasant woman' and, skidding, managed to bring the vehicle to a halt on the edge of the mountain before Fall manoeuvred the car away from danger.

Tony also recalled that he and Jimmy witnessed jaywalking 'local' residents perhaps in an alternate state of mind. He said, 'In some sections of the South American section – particularly Colombia – all the locals were chewing on the root [taking cocaine], and were out of their heads most of the time, so they would wander on to the road.'

Tony saw the excited effect that Jimmy had on the civilians of Peru, the initial stop on the home run. He was known to them as he had secured a hat-trick against their national side eight years earlier.

But Tony felt Team Ford's time on the road since Wembley, overall, had had a detrimental effect on the health of Jimmy and himself. He said, 'Our skin was taking a real hammering. We hadn't eaten any fruit or vegetables for weeks. The lack of vitamins was a real problem and we began to feel very ill.'

It looked from one photograph between stages that Jimmy, dressed in largely dark team overalls with light flashes and the Ford logo on his left breast, was feeling the strain of the whole experience. His head was lowered, a tired expression on his face and a day or two's hair growth around his mouth and chin with the potential to become a beard. Limp-wristed, he was handing an A4 notebook back to an individual who was largely out of frame bar his hand about to grip it. It was certainly in contrast to another image at the start line at Wembley where he was all smiles.

Only 32 cars made it to the Peruvian capital, Lima, which had recently suffered an earthquake. There were tropical monsoons and landslides through Ecuador. And the pair had to survive engine problems in Chile when their car 'broke down in the middle of nowhere'. Jimmy told how he thumbed a lift on a bus back to a garage the duo had passed only to discover it went the wrong way. However, they were eventually able to carry on and complete the final 100 miles to Fortín de las Flores.

Tony and Jimmy celebrated by jumping into a swimming pool with their clothes on. Tony had helped his 'celebrity driver' earn respect in a new discipline.

Graham Hill, the two-time Formula 1 world champion, said at the presentation of medals, 'It is an outstanding achievement for him [Greaves] to finish so high in a field against some of the greatest rally drivers in the business.'

Jimmy was full of praise for Tony and his ilk. He wrote in the book *This One's On Me*, 'If I had realised how hard the race was going to be, I doubt I could have summoned up the courage to face it.

'Those rally drivers are amongst the toughest and most fearless sportsmen I have ever met. There were times when I felt physically sick over the demands of the race, and several times I wanted to quit, but there was no way I was going to let Tony down.'

It all gave Greaves's wife Irene plenty of cuttings for her 30th scrapbook on her husband's sporting achievements, with Tony heavily featured too.

And Patricia Fall, hopefully, enjoyed her Caribbean holiday.

18

John Fennelly

Aficionado

JOHN FENNELLY revealed on 7 March 2022 that he was retiring 'at the end of the season' after close to 40 years working for Tottenham Hotspur. He had been club press officer for more than three decades, working with luminaries from Bill Nicholson to Glenn Hoddle to Paul Gascoigne, and members of the media. From 2015 he was the club's historian.

But before that, former *Tottenham Herald* newspaper reporter Fennelly, born in Dublin and settling in Cheshunt close to Spurs' training ground at the time, was a Lilywhites fan. And during this time he hero-worshipped Jimmy.

He said, 'Whoever once said that you should never meet your heroes clearly did not have the great Jimmy Greaves in mind.

'I had first seen the maestro in action on my debut as a schoolboy fan at White Hart Lane late in the 1965/66 season. It didn't go well as an overall occasion as we lost by the only goal to Burnley. But there was a magician on the pitch wearing a number seven on his gleaming white shirt.

'It was gleaming because it was so clean. Greavsie seldom seemed to have mud on his kit – unless he was barged to the ground by a bemused and befuddled defender saddled with the impossible task of trying to catch mist. And there was even less evidence of perspiration. By his own admission Jim was not a grafter and that apparent lack of industry would give defenders a false sense of confidence. Because when that chance came, he struck like a viper.

'Yet he didn't lack energy, just preserved it. As he often proved, he could go on runs from our own half and beat just about every opposing player before the inevitable rolling of the ball past a grounded goalkeeper.

'Bill Nicholson once told me that when Jimmy scored, the ball rarely hit the net. So, I looked back over many of his televised strikes and there it was. Greaves scored all kinds of goal and power was certainly on the agenda when it needed to be. But accuracy was the Jimmy Greaves speciality and with it little opportunity for an intended or accidental block.

'Yes, he was the club's greatest ever goalscorer and we were all proud of him. He had been first seen at the Lane making his first senior Chelsea start as a 17-year-old in 1957 and scoring – as he always did on his debuts.

'Indeed, he went even further on his first Spurs introduction in 1961 with a hat-trick against Blackpool to send the home fans into raptures. They all thought that the double side could not be improved on. But Jimmy Greaves did exactly that.

'It was goals all the way from then on and, although he never changed his style, he could never be marked out of a game because, no matter how much opponents studied his style, there was no answer to this evasive will-o'-the-wisp.

'He was the same in training at Cheshunt. If the session did not include a ball, he wasn't too keen. Fortunately, he was naturally fit and certainly well capable of doing his job on the pitch.

'I lived in that neighbourhood as a child and Bill Nick's love of a pre-season long-distance run meant that I would often see the squad jogging near my home. And Greavsie would always cut a lone figure way behind the main group!

'Although he had amazing precision and skill, he could also go direct in his pursuit of goals. A boot upfield by Pat Jennings, a customised flick header from Alan Gilzean and Greaves nipping through to slip the ball home. All my fellow Spurs fans of that era can simply close their eyes and easily summon up that vision.

'Losing Jimmy was simply tragic but the pain has been eased by the many tributes paid on television that showed the majesty of the man in his pomp as the goals rained in.

'When he left Tottenham for West Ham in March 1970 I did wonder. Mixed feelings. A school friend was in tears but my loss was tempered by the excitement of the incoming talents of Martin Peters. What would he bring?

'I watched the Peters debut at home to Coventry when he scored on what was a dismal day as we went down 2-1. Typically, Jimmy went one better. As we left the stadium in our gloom, the news came through that Greaves had bagged a brace on his Hammers introduction. That hardly helped the general gloom as we waited at White Hart Lane station for the train home.

'When I finished my apprenticeship as a sports journalist, I would often see him around but didn't speak with him until I arrived as the Spurs press officer in 1984. I remember a lovely handwritten letter from him in reply to my request for any club item that I could auction to raise funds for the Tottenham Tribute Trust.

'In it he explained regretfully that he had nothing left as he had given it all away, so generous was he in response to all such requests from fans. How I wish I still had that letter – what would that raise for our former players of his era now?

'But he was such a humble, generous man, with his time too, and never anything more than gracious as the fans respectfully approached. He was everything I wanted my schoolboy hero to be.

'One of my nicest memories of him had nothing to do with football. It came one Saturday morning when I was walking our two dogs on a small local green. A man was leaning over his garden fence and gave me a call. It was Jimmy Greaves. I didn't introduce myself so that he wasn't distracted from expressing his own canine affections and he could not have been more charming as he fussed over both dogs with a beaming smile.

'Never meet your heroes? Maybe. But then not all are Jimmy Greaves. A special man and a special player, and one who leaves us with special memories.'

19

Jeff Foulser

Television colleague

JEFF FOULSER revealed he worked with Jimmy when our subject was 'at his peak in a TV sense'.

Jeff was 'running live football for ITV' as executive producer when he combined with Jimmy on World Cups and *The Big Match* in the 1980s.

Only 24 when he took over production duties of the flagship programme *The Big Match* in 1976, he went on to become chairman of Sunset+Vine, a leading independent TV sports production and media company.

Jeff, who produced the 1988 Seoul Olympics for ITV, had guided the firm from one with just five employees to becoming an international host broadcaster in over 30 years, and remained active.

But he put the brakes on and kicked back when it came to talking Jimmy. Even the fact he was due to attend a meeting did not distract him as he told an assistant from his office, 'I'll be a few minutes. Start without me.'

Jeff was keen to talk about the football hero he worshipped as a youngster and the colleague he rated as having 'star quality' as a broadcaster. He said, 'Jim was an absolute natural TV performer. He had a fantastically sharp mind, quick wit. So warm and personable.

'As a TV man, I admired what he was and what he brought to television. He was someone who made you want to watch him.

I don't think it was intentional on his part. He was just very, very good at it.

'A bit like Brian Clough, but in a much different way. Cloughie divided opinion much more. People either loved or hated him but always watched him because he was always going to say something.

'But people loved Greavsie when he spoke on screen for his warmth, his sense of humour. I remember the first time I heard him say "it's a funny old game, Saint" when he and Ian St John were talking on the *Saint and Greavsie* programme.

'He was TV gold dust. When cameras were on he was away. He never gave it a moment's thought until the red light went on! And then he was just "Greavsie".

'He had something that few people have: star quality both on the pitch and in front of the camera. Absolutely no question about that.'

Jeff felt Jimmy would be a success given the qualities he had in front of the camera. He said, 'Jimmy was at Central TV but he was so good that he was picked up by the network for whatever it was. The World Cup and, of course, *Saint and Greavsie*. A brilliant double act.

'I never produced the show. That was the late Bob Patience [with Richard Worth] who joined ITV from newspapers. A real Glaswegian who had a great connection with Greavsie and [fellow Scot] Saint and did a great job, although they were so good they didn't really need producing.

'But I was always around because I was doing my live football, *The Big Match*, after Saint and Greavsie were on the air. There was a fantastic buzz around the show. And it got good ratings.

'I was a young producer. It was all fun at the time really. It was in a world where there weren't many channels; ITV, BBC1 and BBC2. That was it. And there wasn't much live football. Shows like *Saint and Greavsie* were shows where people got their fix of football. There were hardly any live matches a year on television, unlike today when there are dozens a week.

'People still talk about *Saint and Greavsie*. You need a bit of light and shade in covering football. The game is very serious. It's about money, power and all those things, but it is still a game and people still like to have a laugh. The programme was iconic.

'The Saint was always seen as the straight man, Greavsie the joker. But the Saint had a fantastic sense of humour and a really quick wit as well. He allowed Greavsie to be what he was – as he had a real appreciation of what Jimmy brought to the double act – but the Saint was the glue which held them together.

'Not surprisingly, I think Jim found it difficult to socialise with people after he stopped drinking. You always got a sense he was holding back a bit. I don't want to be critical about that at all. I think once you've stopped you must spend your whole life trying to keep away from it. He did that. Absolute credit to him. He didn't have a drink for God knows how many years – but drunk a lot of coffee! He was always in the studio going, "Who wants a coffee, guys?" He'd put the coffee on and make coffee for everyone.

'I would say I wasn't a friend. I was a work colleague, always at a distance. Maybe he didn't rate me, didn't like me, I don't know. Unlike Saint. The Saint and I became really good friends. We used to go to the gym together in the West End.'

How would Greaves fare as a broadcaster today? Jeff said, 'Coverage has changed now because there's so much more football, you've got to do something so out of the ordinary to get noticed now, really. It's driven by the data and the graphics. Different camera angles. People want to get more in-depth, why things are happening. The quality of production is really high now. And there are some very good pundits. But you don't want everybody to be like Gary Neville who is a really serious football man. You need someone to lighten it up a bit. It is not like life and death football, is it? Greavsie would have absolutely survived in this environment because he was so good. So would have Saint. He was a very perceptive analyst.'

Jeff's recollections of Jimmy the footballer remained as cherished as they had ever been. He said, 'Jimmy was my first hero as a young boy as a big Spurs fan. He was a god, really. I used to love standing on the Shelf at White Hart Lane with my mates and watch Jimmy. Fantastic memories from those days.

'We used to queue about three hours before the game, and get to our little position in front of a barrier. They were great times. I saw him score some wonderful goals. He was just a magical part of my childhood.

'I played against him once. I was in an ITV side and he lined up in a team of journalists. He got three goals in no time and was on a different level from everybody else. Quite extraordinary, really. I wasn't a particularly good footballer – cricket was my game – but you run around when you are fit and young and think you are all right. Then you play these people, like Jimmy. But it is still nice to say I played in a match with him.

'I will always remember him as my first hero. A fantastic footballer. I've become cynical as I've got older and met all these people. I've been very fortunate in my career to meet some great people such as Muhammad Ali and Franz Beckenbauer. And Jimmy was great.

'In the end they are just normal human beings. Yet when you are young you are impressionable. Jimmy made a massive impression on me. I still revere him as a footballer. He is absolutely a national treasure; the best pure goalscorer this country has ever had.'

Then Jeff prepared to leave his office for that meeting, saying, 'I'd better nip off and join it.'

20

Barry Fry

Manager

BARRY FRY let out a belly laugh when informed that legendary late skiffle singer Lonnie Donegan's recording 'Have a Drink on Me' was played at Jimmy Greaves's funeral (light-heartedly referencing our subject's well-publicised battle with alcoholism).

The ebullient Barry managed Jimmy at non-league Barnet and said, 'Greavsie would have insisted on that! Brilliant. That is Jim and his sense of humour all over. Lovely, lovely, lovely.'

Jimmy moved out of the Football League from top-flight West Ham United in 1971 aged 31 and played in non-league for most of the 1970s. Also performing for Brentwood Town, Chelmsford City and Woodford Town during the decade, Jimmy spent two seasons between 1977 and 1979 with the Southern Premier League club at Underhill.

Barry was impressed with the contribution of Jimmy, who netted 25 in 64 games for the Bees, including a hat-trick against Wealdstone and doubles versus Cheltenham Town, Camberley Town, Dover and Feltham.

The game's greatest top-flight goalscorer in many eyes even scored what he considered the best goal of his life while with Barnet. Greaves said in an interview with the late presenter and commentator Brian Moore, published on YouTube, 'My best goal? It was for Barnet against Grantham. Terry Price took a corner and hit it back 35 yards. I was on my own. And I hit it and the ball went to one corner, swerved and into the top of the other corner. I was so far out but I didn't half hit it well. It was a corker. I went over to the stand and said "take that you lot" and there wasn't a soul in it!'

Barry said, 'What Jim did for Barnet was miraculous. It was a joy and a privilege to be his manager. His attitude was fantastic. He covered every blade of grass. He was kicking it off the line one end and scoring at the other. He wanted to take throw-ins, corners, free kicks. Normally when you have a player like that coming out of the big time, it isn't like that. His enthusiasm for and knowledge of the game was brilliant. He helped so much. We had a lot of young players in the team and he certainly helped them by setting an example with his energy, work rate and, obviously, skill. To have a world-class player like Jim – and no disrespect – at poxy Barnet was brilliant!

'The opposition wanted to kick lumps out of him, as you can imagine. The only times Jim got into trouble with me was when he got sent off for retaliation a couple of times, although I don't blame him. I'd have done the same!

'He gave me a lesson which helped me as a manager. I remember giving him a b*****king once. He got through three times with the keeper to beat and he missed. So I said, "F**k me, Greavsie, when are you going to score?" He said, "The next time I get through, I'll score. The beauty of me is that I might miss 'em but I'll always be there." I've never ever forgotten that. I told all the strikers I ever had – and that is a lot in 32 years of management – what Greavsie said. That it was a case of "keep getting there and by the law of averages you'll score".'

Barry inherited Jimmy at Underhill. The man who was to lead Barnet into the Football League for the first time in 1991 said, 'When [predecessor] Billy Meadows left Barnet, I went in there. Jim was already playing for them. The chairman at the time was Dave Underwood, who used to play for Watford, Liverpool and

Fulham. He knew Jim – they were big mates – and he invited him down.

'I was amazed. Jimmy Greaves was one of my favourite players. A football hero for me. I think he's the best goalscorer ever. I really do. He not so much blasted it in from 30 yards but skipped over the turf, beat players and passed it in. He was absolutely brilliant. I saw him score the best goal I've ever seen. It was at Stamford Bridge. He was about 30 yards out and the ball came over his shoulder from a big punt from the goalie and he turned and swivelled and volleyed it in. I've never seen a goal like that. Timing was perfect.'

Greaves publicly revealed he was an alcoholic during his time with the Bees. He made his announcement in the *Sunday People* of 29 January 1978. He then abstained – bar one drink to celebrate being awarded an MBE in January 2021, revealed wife Irene in a *Daily Mail* article – from the following month until his passing in September 2021.

Barry said, 'I didn't have a clue about Jim's "problem". One day I read the front page, the back page and the middle pages about it. I thought "wow". We all like a drink, but I didn't know it was that bad. He hid it so well. He used to sit at the front of the team coach. Those days you brought a crate of beer on and everyone was having a beer but he never even drank on the coach. And he performed every single time on the field.

'We were only part-time and he didn't always come to training, but that didn't bother me because he always performed on the Saturday.

'I've nothing but love and admiration for Jimmy Greaves as a player, as a man. What he done when he came out about his "problem" was very brave. It shook a lot of people, but he controlled himself unbelievably well.'

Barry remained a member of the Jimmy fan club when his player and 'football hero' moved into television in the 1980s. Jimmy became a national treasure with his wit and charm on the small screen, most markedly alongside Ian St John on *Saint and Greavsie*, and in theatre shows.

Barry, who managed a host of clubs before coming director of football at Peterborough United, said, 'Not only football people did he make laugh, but Jimmy made the ordinary household roar. On that *Saint and Greavsie* TV show he was brilliant. Just a natural; off the cuff. He was fantastic.

'It was the greatest football show that there will ever be. Every lunchtime when my players were having a pre-match lunch somewhere we saw it. We fell about, p***ing ourselves. Why the f**k that show got stopped, I'll never know. Everybody in football and everybody who weren't in football in the whole country loved that show because of Greavsie's quick wit – and he didn't give a f**k what he said either. He'd just say it – and Saint would go under the table!

'As a player, no matter who you played for, who you supported, Jimmy Greaves was the best striker in the f***ing country. But more than that, when Jim was on the telly, he was the best comedian on the telly. It was the way he told them.

'Whenever Jimmy Greaves's name comes up it makes me smile. A wonderful man, on and off the pitch. When I phoned him and asked him to do me a couple of favours – to do a couple of after-dinners at Peterborough – he did. He was so good. Talking, signing autographs, having his photograph taken with everyone there. Those events raised much-needed revenue. He never refused me anything. He was always absolutely great every time I spoke to him.

'He also did a lot for Jimmy Hill, chairman of Goaldiggers, a football charity set up to help under-privileged kids. Elton John was involved in it. He was very good like that, Jim. He'd help a lot of people out, including those at Barnet Football Club. A marvellous man. But a lot of top players like Jim got stick from newspapers even if you give them 99 good things they'd done.

'The beauty of Jim, also, is that he was just a normal guy. No airs and graces. I've been very lucky to manage Jimmy Greaves and, at Dunstable, George Best [a Manchester United youth team-mate of Barry's]. George played five times for me as a guest. To have those two legends play for you, well, what an honour.'

Barry believed Greaves 'would grace the game today'. He said, 'You would struggle to put a price on him now when it is £100m for this player, £150m for that player. He'd be worth 500 f***ing million. He'd be top dog. The very top. He'd probably be the best f***ing player in the world. The way he used to glide by players! Even when I was Barnet manager, when Greavsie got the ball, I sat on the edge of my seat because I anticipated him gliding over the ground, beating a couple and either playing a good ball in or putting it in the net. He made it look so easy.'

Barry remembered later working with Jimmy while in charge at Birmingham City. He said, 'Jimmy made a great career out of television in the Midlands. Talking football, Greavsie was the main man. He was always on this midweek show [*Central Sports Special*] with presenter Gary Newbon. I came on it spasmodically.'

Just before those days, Barry took a call from Jimmy. It was the spring of 1993. Barry had just managed Southend United to second-tier safety at the end of a tense 1992/93 campaign before leaving for Birmingham. And he had explained publicly how Greaves's son Danny was the individual to thank for keeping Shrimpers up.

Barry said, 'I went from Barnet to Southend. It was on April 1 – I know I shouldn't have gone there! We had nine games left, bottom of the league by a mile. We won six of them and drew two, and we managed to survive. When I left in January the following year we were second.

'I wrote an article in the Southend paper, in my book, or summat, and what I said was we couldn't have avoided relegation without the enormous help of Danny, who was youth-team manager at the time. He marked my card on every player there and was spot on. He was brilliant. Jim rang me up when he read it, telling me, "I really appreciate that because there's not too many managers who would give credit to somebody else."

'But I said to Jim, "Danny deserves it. Without his contribution, we wouldn't have stayed up. Just stating a fact, mate." He said, "No, I appreciate that."

'I know Danny very well. In fact, I tried to get Danny to come and be a coach for me at Peterborough but he had to look after his dad. Danny looked after him for years and years.'

21

Alan Gilzean

Team-mate

ALAN GILZEAN, who died in July 2018, was one half of a prolific striking partnership with Jimmy Greaves at Tottenham Hotspur.

Spurs duo Harry Kane and Son Heung-min created a new record for Premier League goal combinations when the former supplied the latter in a 4-0 victory over Leeds United in February 2022. It took their all-time number up to 37 and pushed them one ahead of Didier Drogba and Frank Lampard of Chelsea. Interestingly, Spurs twosome Darren Anderton and Teddy Sheringham were fifth on 27 behind Manchester City's Sergio Agüero and David Silva, and Arsenal duo Thierry Henry and Robert Pires, both with 29.

But the Gilzean–Greaves axis impressed in front of goal decades before all of them. The pair were known as the G-Men, an expression still common, and used as recently as March 2022 by a punter telling his son about the hot combo while pointing to the cover of your author's official biography of Alan on the bookshelves of the Spurs Experience Shop.

And the Spurs fans loved them, chanting, 'We've got the G-Men in Greaves and Gilzean. They are the world's best goalscoring machine.'

Alan, who oozed class and guile, replaced the more bullish though skilled Bobby Smith alongside Jimmy for Tottenham in

December 1964. A prolific goal-getter for Dundee, Alan adapted his game to provide quicksilver Jimmy with a plentiful supply of chances, either with a flick of his boot or head.

I wrote in *King of White Hart Lane*, the biography of Alan, that they were, 'Clearly the perfect foil for each other, Gilzean largely supplying the bullets and Greaves squeezing the trigger.'

The fact Jimmy was the club's top goalscorer year on year – even in the 1965/66 season when he missed the opening three months of it laid low by hepatitis – was testament to the effectiveness of his partnership with Alan.

Alan's memory was pin-sharp when he recalled the double act he formed with Jimmy at a live *Spurs Show* podcast in 2013.

He said, 'When you lined up with the guy, he was so unassuming. No big-headedness at all. A right down-to-earth guy, but when he got on the park he was, ah, quicksilver. His awareness, calmness under pressure, and I've said recently that when I watch Lionel Messi now, that was like watching Greavsie all those years ago.

'I can remember watching Chelsea on the television. Their two strikers were David Cliss and Jimmy Greaves and I remember saying to myself [about Greaves], "This guy's some player." A few years passed and I went to watch Scotland playing at Wembley and England thrashed us 9-3! Greavsie ran amok. The following week, he was away to Italy.

'And the next time I bumped into him, I played for Scotland under-23s at Aberdeen and Greavsie was in the opposition. And again they beat us.

'It broke my heart the day he left Tottenham. I think he was rushed in to leaving Tottenham in a swap with Martin Peters.

'I had five wonderful years with the little maestro. And it was a pleasure to play with him.'

Alan pointed out that Jimmy was the best striker partner he ever had, and was even quicker than Messi, in a 2016 interview with Alan Pattullo for *The Scotsman*.

He said, 'The question I get occasionally – I played with Denis Law [for Scotland] and I played with Jimmy Greaves, who was the best player? In my opinion it is Greavsie. That's a shame because Denis is a Scot. I got on well with Denis, he is a great friend. But if you give a boy a ball and had to put a house on him scoring, it would be Greavsie.'

Jimmy credited a debuting Alan for making both his goals in a 2-2 league draw against Everton at White Hart Lane in December 1964. They netted one apiece in the next home game, a 4-0 victory against Nottingham Forest and shared four, with Jimmy bagging three, in a 5-1 FA Cup win entertaining Torquay, following it up in the same competition by firing five between them – Greaves scoring another hat-trick – in crushing Ipswich. Gilly struck a trio and Greaves two in a 5-2 win over Blackburn Rovers. There were countless other occasions that the G-Men were in full working order.

It was not all sweetness and light for the dynamic duo, however. There was frustration when Spurs, as a result of winning the 1967 FA Cup, returned to the European competition they won in 1963, the Cup Winners' Cup.

After the pair helped Spurs pip Hadjuk Split, they faced Lyon with the first leg – a 1-0 reverse in France – described by *London Evening News* reporter John Oakley as the 'Battle of Lyon'. Five Spurs players were injured, including Alan. Spurs' Alan Mullery and the hosts' André Guy were sent off.

Jimmy and Alan played in both legs. Greaves scored twice and Gilzean once as Spurs won the second leg 4-3 at White Hart Lane, but Tottenham lost on away goals.

Alan joked at the *Spurs Show*, 'The first leg was an enjoyable match! It was really funny [in the second leg]. I remember coming into the dressing room afterwards. Bill [Nicholson] got hold of Greavsie and me and gave us a right rollicking. We had scored four goals and the defence had lost three and Bill Nick blamed the forwards! Funny old world, isn't it?'

Overall, the pair were headline news together throughout their five years and four months alongside one another. Jimmy and 'his favourite strike partner' had a 'telepathic relationship' on the field.

Alan's son Ian, later a striker at Spurs, said, 'Dad became more a creator than he'd been at Dundee. He still scored a few but mainly he was the foil.' The pair's relationship off the field was limited due to not living near each other largely and it resulted in them eventually not seeing each other for over several decades after their playing days were over.

Jimmy had his personal problems in the 1970s before launching a two-decade television career, while Alan took a job outside the game in transport before moving down to Weston-super-Mare.

But through former Spurs team-mate Steve Perryman they reunited for a Sporting Club dinner event on Guernsey in May 2013.

In a story eye-witness Perryman elaborates on in a later chapter, they met up in a car park outside the hotel, 'showing their love and respect for each other'.

The G-Men also got together again following Jimmy's major stroke. In another tale covered in more depth elsewhere in this tome by Pat Jennings, Gilly and the goalkeeping legend visited Jimmy at his Essex home. The pair were making up for lost time but they had already built up a store of memories together which lasted them a lifetime. RIP the G-Men.

22

Ron Harris

Club-mate, opponent and colleague

THE SCHOOLBOY Ron Harris felt 'fortunate' to be a Chelsea ballboy as he was able to study the emerging Blues prodigy Jimmy Greaves from the closest of ranges pitchside.

The Stamford Bridge record appearance maker was to develop an on-the-field rivalry with Jimmy when the striker supreme played for Tottenham Hotspur in the 1960s, which Ron described as between 'the best English goalscorer of all time' and someone who was 'proud' to clip his wings.

And, eventually, Ron became a guest act for Jimmy on theatre tours, with his old club-mate having turned into a popular on-stage stand-up and raconteur in his later years. But Ron's earliest sightings of fresh-faced Jimmy burned deep in the memory of the defender who earned the nickname of 'Chopper' through the on-the-field 'treatment' he dished out to opposing attackers.

Ron was en route to joining elder sibling Allan on the Chelsea payroll. He recalled, 'I used to go to games with my brother Allan who was taken on the staff a couple of years before me.

'I would earn 7s 6d each match for being a ballboy. And I learned a lot from Jim and the other players. Apart from running after the balls and throwing them back, you were that much closer than the crowd and you could see things happen that much better. I was fortunate.

'Jim was in the team at 17 and you could see back then that he was an out-and-out, natural goalscorer. If you look at his track record it is second to none.'

Jimmy proved Ron had a point by scoring 132 times in just 169 first-team appearances for the Blues.

Jimmy was among what they called Drake's Ducklings, named after manager Ted Drake, a young group which included and was to include the likes of Peter Brabrook, Peter Bonetti, Barry Bridges, Ken Shellito, Bobby Tambling and Terry Venables. It provided the foundation of the team over the following decade and came in following the break-up of Drake's 1955 championship-winning side.

But Jimmy was an exceptionally precocious talent, making a scoring debut for Drake's team at 17 years of age in a 1-1 draw against Tottenham Hotspur at White Hart Lane in August 1957. He flew the nest to AC Milan in 1961 as Ron and his brother helped Chelsea win the FA Youth Cup.

Ron became an opponent when Greaves joined Tottenham Hotspur after a handful of months in Italy in an on-the-move year for the son of a Tube train driver.

And when the Blues and Lilywhites met between 1963 and 1969, it was mostly Ron who was commissioned to stem the flow of Jimmy goals. A daunting task.

But Ron, who went on to make a record 795 Chelsea appearances, was up for the challenge. He said, 'I knew, of course, that Jim could score for fun, and that he was quicksilver over ten yards. So I used to follow him everywhere. All I was doing was standing shoulder to shoulder with him. If he went out on the right wing, I'd be next to him. If he was on the left wing I'd be two feet behind him. I didn't worry about getting involved in the Chelsea build-up because my job was to stop people from scoring. I did that to people like Denis Law of Manchester United and Peter Thompson of Liverpool, and once [48-year-old England legend] Stanley Matthews playing for Stoke. I did ruffle him up, Stan.

The first time I ever got booed by the Chelsea fans, but, as I said, that was my job.

'Yes, Jim might have been quicksilver over ten yards, but you could tackle people from behind years ago, something you can't really do now. My motto was "you can run but you can't run without legs". Did I get Jim a few times like that? Oh, yeah. I used to try and get in nice and early when I followed him everywhere.

'We never spoke much at a match. He might have shaken my hand at the end, given me some verbals during the game. A few choice words. Probably called me a few names. That was it.

'It was only when we started working together on the theatre circuit that we became more and more friendly and I discovered you could not meet a nicer fellow'.

Ron reckoned he was 'taught a lesson' when Jimmy tricked him, to score in an early meeting between the pair.

After Ron had denied Jimmy a goal for three matches, Greaves was on target for a consolation goal as Chelsea overcame hosts Spurs 2-1 on 1 February 1964.

Harris, then 19, said, 'I hadn't been playing that long and we'd conceded a free kick. I was standing shoulder to shoulder with Jimmy and bear in mind I was a raw youngster. He said, "You are doing ever so well son and, I'll tell you what, have a look at the sky, Chop, it looks like rain." And of course – like an idiot – I looked up, didn't I? A Spurs player floated the ball to the near post and Jimmy scored with a header.

'It taught me a lesson and after that I just ignored him when he spoke. Once bitten twice shy. Off the field, fine. But I never got involved in conversations during the game. I didn't speak to anybody from the opposition.'

Jimmy became like a failed Houdini as he struggled to perform an escape act and hit the net again when shackled by Ron for the rest of their on-the-field rivalry. Ron said, 'I'm quite proud of that. I like to think I did a good job because of all the years I played against him and marked him. Maybe I need a pat on the back!'

One match in which Ron denied Jimmy was the 1967 FA Cup Final at Wembley. Ron became the youngest ever final captain, aged 22, and ended up on the losing side with Spurs winning 2-1.

The man who led Chelsea to the trophy in 1970 and the European Cup Winners' Cup a year later said, 'I was there to mark Jim and follow him around, which I did. We might have got beat 2-1 but maybe I got a bit of credit because he never scored a goal that day, did he? If I stopped him from scoring I'd like to think I'd done half of my job.'

Ron underlined that he was particularly 'proud' of his performances against Jimmy. He said, 'I think, as I've said, Jimmy Greaves is the greatest goalscorer this country has produced. Simple as that. The best goalscorer of all time. Jim would always be in my best XI. He's a lot of people's favourite player. If you chose your best ever Spurs team, for instance, he would be in it. Jim, Bestie and Denis Law were from an incredible era for football and would walk into a lot of people's best ever XI. What would he be worth in the market today?

'If you ask anybody from any football club for a list of top goalscorers, Jim would always be the number one. Scoring was what he was all about. He used to say, "Do you want me to chase the full-backs and not score or score two or three goals a game?"

'With the pitches he played on, it'd be more than likely he would have a field day on the carpets they have today. You played in the snow and frost at times back then. At Chelsea, half the pitch could be frozen solid [in the shadow of a stand] and the other half was soft. You would play at Wembley after the Horse of the Year Show had churned up the turf. Disgraceful! You just got on with it.

'Look at the number of goals Greavsie got when people used to slide in, tackle from behind. I'd like to see some of the goalscorers today being man-marked by Tommy Smith, Norman Hunter or myself. I bet they wouldn't score half the goals they score. Nowadays the football is pretty much non-contact.'

Ron, who had only missed a couple of games in the last 20-odd years as a Bridge matchday host, reasoned why he considered Jimmy so highly when comparing him to the Chelsea forwards of recent times.

Romelu Lukaku and Kai Havertz scored the goals as the Blues defeated Palmeiras of Brazil 2-1 to lift the Club World Cup in Abu Dhabi in February 2022.

And their strikes ensured the club completed victory in every competition open to them in the wake of Russian billionaire Roman Abramovich buying Chelsea in 2003.

Havertz was also the match-winner as Chelsea lifted the 2021 Champions League by beating Pep Guardiola's Manchester City in the final, but Ron believes Jimmy was better than the Blues' modern-day front runners. He said, 'They couldn't lace his boots. Football is completely different. Jimmy's role was purely to score.

'Everybody seems to play the same way. If goalkeepers make a save, you never see them pump it up the middle. They'll throw it to the full-backs and there's ten passes and their team doesn't get out of your own penalty area.

'Jimmy would be shouting "get the ball up early". Not only Jimmy. Denis Law, Peter Osgood and others would be doing the same.'

Ron appreciated getting to know Jimmy on a personal level when the pair came together for those theatre shows. He said, 'Jim used to be the first one on stage. He'd spend 25, 30 minutes talking about his career and then he'd say "got a special guest today, Ron Harris". I'd come on and we used to do a little session throwing questions to each other and then open the floor to people. There was always lots and lots of people there. They were there to see Jimmy. I was just a "special guest".

'It was something different. I enjoyed it and I'm sure Jimmy did. Good fun. He did it a lot longer than me. Getting paid for something you enjoy was good. We used to travel around the country. I was lucky to work with him and Terry Baker for a few years. He could have been a big-time Charlie with what he achieved in the game, but Jim was this terrific fellow who got on with everybody. He'd go out of his way to sign things. And he had a great sense of humour.'

23

Glenn Hoddle
Aficionado

GLENN HODDLE took his place in the gallery overlooking the ball court at White Hart Lane. Glenn would go on to be 'voted many times over the years as our greatest player', in the words of the official Tottenham Hotspur website. He won 53 England caps, played in two World Cups, managed the club and, in the global tournament, his country.

This day he was an up-and-coming 15-year-old looking down on 22 seniors battling it out in cramped conditions. The court's pitch was suitable for small-sided games. But 11-a-side? Well, that was another matter.

And there was one figure who caught his attention, triggering a lightbulb moment in the youngster's imagination. That figure was Jimmy Greaves.

Jimmy was preparing for his testimonial match against Feyenoord under the lights at White Hart Lane on Tuesday, 17 October 1972, in which he was, of course, to score, to the delight of 45,799 supporters.

Glenn, who signed schoolboy forms for Spurs that month, became an apprentice in 1974 and, a year later, a professional, making 490 appearances for the first team over 12 years.

But that day at the ball court remained ingrained in his memory half a century later. He said, 'I remember when Jim came back for the testimonial. He'd finished playing not too long before. He trained for a week. I remember watching him on the ball court from up top in its gallery; the amount of goals he got in such a short period of time in this 11-a-side in this gym. And the ball court wasn't a big area. You can imagine how tight it was. It was amazing to watch him.

'I learned off him that day. That he had a radar about him. He was forever looking over his shoulder to see the space behind him, looking to see where he was in relation to the goal. From my ten minutes watching him he must have scored about seven or eight goals. He was quite amazing.'

It came at a time Tottenham's all-time record goalscorer was 32 but had been retired as a professional for 15 months.

Yet Glenn believed Jimmy to be 'naturally fit'. He said, 'Jimmy was a genius at what he did, but I don't think he was somebody people would say drove himself fitness-wise. He was naturally fit, looking at his physique. He had that change of pace. That was born.

'Certainly when I watched him on the ball court that day he was still very lean and sharp. That's what he had. Also, his mind was quick. His feet were quick. He got away from defenders. Like every good striker he had this sixth sense, really, of where the ball was going to drop, where he'd be related to where the ball was going to go in the penalty area. My word, he had a wonderful finish. Two feet. He was left-footed but his right foot was as good as most people's. He had that natural goalscoring ability too.'

Our conversation meandered further back in time from Glenn's recall of the 'radar moment' to when his Spurs-supporting dad Derek first took him to White Hart Lane aged eight. Glenn first saw Jimmy live and the striker had a galvanising effect on him while watching behind a crash barrier on a packed terrace, along with those around him.

Glenn said, 'That really was the time I became a Spurs fan. I watched the reserves too. Dad used to take me up until I was 11 when I began to train with the club and was able to get passes into the games.

'I had a lot of memories as a kid watching Jimmy play. My dad and I saw big games against Liverpool, Nottingham Forest and Manchester United. It was such an era. Besides Jimmy, Manchester United had George Best and Denis Law. It all sticks in my memory.

'The thing about Jimmy was there was an expectation when he picked the ball up in the stadium. In that era, Georgie Best had that. Bobby Charlton had it. The atmosphere in the stadium changed when Jimmy was in possession. Things were going to happen. I remember thinking that as a kid. I think that says it all about Jimmy.

'He was a wonderful player. I was still a kid, wet behind the ears, watching football through the eyes of an eight-year-old, but you could tell he had that finishing touch. You don't gain that. Nobody coaches you that. Jimmy was a born goalscorer.

'Dad was an amateur footballer and a big Spurs and Jimmy Greaves fan. We moved out to Harlow. I had an older mate from round the corner who was a big Spurs fan and that was when Dad started to take me to see them. White Hart Lane wasn't too far.

'When people think of Tottenham, you think of Jimmy Greaves, Danny Blanchflower and their team-mates, when Bill Nicholson was the manager. All that era. They are the players people who saw them relate to, like the generations relate to players who played in my era. Now the current generation will probably be relating to Harry Kane in future years.

'When you think of Tottenham's history, Jimmy didn't play in the team that won the double but he was in that very successful period of time when Spurs were dominating. They were the best team in Europe to a certain degree as they were the first British club to win a major European trophy after, of course, being the first to do the double in the 20th century. And you think of Jimmy Greaves through that period of time. The focal point.

'Jimmy played in matches that were part of history with Tottenham. Other players come and go but Jimmy will always be remembered.'

Glenn has been voted as Spurs' all-time best player by many polls, but Spurs TV – the club's in-house channel – described Jimmy in such terms. 'That says it all,' said Glenn. 'Jimmy was a wonderful, wonderful player. He was unique. It was very sad when he left Tottenham. I don't think he was ready to leave. Probably a couple of years too early, to be honest. He achieved a lot at Tottenham. I think he probably wanted to achieve a bit more than he did, actually, getting there just after the double. But he had a couple of cup wins; yet as a finisher his record just speaks for itself. It is just incredible. He should always be looked at as one of the best player Spurs have ever had, if not THE best.'

Harry Kane has chased Greaves's Spurs all-time record goal tally in competitive matches of 266 in recent years and moved himself one spot behind our subject during the 2020/21 season, ending the following campaign on 248.

Glenn revealed he felt the duo would have made a good combination up front for the Lilywhites if the timing of their careers had coincided, 'Can you compare the two players? Not really. I don't think you can compare anyone to Jimmy, to be quite frank, as a finisher. And their styles of play are completely different. But they would have made a good balance if they'd have been able to play together.'

Glenn managed the likes of prolific strike duo Alan Shearer and Michael Owen, who helped his England team reach the last 16 of the 1998 World Cup. Shearer, who scored a record 260 Premier League goals, also guided his country to the 1996 European Championship semi-finals.

In total, Shearer managed 30 in 63 and Owen 40 in 89 for England. Greaves netted 357 top-flight goals and 44 in 57 for the Three Lions. So would Glenn have put Greaves in ahead of them for his England squad? He replied, 'Jimmy would have been at the top in any England team selected at any level. His record really does speak for itself. The records are there for Alan Shearer and other England strikers. But Jimmy is a cut above. Look at the amount of games he played. He didn't need over 100 games to score those goals [all-time leading England scorer Wayne Rooney posted 53 in 119]. His ratio of scoring is phenomenal. Forty-four in 57 games. No one is ever going to do that again.'

When asked where he would place Jimmy on the list of the game's goalscorers, Glenn said, 'Well, the thing is, with any great player – and Jimmy was a great player – you look at different eras in football. You just know Jimmy Greaves would be scoring a bundle of goals whether it was today or in the 80s when I played or in the 90s. Every era. Even before he made it through. Going back to Stanley Matthews's day. Back then, Jimmy would have been scoring goals because he was a natural.

'It's a little bit, like I've said about myself in many ways, I didn't choose football. I don't think Jimmy chose football, football chose him. He could have played in any team.'

Would England have won the 1998 World Cup in France with Greaves at his peak? Glenn said, 'Well that's a big hypothetical question! We would have had more of a chance with players like Jimmy Greaves in our side, of course we would. But it doesn't guarantee you, does it? It would have been lovely to have worked with someone as good as Jimmy. Every era you've got quality players. And that will continue in the future.'

Glenn sympathised with how things turned out for Greaves in the 1966 World Cup, and how he missed out on a place in the final having been injured during the group stage. He said, 'That it didn't happen for Jimmy was something very sad for him. I know Jimmy Greaves and Geoff Hurst eventually played together at West Ham, but they would have been a fantastic blend as a strike force. Roger Hunt was a good player as well, but you look at the attributes of

Jimmy and Geoff. Those two as a unit together would have been absolutely a perfect balance.'

A feature of England's World Cup success was Ramsey's decision to play without wingers, adopting a 4-4-2 formation that was more about the team than individuals. But Glenn remained convinced Greaves would have still thrived in it. He said, 'Alf had England playing in a very rigid 4-4-2, no wingers, but Jimmy would have been lethal in any system. It wouldn't have mattered to him. He would have scored goals. If he hadn't have got injured he could have scored as many goals as anybody else.'

Jimmy and Glenn both played abroad during their careers. Jimmy moved from Chelsea to AC Milan for £80,000 in June 1961 before returning to England and Spurs by the end of the year.

Greaves wrote about his largely unhappy time with *I Rossoneri* in his autobiography, 'I'm a home boy ... the simple pleasures of London life. I had got involved with Milan for mercenary reasons.'

Hoddle enjoyed four years at Arsène Wenger's Monaco after leaving Spurs in 1987. He said, 'I went abroad for different reasons to Jimmy, I think. I went at what was at the back end of my career – or rather in the middle of it really – at 27, I felt experienced enough. For Jimmy to go back then was tougher. It was probably the nature of Jimmy. The way he was with playing club football in England, the team spirit, the team-mates. I think he would have lost a bit away from all that. If you are not happy as a person you are not going to be happy as a player. You are never going to get the best out of yourself.

'My experience was totally different. My arms were opened up for it. I was embracing it. It was something I wanted to do – challenge myself in a style of football abroad that was going to be more conducive to me than it was in England, in an English system. I was delighted to go, and very, very pleased I went. I enjoyed every second of it. When looking back, Jimmy probably thought that it was a mistake to go. But it wasn't. It made him feel it was so much more worth coming back to England and playing in English football. You learn from every experience.'

Glenn followed Jimmy into broadcasting and the former was impressed with the way Our Jim adapted to become a television presenter, commentator and pundit, especially on the legendary *Saint and Greavsie.*

Glenn, who has worked for ITV, ESPN and BT Sports, said, 'Jimmy was a bit of a pioneer. He worked with Ian St John quite a bit. I didn't really work with Jimmy. I might have shared punditry of a game but if so that could not have been many times. Jimmy was great fun to watch on television. He did it in his own unique way.'

Glenn was impressed by the strength of character displayed by Jimmy to come through the dependency he had developed on alcohol in the 1970s to forge his broadcasting career. He said, 'There's a multitude of reasons why people go through that [the drink problem] – maybe through one or two other problems, but, at the end of the day, the main thing was Jimmy came through it. He showed his mettle, his frame of mind, his character.

'When you are a top sportsman like Jimmy you can't not have a strong character. You wouldn't make it as a sportsman if you didn't. I think he showed a lot of people the way. He was a great, solid and positive example. Credit to him.'

Glenn believes Jimmy's memory will live on. He said, 'I met him a few times at his golf days. We'll still continue doing a few golf days, I think, for the Jimmy Greaves Foundation's charities.'

24

Sir Geoff Hurst
Team-mate

SIR GEOFF HURST sat in the yellow glow of a bright electric light in his backstage dressing room talking Jimmy Greaves. It was around half an hour before show time and followed a meet and greet on stage with guest fans. The illumination exposed how he had defied the ageing process, having reached the 80-year milestone. Lean, dapper, in a grey suit, light blue shirt and matching diagonally striped tie in a darker shade, and eyes that twinkled; you could also see in those peepers and his body language as clear as a sunny-blue-sky day that he meant every word. The Jimmy he knew was important to him and he was expressing that importance in affectionate, erudite and honest fashion.

Geoff and Jimmy were international and club team-mates, for England and West Ham United, experiencing contrasting fortunes in the triumphant summer of 1966.

Geoff was immediately installed as a national hero after scoring a treble in the World Cup Final, became a Sir in 1998, and enjoying life as star of the show on theatre tours, sharing memories and views to entertain and captivate audiences around the UK.

Geoff, who was getting ready for a show at the New Theatre in Peterborough, said, 'The Jimmy Greaves I knew, of course, is one of the greatest goalscorers we've ever seen, if not the greatest. His record just speaks for itself. Absolutely astonishing. You don't use the word genius in many walks of life, but you'd have to use the word genius when it comes to Jimmy for scoring goals.

'The Jimmy Greaves I knew personally was one hell of a nice guy, with an unbelievable, wicked sense of humour which came across. Terry [Baker, master of ceremonies at Hurst's shows] did a lot of stage shows with Jimmy. And Terry [in a baggy T-shirt displaying the image of late musician Jimmy LaFave as he'd left his suit behind on the previous stop on the road] talked earlier at the pre-show meet and greet tonight about not being particularly well dressed when he spoke to the guests. If he'd have been with Jimmy and that had happened, Jimmy would have taken the mickey out of him. And Jimmy would have been so funny doing it. I said to Terry, "It doesn't matter how badly you are dressed, I wouldn't have been able to have a go at you like Jimmy. I'm not as clever as that."'

Geoff told of how Jimmy had been a 'boyhood hero' and that he displayed his doe-eyed devotion to him when he randomly met the person he had put on a pedestal the year before establishing himself in domestic and global folklore.

He said, 'I remember bumping into Jimmy in October or early November 1965. It was before I'd played for England, while he was a world-class player. I can tell you where it was – Romford in Essex.

'I was shopping with Claire, my daughter, who is sadly no longer with us, and had just been born. I passed this shop. It was a tobacconist shop. Jimmy smoked a bit, as we know. I saw him, went in there, said hello and started talking to him. I was so engrossed, in awe of Jim really, being a non-international while Jim had been playing at the top level for about eight years. One of the greats. Just fantastic, a boyhood hero. I walked out the shop having been talking to him and I'd left my daughter in a pushchair in the shop!'

Geoff and Jimmy are, of course, inextricably linked in English football's most famous story; 1966 and all that, to nick the title of the hat-trick hero's autobiography.

And he was telling me all about it in those last moments before he hit the stage. 'It is always a pleasure talking about Jim,' he said.

Geoff had written his name in the record books with that most famous of hat-tricks at Wembley on Saturday, 30 July 1966, with Jimmy looking on from the sidelines. He had taken over from Greaves after our subject had helped his country qualify for the knockout stages, and kept his spot through to the final after scoring the lone goal against Argentina in the quarter-final and aiding a 2-1 semi-final victory against Eusébio's Portugal after Greaves was left nursing 14 stitches in a deep shin wound sustained when France midfielder Joseph Bonnel's studs raked his leg in the final group match, which England won 2-0 to go through.

Jimmy had hung on to what he thought was a mere 'one per cent' chance of making the team for the final. But the fact Geoff got his trio of goals – the first with his head, the second with his right foot and the third with his left – against West Germany obliterated any argument as to whether he should have played.

It was just that Jimmy was THE goal king of his age – of any age – and loved by English fans no matter the hue of their club's colours; no wonder, having scored 43 in 54 internationals going into the finals.

Jimmy himself later said Alf Ramsey was right to keep the side which had performed so well in his enforced absence.

But it didn't stop him feeling 'devastated' at missing out as the inventors of the game sealed its most prestigious trophy for the only time to date. And he skipped the celebration dinner because, dispirited, he did not want to be a party pooper.

A lot of water has flowed under the bridge but the ins and outs of the tale have retained an endless fascination.

Geoff said, 'There must have been unimaginable disappointment for Jim that he wasn't playing but I was just thrilled to have a chance of coming back in the team. Not for a second would I feel "poor Jimmy" because it was part and parcel of the game as it was then.'

Geoff said that 'not for a second' did Jimmy's injury take the edge off his feat, adding, 'We didn't speak about his injury. Never, ever remotely touched on it. The strange thing about Jimmy and I; I admired him tremendously but we never spoke about injuries, about why he was out, how he felt. I read, naturally, about how he felt. He wanted after the final to just go and leave, get away from the whole thing. Even when Jim came to West Ham for a season or two, it was never ever discussed. We probably didn't do so because at the time we played in, injuries, illness and form were just part and parcel of the game. But I know he must have been bitterly disappointed.

'Jim's performances in the qualifying matches were fine. Jimmy said himself he'd lost that extra yard after contracting hepatitis in the lead-up to the 1966 finals. It was, I think, quite a significant illness for him. Anyone with hepatitis would know. Physically you are not quite the person you had been. In football terms, which Jimmy talked about, if you lose that half a yard even, it makes a difference to scoring goals and not scoring goals. And that was leading up to the 1966 finals, although he was in the team. I still think he would have played in the final had he not been injured against the French before the quarter-final.

'So as much as Jimmy was slightly off his best because of that serious illness, there was no question at all of him being left out. I mean to such an extent it would have been a huge risk from Alf Ramsey's point of view to leave out one of the greatest goalscorers there's ever been if he had been fit. The repercussions would have been very difficult for Alf had we got beaten. Remember, there were no substitutes then.

'I've never heard before, during, after or since, there was any kind of rift [between Jimmy and Sir Alf]. All I would say is – and this is just a guess – that Jimmy was such a laid-back, fantastic character with a great sense of humour and that in itself may not have quite fitted Alf's unbelievable discipline.

'We've certainly never had a goalscorer like Jimmy. No one has. He was world-class. We were lucky to have a backbone of world-class players in 1966. It is correct and absolutely spot on to state Bobby Moore, Gordon Banks, Ray Wilson and Bobby Charlton, with Jimmy, were. We've had some great players over the years. People like Frank Lampard Junior and Steven Gerrard. Wonderful players. But have we had a backbone as good as the one we had? I'd say probably not.'

Geoff revealed how Greaves almost helped increase his chances of scoring even more than three in the World Cup Final, 'We might not have discussed some things, but one thing we did touch on was what boots to wear. We did have that conversation. Jimmy felt ones with moulded soles gave him an extra half a yard. That was his line. So I wanted to wear them in the final.

'I didn't in the end because it rained on the morning of the game and the pitch was quite cut up. I did, though, always try to wear moulded soles when I could and they appeared to work.'

Hurst had been the odd one out of three when Ramsey named Greaves and Roger Hunt – who both passed away within eight days of each other in September 2021 – as his front two in a 4-4-2 system for the opening game of the finals against Uruguay, which ended goalless.

He said, 'I was vying with two of the biggest players, at two of the biggest clubs, you've ever had in Jimmy and Roger, who were, of course, with Tottenham Hotspur and Liverpool respectively.

'Looking back, there were two things. I never believed I'd play for England anyway. That was never on my radar. And I was competing for those two spots with those other two players. I probably thought I was best suited to playing with either Roger or Jimmy. I was taller and better in the air than either of them. So it would probably have been a better balance.

'Alf went with Jimmy and Roger. I hadn't scored that many goals in the warm-up games. Jimmy and Roger had got a few. I got one in my second game, a 4-3 win in Scotland, playing with Roger, who got a couple. I played with Jimmy in the next game. It was against Yugoslavia and he got a goal in a 2-0 win for us. I also played with him in a win against Denmark. Jimmy got four against Norway playing with Roger. But I got in, of course, when Jim was injured.'

It had seemed as though Jimmy might, though, have had a shout of partnering Geoff internationally at the 1970 global jamboree in Mexico as late as the previous summer, after finishing top of the top-tier goalscoring chart for a record sixth time.

But Geoff was unable to test any theory that a partnership with Greaves in England's defence of the World Cup in Mexico would have the edge over one with Hunt, as neither made the squad. 'Sir Roger' had moved down to the second tier to join Bolton Wanderers in December 1969, while Jimmy was axed by Spurs following a disappointing FA Cup performance against Crystal Palace and later reflected, 'Deep down I knew there was little chance of Alf giving me a telephone call.'

Jimmy was stuck in the reserves, committing to compete for Ford in the London to Mexico World Cup Rally and joining Geoff at West Ham.

Geoff and Jimmy – and England captain Bobby Moore – got together at club level in March 1970. Jimmy, who began his Spurs career in a reserve game at Plymouth Argyle, signed it off in another against the Pilgrims, having been unable to regain his first-team spot after that FA Cup defeat to Palace.

Jimmy joined Geoff and Bobby at a struggling West Ham in a swap deal for Martin Peters, who made up the east London club's contribution to England's World Cup success.

Jimmy scored twice on his Hammers debut in a 5-1 win against Manchester City at Maine Road, while Hurst also netted a double, on Saturday, 21 March 1970. He went on to amass 13 goals in 36 starts for West Ham before calling time on his full-time professional career at the end of the 1970/71 season.

Geoff said, 'Maybe Jimmy didn't want to be part of the deal with Martin going. I don't think he was totally happy. I think that was quite evident. He's a Spurs legend, I understand that, particularly in light of the bit of rivalry between Spurs and West Ham. But, the clubs had the power in those days. Players didn't possibly have the power and strength to stand up to them. Jimmy didn't with his move from Spurs. I had a similar situation myself when Manchester United offered big money for me and the club just said "no", something that has never been an issue for me at all, though.

'Whereas today the players have more of the power with the moves. If it had been today, both Jimmy and I probably would have said, "No, we're under contract with our clubs and don't want to move."'

Geoff felt that Jimmy was fading as a player when he joined the Hammers, 'He was getting to an age. He'd the hepatitis which I think affected him. Also, he'd been at the top since he was 17, playing top-class football at an unbelievable level. By then he'd had quite a long career and so nature plays its part, particularly as a front player. You lose that half a yard. It happened to me.

'He had a fantastic career. Whatever age he finished, he still had the most unbelievable career. Look at Bestie [George Best] who retired around 27 which is normally the peak of a player's career. You can't knock Jimmy at all because he was absolutely unbelievable. His record at Chelsea, Spurs and England is just phenomenal. Even at West Ham. You used the word fading, but I think he got 13 goals in 30-odd games. These days if he scored 13 goals in 30-odd games he'd probably be worth about £200m.'

Jimmy revealed his addiction to alcohol in 1978, but Geoff was adamant that he 'never heard any whispers at all' until then; 'I didn't have any knowledge whatsoever about Jimmy having a drinking problem until I read about it in the press. The fact I had absolutely no idea whatsoever goes back to what I was saying earlier. Important subjects between players like drinking, loss of form or injuries were not talked about. Not for one second.'

Geoff has come through hard personal times and lavished praise on Jimmy for being able to control his addiction and go on to successful careers in television and entertainment. He said, 'What he achieved to come back and stop drinking and become a celebrity on *Saint and Greavsie* and the column he wrote was just absolutely fantastic; you can't possibly give the man enough credit for the way he got himself out of that awful alcoholic problem. It showed a strength of character, personality and determination.

'It is amazing that someone with that problem can just say, "I'm not drinking anymore." He didn't drink at all from that point and had fantastic careers on television and theatre, as well as getting his family back.'

For Geoff, Jimmy will always remain one of the greats in football. He said, 'As I've said, he was world-class. And with the record of goals he got, you would have to put him up front in any all-time best England team. Without argument.

'As well as his international goals record, and up until Cristiano Ronaldo passed the figure a couple of years ago, his total league goals of 357 was the best in all of Europe's major leagues. He had a great career with Spurs but not much is touched on about his time at Chelsea. He was only 17 when he got in their team and got 130-odd goals in 160-odd games. Astonishing, as he was so young. And he'd scored millions of goals as a kid for the Chelsea youth team. He was so natural.'

Geoff connected with his audience at Peterborough's New Theatre in a light, easy-going, humorous style; a class act. After the show, which helped raise funds for the Jimmy Greaves Foundation, it was straight out of the stage door and a drive to the next stop on the tour to spread the word of an extraordinary football life mixed in with another at least as extraordinary.

25

Pat Jennings
Team-mate

PAT JENNINGS OBE had just returned from a sunshine golf trip to South Africa, happily chatting in a circle in the newly opened lounge at Stevenage Football Club. Spurs' most feted goalkeeper was impeccably dressed in a suit, club tie and crisp white shirt; instantly recognisable, with his thick hair over his ears, despite having retired as a player 35 years earlier.

Pat wanted to be there to support his friend and former team-mate Jimmy Greaves at a film night – the only public screening of BT Sport's *Greavsie: The Jimmy Greaves Story*, to help raise funds for Jimmy's health battle. It was 20 February 2020, Jimmy's 80th birthday.

Less than a month later, the country was in lockdown due to the Covid-19 pandemic, which remained prevalent into 2022.

But in between, sadly, we lost Jimmy, and Pat was there in support at the funeral in the deceased's Essex heartland on 22 October 2021.

The charming Pat, one of nature's gentleman and the ultimate template for an idol, is one of the most supportive of people, attending charity functions every day in the week leading up to that Christmas.

But Jimmy gave Pat a special, personal reason for wanting to support him. It goes back to the summer of 1964, when Spurs were in transition after the most glorious period of their history. Teenager Jennings joined the club for £27,000 from Watford; one of the new boys on the block, with Alan Mullery, Cyril Knowles, Jimmy Robertson and, in the December, Alan Gilzean charged with somehow trying to help Bill Nicholson develop a side capable of emulating the Glory Boys who had immediately preceded them. A daunting task for anyone, let alone a wet-behind-the-ears goalkeeper.

But Jimmy, a star member of the Glory Boys, gave Pat the 'confidence booster' which helped transform him into one of the world's greatest stoppers.

Six decades after his arrival in London N17 aged 19, Pat remained forever grateful for the backing Jimmy gave him.

He had had just 12 months of experience of English football, of living in the country after leaving the family home and his first club in Newry, Northern Ireland, when Jimmy and co at the Lane first clapped eyes on him. He was thrown in the deep end.

Pat attended the funeral of John White, the lynchpin in Spurs' league and cup double-winning side, immediately on joining the club. And just under a month later – at White Hart Lane on Saturday, 22 August 1964 – he made his debut in the season opener against Sheffield United, alongside Jimmy, who scored, as Pat managed to keep a clean sheet.

But more erratic displays followed, and he was in and out of the team, sharing the number-one berth with Bill Brown, the stopper who had been part of the Spurs side to achieve the double in 1961.

Yet Jimmy was there for Pat; a crutch for the rookie Irishman to lean on exactly when he needed it.

And, to underline the point, Jimmy's efforts helped lay the foundations of the greatest of careers which might have floundered but for his intervention.

Pat said, 'Jimmy was a proper gentleman, a lovely, lovely man and I'll always thank him for what he did for me when

I arrived at White Hart Lane as a teenager. It was such a confidence booster.

'I had been playing in the Irish B League 15 months earlier and joined Watford who were a struggling Third Division [today's League One] team. All of a sudden – aged 19 – you are joining Tottenham of the First Division. They were so good at that time, just coming off being the best team in the country. That gave you an idea of what I was up against.

'There weren't any goalkeeping coaches in those days and I'd had no experience, really. You just had to learn through your mistakes. I'd be parrying shots instead of holding. You might have got away with that in the Third Division, but not the First. People at that level always cashed in on your mistakes.

'One day, Jimmy came over and told me, "Don't worry, you are going to be the best." It was a learning process for me at that stage and he could have pointed out something in a game and said, "You should have done better there." But he didn't.

'What he said meant the world to me, coming, as it did, from someone of his stature, the world's greatest goalscorer. To say what he said gave me all this confidence. You don't usually expect those sort of people to be so down to earth and thoughtful. It was incredible for me.'

Pat felt 'everybody loved' Jimmy. He said, 'Not only because he was a fantastic goalscorer, a fantastic player, but just for the person he was. I don't know anybody who has had a bad word to say about Jimmy Greaves.

'When he went on to TV and did *Saint and Greavsie,* people loved him. He was a complete natural at that as well, always brilliant on the interviews, always easy-going. Never had a bad word to say to anyone even to knock a reporter back. His sense of humour was always there.'

Pat compared and contrasted the characters of Jimmy and the goalkeeper's Northern Ireland team-mate George Best, another

Frank Blunstone with Greaves and Chelsea manager Ted Drake (A)

Barry Davies (The Barry Davies Collection)

Terry Dyson and Greaves, European Cup Winners' Cup heroes with trophy (A)

Mike England celebrates 1967 FA Cup triumph with Greaves (A)

Tony Fall with rally co-driver Greaves (A)

John Fennelly (TH/GI)

Jeff Foulser (second right) with (from the left) Brian Moore, Jim Rosenthal and director Ted Ayling
(The Jeff Foulser Collection)

Barry Fry with Jimmy Greaves (Peterborough United)

Alan Gilzean and Greaves reunite (The Steve Perryman Collection)

The G-Men (TBC)

Ron Harris (far right) next to Greaves with Steve Perryman and Alan Gilzean looking on (TBC)

Glenn Hoddle (far right) with Greaves (second left), Daniel Levy, Cliff Jones and Martin Chivers plus (in front) Steve Perryman at Bill Nicholson's memorial service at White Hart Lane (A)

Geoff Hurst and Greaves at West Ham (A)

Geoff Hurst with Greaves (TBC)

Greaves with World Cup winners, including Martin Peters (back, far left) and Roger Hunt and Geoff Hurst (far right) (TBC)

Pat Jennings with Greaves at Spurs (A)

Cliff Jones and Greaves (A)

Harry Kane (TH/GI)

Dave Kidd (The Dave Kidd Collection)

Dave Mackay hugs Greaves with Gordon Banks and Bobby Charlton looking on as the Royal Mail issues stamps of them and seven other 'Football Heroes' to commemorate the 150th anniversary of the FA and 140th of the Scottish FA in 2013 '(GI)

Bobby Moore meets Greaves in a British embassy house in Mexico '(GI)

football legend who our subject shared a theatre stage with after they had retired from playing. Pat said, 'George was a lovely fellow as well. You couldn't help but like him. And also, like Jim, such a down-to-earth person as well. They were just different characters. George was a bit of a loner. Jim loved a sing-song. He couldn't wait to get singing whenever the sounds broke out, performing the likes of 'Maybe it's Because I'm a Londoner'. You can imagine the banter with all the English, Irish, Welsh and Scots boys at Spurs!'

Jennings felt it would take a phenomenon to overtake Jimmy's 357 English top-flight league goals, a European record only overtaken by Cristiano Ronaldo in 2017 when the Portuguese superstar was at Real Madrid.

Pat said, 'When you consider players of today like Cristiano Ronaldo still playing at 36, 37, while Jimmy packed up at 31, it gives you an idea of how far ahead he was in the first place. Added to that are the perfect pitches nowadays compared to the ones Jim and I played on together. He often had to wade through six inches of mud. Opponents cannot kick you out of the game like they did in our day. In fact, nowadays they cannot lay a hand on you. But he was able to do what he did despite it all.

'When you saw him one on one with the goalkeeper you thought, "Right, that's it. That's a goal." He was that good. He was a world-beater then and would be even more of a world-beater today. Would he have doubled his total of goals today? Absolutely. Nobody would get near him.'

Pat stood in awe as he saw Jimmy the goal machine at full throttle – as a team-mate and an opponent.

He said, 'I remember one game when we were a goal down with a few minutes to go at White Hart Lane against the great Manchester United team of George Best, Denis Law and Bobby Charlton, who all played this day [10 September 1966 at White Hart Lane]. We scored two goals in the last three or four minutes from nowhere. Gilly got the equaliser but Jim scored the winner.

That was what Jim did. All of a sudden he sets off and the next thing, it is in the net.

'There was also the match in which I remember Jim putting three past me. It was my full international debut for Northern Ireland in Belfast [3 October 1964]. Jim netted his hat-trick to put England 3-0 up at half-time. It was the first time I'd played against him.'

Pat also endured Jimmy scoring against him in a club game after joining West Ham United, which illustrated a couple of qualities the frontman possessed: finding space and timing. It happened when the ace returned to N17 on 15 August 1970.

Pat said, 'Jim always had the knack of turning up in the right place. He knew where the ball was about to fall, especially in the opposition box.

'That first game when he came back to us at White Hart Lane from West Ham showed it. We were one up. West Ham had a corner and all of a sudden a gap appears. Who's there? Jim. Next thing I know I'm picking it out of the net. That was him every week with Spurs.'

Pat believed speed off the mark, bravery and sharpness of brain, besides his timing and sixth sense, helped Jimmy amass his staggering number of goals.

He said, 'Jim's skill and speed were major assets, but he didn't need to train too hard. He did the same as everybody else, but was naturally fit. A fantastic athlete. He would step it up if there was a competition prize, especially if it involved sprints. That's where his strength was, over ten to 15 yards. He was so quick that the moment he picked the ball up he was away.

'Jim didn't like long-distance running. But sprinting, as I suggested, he was lightning quick. On Fridays, the day before a game, we'd end up with nine or ten sprints. Bill would say whoever wins the next one goes in to change – and you could be sure that would be Jim.

'He also had courage, when the boots were flying around, particularly in the penalty area. You couldn't kick him out of it.'

Pat remembered Jimmy's willingness to be brave on the ball was prevalent even in small-sided matches on small pitches, like the practice court at White Hart Lane.

And, on one occasion, it ended with Jimmy having to have stitches in a gash on his forehead when he and Pat were both left bloodied after clashing heads. It also revealed how Jimmy thought of the team before himself. It came on the eve of a league fixture against Stoke City at the Lane.

Pat, who was playing outfield the day of the bloody collision, picked up the story, 'It was a training accident on the ball court this Friday morning. Jim is through and I'm going out to mark him. He sells me a dummy and I bought it and we clash. I limped off with Jim. I could feel the blood coming out of my eye. Jimmy was also cut. We were both lucky the club doctor [Dr Brian Curtin] was there every Friday morning in case there were any problems. He stitched us both up. But Jim said to him, "Look doc, look after Pat. He's more important than me for the team tomorrow." What a compliment that was! That is what Jim was like. We were both able to play; I remember Jim had cross stitches in the middle of his forehead. And I think we won the match.'

Pat believed himself and Jimmy were part of a 'family' at Spurs, nurtured by Bill Nicholson, who carefully reconstructed his second great side with Pat himself, Alan Mullery, Alan Gilzean, Cyril Knowles, Mike England and Jimmy Robertson coming in to accompany survivors of the first, Dave Mackay, Cliff Jones and, from December 1961, Jimmy. The plan culminated in Spurs lifting the 1967 FA Cup.

He said, 'Players spent much more time together then than they do now. You spent careers with players. Jim was at Spurs for nearly ten years, I played 13. We were more like a family than to what it is like nowadays. The club meant so much to you. That was reflected when we were playing in local derbies. It was just all part of that togetherness we had as a club under Bill Nicholson. That was the way it was.'

'Family' break-ups can be that much harder, as was evidenced by Pat when Jimmy left for West Ham in exchange for World Cup Final goalscorer Martin Peters in March 1970.

Pat said, 'There was no way Jim should have been allowed to leave Tottenham. He was still scoring for fun. And it was the same in the testimonials he played in years after, packing up far too early at 31.'

Jimmy scoring in his own against Feyenoord on 17 October 1972 made Pat's point. He said, 'There were over 45,000 supporters who turned up on the night of his testimonial against Feyenoord to show what they thought of Jim after he'd been away from them for a couple of years. And he scored. I wasn't able to go because I was in an international match that week but when it came to my testimonial [against future club Arsenal on 23 November 1976] a friend of Jim asked if Jim could play in it. You can imagine my reaction! Where would you like to play, Jim?! That was brilliant for me that he wanted to play in it – and he did. He scored twice. He played in a lot of testimonial matches and, all those years after packing up, was able to score whenever he wanted.

'There's no doubt given full-time training in a good squad, a good team, he could still have been sticking the ball in the net for us in the first team. You don't lose the skill he had overnight. He could still have done a great job for us. It could have been the same with Dave Mackay when you see the job he did for Derby after he left us.

'It was one of the worst days of all at the club when we heard Jim was leaving. The dressing room was like a morgue. Those of us who had been with him week in week out couldn't believe what was happening.

'Without a doubt it was tempting to get Martin Peters, who proved brilliant for us. There should have been some way we could have got a great player like Martin in without letting Jimmy go. I wish there had been. But that's the way football was in those days.

'You can't criticise Bill Nick. He was an unbelievable manager. I have never heard anything new in terms of coaching that I hadn't heard from Bill all those years ago. Just the basic stuff. Some of today's teams are playing what we were brought up to do.'

Jimmy felt worse about leaving Spurs than missing out on England's 1966 World Cup Final triumph against West Germany. And Pat said, 'Yes, that is believable. Jim absolutely loved the club. I couldn't believe Bill let him go at that stage because he loved Jim.

'Bill Nick got us tickets for the World Cup Final. I was really disappointed a player as good as Jim didn't actually play. He'd been injured against France in the match which qualified England for the knockout stages. I've actually got one of Jim's 1966 caps. Something we did in those days was swap caps. I've got a Welsh cap from Cliff Jones. We all gave away international stuff whenever one of the boys was having a testimonial.'

Pat felt something similar to the disappointment Jimmy experienced after England's Jules Rimet Trophy triumph when Spurs let him join north London neighbours Arsenal in August 1977. He helped the Gunners win the 1979 FA Cup and reach the final in 1978 and 1980, when he also guided them to the decider of the Cup Winners' Cup, all under his former Spurs boss Terry Neill. Pat's spell at Highbury also saw him become the first professional player in English football to make 1,000 senior appearances.

But his heart always remained at White Hart Lane, which is perhaps one reason he escaped the wrath Spurs' England defender Sol Campbell experienced when he switched from white to red in 2001.

Pat returned to the Lane in 1985 to make it 15 years as a player. He went on to spend 24 years coaching at the club and serving Spurs in matchday hospitality as he closed in on 60 years from when he first signed, while supporting multiple charity fundraisers.

He said, 'I'd won the PFA Player of the Year trophy the year before I was sold to Arsenal – and still the only goalkeeper to win that AND the Football Writers' Player of the Year award. I thought I was going to go on and make the most appearances ever of anyone in a Tottenham shirt. I had just taken over Ted Ditchburn's club record [for a goalkeeper]. I thought I was going to go on to the all-time record and it was a big disappointment for me it didn't happen.

'When I went to sign for Arsenal, the secretary of the club came with me and went, "Are you sure you want to be transferred?" I said, "What are you talking about, I've been sold." He said, "Hold on, don't do anything." He made a phone call and got back and said, "I can't believe what they have just told me."'

The 1967 FA Cup Final triumph in front of 100,000 was Pat's lone major trophy alongside Jimmy, although they also combined for Spurs to share the 1967 FA Charity Shield with Manchester United – with the goalkeeper on target thanks to a long clearance, and not his striking colleague.

Pat still treasured the achievement of that 2-1 Wembley win over Chelsea, but the moment that Greaves learned to control his addiction to alcohol filled him with more pleasure.

Jimmy enjoyed a legendary partnership with Alan Gilzean, one he described as the 'best of my career'.

Pat and the other half of the G-Men, whom the former had helped reunite with the club after three decades, visited Jimmy in his Essex home after their old team-mate had suffered his second, and major stroke.

He said, 'One night we got chatting. I said to Gilly, "Do you want to meet Jim? I think I can organise to go down to his house to see him." I rang Danny, one of Jimmy's sons, and Danny said, "Yeah, Dad would love to see you." So we organised to pay him a visit. It was just brilliant to see Jim after all those years, but so sad. He was in a wheelchair. Terrible to see him in that situation, but lovely to get the opportunity to go and see him again with Gilly. Jim absolutely knew who we were.

'Another time, Spurs had opened the new training centre. I got a call from the chairman's wife at the club who said to me, "Would you be about because we are expecting Jimmy up at the training ground. We want somebody around to say hello to him." Gilly came up that day too. Five or six of us went to meet him. That was brilliant.

'Jim was right there with us. Again, he knew exactly what we were saying. It was good to see him, and probably the last time I saw him.

'I talked to Danny when Jim passed away. I think Danny said at that stage that Jim had done brilliant to get to where he was considering the situation he was in. I think he had just had enough. It was lovely to be able to go to his funeral service and pay our last respects to him. For people like us he'll be remembered forever. Anybody who played against him would be the same. He was not just a fantastic player, but also a fantastic bloke.'

26

Cliff Jones

Team-mate

JOAN JONES, in her cheery, upbeat way, answered the phone. Her husband, Cliff, had just popped down to Tesco to pick up 'a bit of shopping before Rob and Linda turn up to take us out for lunch'.

Rob was the son of John White, and Linda the widow of Peter Baker; White and Baker being team-mates of Cliff when the three helped Tottenham Hotspur become the first club to complete the same-season double of the First Division and FA Cup in the 20th century.

But the reason for my call was about an individual who joined the trio in the team and improved it: Jimmy Greaves. Together they were part of the first British team to win a major European trophy, the Cup Winners' Cup, after retaining the domestic prize and going within an ace of a back-to-back double. Jimmy said on the *Spurs Show* podcast that the group was 'one of the greatest teams the world has ever seen'.

Cliff was a superstar in his own right, speeding Usain Bolt-like with grace, balance and purpose to either score or lay on chances for Our Jim and others, many times over a quagmire of a pitch surface. Juventus, who supplied Spurs with Rodrigo Bentancur and Dejan Kulusevski in January 2022, were understood to have had a world-record £125,000 bid turned down by Tottenham in 1962.

He also earned 59 caps for Wales and performed in the 1958 World Cup finals alongside legends John Charles and Ivor

Allchurch, while facing match-winner Pelé's eventual champions Brazil in the last eight.

If there was another player in that Spurs team who could excite your author squeezed among the terrace throng at White Hart Lane as much as Jimmy did, it was Cliff. He was so brave. And, as I have discovered in recent years, a charming man with a charming family.

Cliff adored Jimmy as a footballer, friend and, when alcohol became a problem for the Welshman, supporter.

Having seen what his team-mate could do close up, Cliff is unequivocal in declaring Jimmy as football's all-time best goalscorer.

He said, 'I never really knew Jim personally until he joined the football club, but I certainly knew of his reputation. From his Chelsea days when he was always scoring goals. That he'd gone to Italy and it hadn't worked out for him. That Bill Nicholson went over there and rescued him. There was a great buzz of excitement about the fact that he had signed Jimmy Greaves. And he proved himself to be the greatest goalscorer there has ever been. Whenever anybody asks me about Jimmy Greaves I'd say that.

'The game came easy to him. A scorer of tap-ins; a scorer of great goals. He was just a natural. Everything came instinctively to him. He loved to score goals. He'd rather have a stinker and in the last minute toe-poke one over the line than have a great game and not score. He just had to score. If he scored goals he was happy. If he didn't score goals he wasn't so happy.

'I have to say he wasn't the best of trainers. He used to drive Bill Nick a bit mad, really. He didn't like the slog.

'It was a long season. These days the pitches are totally different than they were when we played and you just had to train for that.

'But although Jim wasn't the best of trainers he was just naturally fit. Yet if he needed to do something extra he would do it. Bill Nick would see to that! He ran the club from boot room to boardroom.'

Cliff recalled matches against Leicester City as examples of Jimmy displaying his predatory instincts and, in one, a certain mischievousness.

There was a 4-0 victory over City at White Hart Lane on Saturday, 3 November 1962 which maintained Spurs' position at the top of the table while showing the imperious form that led BBC commentator Kenneth Wolstenholme to predict, 'I reckon they'll still be top at the end of the season.'

An unmarked Jimmy put Spurs 3-0 up after a Blanchflower penalty and Terry Medwin strike. It was a simple finish, sweeping home a half-volley from a Les Allen cross. But his second, ten minutes from time, was a thing of beauty.

A long kick from goalkeeper Bill Brown was put out of play midway between the halfway line and goal line. A quick throw found Terry Dyson, who pushed the ball forward before laying it back to Jimmy to his right. Jimmy controlled it with his right foot and switched it on to his left and moved to the left towards the edge of the Leicester penalty box before suddenly switching direction and bursting through between two defenders. With the ball a yard or two in front of him, he switched on the afterburners to beat a covering defender before jinking it with his feet to take the ball round Gordon Banks and tapping into the net. Match commentator Wolstenholme declared, 'An incredible goal, a sensational goal by Greaves. They don't come better than that, do they?'

Son Heung-min's wonder goal for Spurs against Burnley in December 2019, which won the Premier League Goal of the Season prize and FIFA's Puskás Award, would have given it a run for its money; the South Korean running at pace from his own into his opponents' penalty area, slicing through the Clarets' defence like a knife through soft butter. But better? Not to these eyes who saw them both live. Nor to Cliff, it seems.

Cliff said, 'I always remember that one. He picked the ball up from a way out and gone past three defenders. Gordon Banks has come out. Jim's dummied him and rolled it into the back of the net. Then he looks back and there's three defenders on their arse, plus Gordon Banks. The crowd were going potty. And there was Jim just trotting back to the centre circle. Like "job done".'

Jimmy seemed to save his best goals for Leicester, such as at White Hart Lane when he outfoxed the Foxes yet again on Saturday, 5 October 1968, the month Cliff joined Fulham after ten years a Lilywhite. And again it was another of City's goalkeeping legends who suffered – Peter Shilton.

There were no video cameras. The only visual evidence is the stills produced by snappers pitchside. One shows four outfield Leicester players – two on their knees – in Jimmy's wake as he slides the ball to the right of Shilton and into the net. In my memory there were more floundering Foxes, but perhaps that is wishful thinking. Jimmy completed a hat-trick in a 3-2 win.

Cliff recalled another game against Leicester in which Gordon Banks suffered once more at the hands, or rather feet, of Jimmy. This time it was down to Jimmy's sense of fun and instinct for non-conformity.

It was on Saturday, 24 April 1965 at the Lane. The Welsh wonder had completed his hat-trick, while Jimmy had already netted when Spurs were awarded a penalty at 5-2, ten minutes from the end of the encounter in front of 33,000.

The spot-kick upset Banks. Greaves, for a bit of fun, put the ball in the opposite corner to where the stopper was preparing to take his position. The crowd laughed but the referee awarded a goal. Banks protested and the official explained to him he had played the advantage rule.

Cliff remembered, 'Jim tapped it in and the ref gave a goal? Yes. he did. He just had this knack of doing things that were unorthodox. Certainly did that to Gordon Banks that day.'

Jimmy's arrival at Spurs for £99,999 from AC Milan in late 1961 meant a member of the double-winning team would lose his spot.

It seemed a tad harsh on anyone who had played a role in such an historic achievement, but Cliff believes that was the way it had to be.

He said, 'I felt sorry for Les Allen. He was part of the double side. He had weighed in with about 20-odd goals and then Bill goes out and signs Jimmy Greaves. In many ways you couldn't argue about it because he's the greatest goalscorer there's ever been. But I did feel sorry for Les Allen as he had to make way for Jim for the most part.'

Cliff believed the way Jimmy was as a bloke helped him fit in straight away in London N17. There was no trace of the Big-Time Charlie about this marquee signing who used to watch Spurs from the terraces as a kid.

The World Cup winger, who played in the 1958 World Cup finals under Welsh skipper Dave Bowen, said, 'He settled in so easy, Jim. He was a great lad and so easy to get along with. There was certainly no jealousy. In fact, there was a great air of excitement when Bill went out and signed him.

'He made a good partnership with Danny Blanchflower. Jim loved Danny, loved talking to him. Danny had a way with words. Jim liked that. They got on very well together, Danny and Jim.

'There was certainly no jealousy. In fact, as I've said, there was an air of excitement around the place when Bill went out and signed him. We were so pleased he'd signed.'

Cliff also developed a friendship with Jimmy. He said, 'Jim became one of my best mates. In fact, we used to room together on away trips. He was a very good room-mate but he wasn't impressed with me, I don't think. I was always messing around. John White and I were always up to some sort of prank, silly things like when we pretended to be ice-cream salesman. But it didn't faze Jim too much.'

Cliff and Jimmy also hooked up well on the field, although there was banter between them. The 'Swansea Jack' used to go on long dribbles at pace with the ball seemingly glued to his boots.

Cliff said with a smile, 'Yes, Jim and I did have a few words every now and then. He would say, "The ball is round and rolls." And I would say, "What do you mean, Jim?" He would say, "Could you pass to me once in a while?!"'

Cliff adapted, adding, 'I changed my game as far as Jimmy was concerned. I couldn't run with the ball so much so used to pass it a bit more.'

Cliff revealed he and Jimmy were on the same page regarding their opinion of Bill Nicholson's management. He said, 'We both certainly agreed with Bill on how the game should be played, and his philosophy: keep it simple and entertain the fans.'

Cliff believes he and Jimmy were part of a great team which coalesced under a great manager. He said, 'I have always said when I think about the double team that we had three midfield players in particular we bounced off and they were John White, who we unfortunately lost because he got killed by lightning on a golf course, Danny Blanchflower and Dave Mackay. And then along comes Jimmy Greaves.

'Did he make it better than the double side? I suppose you could say that. But if you win the double one season, you've got to have had that edge to do that somewhere along the line. There was hardly any difference in the two sides.

'With Jim, we should have won the double again the following season, Jim's first with Spurs, of course. We got beaten twice by Ipswich, who were a good side under Alf Ramsey and went on to win the league. I believe if we had got something out of those two games, we would have been champions again.'

But Spurs retained the FA Cup, with Jimmy and Cliff in harness on the goals front en route. The pair had both scored in the semi-final win over Manchester United, with Jimmy upping his overall total in the competition that season to eight.

And Cliff, who scored four on the way to Wembley, remembered Jimmy's prediction, which became reality in the 3-1 final win against Burnley, then one of the country's leading sides and champions in 1960.

Jimmy always scored on debuts, netting a hat-trick on his first league outing for Spurs alongside Jones against Blackpool at White Hart Lane as one example. And his first appearance in the most famous and traditional domestic knockout final would be no exception.

Cliff took up the story, 'It was a tradition on the day before the final that we'd always go to Wembley and have a look round it. Of course, Jim was there. At the end where the players came out from the dressing rooms, Jim said, "Tomorrow the ball is going to come to me here," pointing to a spot on the pitch, "and it is going to hit the back of the net." And it more or less panned out exactly the same way.'

The FA Cup victory, completed with goals from Blanchflower and Bobby Smith, secured a place in the European Cup Winners' Cup campaign of 1962/63, which created British football history.

Cliff made one of Jimmy's double, as Spurs, in all white, defeated Atlético Madrid 5-1 in the final in Rotterdam to become the first team from the land that invented the game to lift a major European trophy.

Jones said, 'It was a special time. Jim got his two goals and so did Terry Dyson. When you become the first team to do something, that's special. Being the first to win things is what we were about. British teams have won the double and major European trophies since but there's nothing like the first time. You look at the likes of Roger Bannister running the first mile inside four minutes. Jim was very much a part of it after the double.'

Jimmy nominated Dave Mackay as the best ever Spurs player, while Cliff rated him the most 'influential'. But the Scottish talisman was absent through injury.

Jones said, 'Heartbreaking for Dave that he wasn't playing as he was instrumental in getting you there to the final in Rotterdam.

He was an absolute winner. Jim felt the same way about him, certainly.'

The European Glory Glory Nights are very much part of Spurs' DNA from the 1960s – and the 70s, for that matter. Spurs wearing all white in white-hot atmospheres at White 'Hot' Lane were unforgettable experiences for those who bore witness, my late father for one.

Cliff hit the perfect hat-trick of goals scored with his left foot, right foot and head, as the Lilywhites debuted in major continental competition in the European Cup. Polish visitors Górnik Zabrze were shocked 8-1 in the electric atmosphere generated by the Lane crowd, which chanted 'Glory, Glory Hallelujah'.

Jimmy had joined by the time Spurs reached the semi-finals against Portuguese champions Benfica and was straight in the deep end, but he hit the ground running. He found the net in the away and home legs but had his efforts controversially ruled out for offside as his side were edged out 4-3 on aggregate.

Cliff said, 'With the greatest goalscorer there's ever been having those goals disallowed showed decisions went against us. We just didn't get the run of the ball. I knew whoever won that semi-final would win the European Cup. Benfica were a terrific side and beat Real Madrid in the final. I think we'd have done the same.'

Cliff and Jimmy helped Spurs reach the 1967 FA Cup Final through victories over Millwall, Portsmouth, Bristol City and, in the semi-final in which our subject scored, Nottingham Forest. Jimmy managed six goals on the way to Wembley.

Cliff witnessed Jimmy collect his second FA Cup winners' medal as one of the first two substitutes to be named in the decider – the other was Chelsea's Joe Kirkup – after replacements had been introduced to the Wembley occasion for the first time.

He regularly faced his Spurs team-mate on international duty, when Jimmy was often in prolific form. Their first senior international showdown was when Jimmy netted for Walter

Winterbottom's team in a 1-1 draw at Cardiff's Ninian Park in front of 62,000 on 17 October 1959 in the British Home Championship.

Our Jim got a double in their next meeting, a 5-1 England win in the same competition at Wembley the following November, and he helped himself to one in a 4-0 win for the Alf Ramsey-managed visitors at Ninian Park on 12 October 1963.

Cliff remembered good times with Greaves and the rest of the Spurs party on tours to South Africa, Israel, Spain, Switzerland, Greece and Cyprus.

He said, 'Bill used to take us on tours. We always enjoyed ourselves. You didn't want anything too clever, too demanding, after a long, hard season. And they were easy-going trips.'

Cliff was impressed with Jimmy when his old team-mate and friend became a broadcaster in the 1980s. He said, 'Jim had a great strike partnership with Alan Gilzean on the field – and he had a great one with Ian St John on *Saint and Greavsie*. And he went on to do a good stage show. Jim was quite brilliant and I've got a great deal of respect for him getting himself back on track and establishing new careers.'

Jimmy had to control an addiction to alcohol prior to launching his time in TV and helped Cliff deal with similar troubles. They regularly kept in touch after their playing days and could often be found enjoying a round of golf.

Cliff was grateful he still had a friend when it came to his battle with booze, which the former winger revealed in his autobiography *It's A Wonderful Life*, leading to him joining Alcoholics Anonymous after speaking to Greaves. He said, 'Jim helped me out there big time. He just gave me the right words and understanding. I just followed what he said. And he was right. He was a big influence for me there; certainly changed my life.'

27

Harry Kane

Aficionado

HARRY KANE revealed how he has been inspired by Jimmy Greaves, Tottenham Hotspur's all-time leading goalscorer.

Kane moved into second spot in the 2020/21 season and his goals-to-games ratio for England is comparable to our subject's international record of 0.77.

He also chased down other extraordinary goal targets set by Greaves by the end of the 2021/22 season as he looked forward to the 2022 World Cup.

Kane, who captained his country to the 2018 World Cup semi-finals and 2020 European Championship Final, said to the club, 'His achievements at Spurs and his goal record for club and country are certainly things that I aspire to.' He added on his Twitter account, 'A proper legend who knows a thing or two about scoring goals.'

Harry met Jimmy at Spurs' state-of-the-art-and-then-some training ground in Hotspur Way, Enfield, in October 2017.

Jimmy had been invited along and Harry displayed reverential respect to the greatest predecessor to his title as Spurs goalscorer-in-chief, in front of a framed mono picture of Greaves at his baggy-shorted peak going round a grounded goalkeeper, when he said to the club, 'It was an honour to meet Jimmy.'

Harry discovered that day that Jimmy might still have retained the ability to make a room laugh with his never-lost sense of humour despite the limitations imposed by the major stroke he suffered two years earlier.

But perhaps, more importantly, the meeting might have lit an extra spark in Harry and that Jimmy was, perhaps, officially passing the baton to the player who, at 24 and on 110 strikes not out, was already striving towards overtaking the goals total set by the greatest striker in the club's history six decades previously.

Jimmy scored 266 in only 379 games for the Lilywhites from 1961 to 1970, plus his 44 in 57 for England.

At Chelsea, he fired 132 in 169 first-team appearances, and 13 in 40 at West Ham, not forgetting his nine in 12 at AC Milan.

Jimmy said to your author in 2003, when asked about his overall record and status as a goalscorer which saw him set so many milestones, 'You've got to consider yourself up there. You can't have any false modesty about it. The record speaks for itself. Scoring gave me a big satisfaction.'

Harry revealed he was under no illusions about the Everests he was climbing. He said to Sky Sports, 'Jimmy was an incredible player, an incredible goalscorer, a legend for club and country. He had incredible, frightening numbers, really. How good a player he was, the goals-to-games ratio that he returned, the goals he scored year in, year out. For someone like me to look at those numbers and try and achieve those numbers and, hopefully one day, go on to better those numbers would be incredible.'

But Kane was clearly up for the challenge, adding, 'I've never backed down from a challenge. I always want to prove a point, prove people wrong, prove it to myself. I want to be the best in my position and have full belief in myself and my ability.'

Echoing the fact Jimmy managed to top the English top-tier goal charts six times, he added, 'Milestones are great when you can do it year on year against tough opposition.'

Harry had first been linked with Jimmy when, in his early 20s, he started to score goals for fun in a Spurs shirt, beginning his upward climb to join the pantheon of leading goalscorers at a club 140 years old in 2022. The ties that bind them grew ever tighter as Harry continued to hit the back of the onion bag on a regular basis, sharing the same attitude to scoring goals as Jimmy.

Jimmy said in his autobiography, 'I didn't like it [scoring goals]. I loved it. A lot of players worry about missing a goal. I never did. If I didn't I knew I'd be there again later in the game.'

On the same theme, Harry said, 'Scoring is one of the best feelings in the world. It's not about how many you miss. It is always about the next one. I stay ready for it.'

The chant of 'he's one of our own' grew ever louder as Spurs youth product Kane, born round the corner in Walthamstow, closed the gap between himself and the individual whose flag had been planted on top of the mountain for more than 50 years; a song, incidentally, which could have been performed for Jimmy had the club followed up an initial interest prior to him joining Chelsea and then AC Milan. Of course, it did not prevent him being loved by the Tottenham faithful as if he were a product of the club, like Kane.

28

Dave Kidd

Newspaper colleague

DAVE KIDD got to know Jimmy through working with our subject for years on his popular newspaper columns.

Kidd, the chief sports writer on *The Sun*, wrote, 'It's probably best to begin with the ending. It was April 2015 and I was in Las Vegas, covering "Fight of the Century" between Floyd Mayweather and Manny Pacquiao, which really ought to have been billed as "The Least Interesting Fight of the Century".

'While in Vegas, I'd heard that Jimmy Greaves had agreed to be inducted into the Tottenham Hotspur Hall of Fame. This might sound like a standard piece of news. After all, Jim was Tottenham's all-time record goalscorer and undoubtedly one of the club's greatest players. Yet knowing Jim as I had come to do so well, as his ghostwriter for the *Sunday People* between 2009 and 2014, I realised that accepting this invitation would have been quite a leap.

'Jim had been largely "estranged" from Spurs since his controversial departure way back in 1970. Back then, manager Bill Nicholson had used Jim as the makeweight in a swap deal with Martin Peters of West Ham. This shocked Jim and broke his heart. After nine years at the club, still an outstanding striker, and having only just turned 30, he felt he deserved better.

'While there is a common misconception that missing England's triumph in the 1966 World Cup Final – after he suffered a gashed shin during the group stage – had been the greatest sadness of his career, that departure from White Hart Lane cut far deeper and proved the beginning of the end of Jim's playing days. He did not enjoy his one season at West Ham, despite the presence of his great friend Bobby Moore, and he quit the professional game the following summer with 357 goals in the English top flight.

'It would be unfair to say that Jim held a grudge against the club where he'd spent the majority of his career but it became obvious, during our wonderfully long, usually joyous weekly chats, that he still felt wounded by his Tottenham exit, four decades later.

'So I was glad to hear that he'd made his peace with Spurs and had agreed to attend a celebratory dinner at the Lane where he would be inducted into the Hall of Fame, along with another great friend of his, Tottenham's record appearance maker and FA Cup-winning skipper, Steve Perryman.

'I had moved to the *Daily Mirror* the previous year, so while I was still in regular contact with Jim, our conversations had been less frequent. I rang him from Vegas and asked if I could take him to lunch at a regular haunt of ours, the Lion Inn in Boreham near Chelmsford, and wondered if he'd mind doing an interview with me before the Hall of Fame evening. It sounded as if Jim was reluctant about the whole affair.

'"You know me, Dave, I hate a f***ing fuss, I'd really rather not do an interview, I'm sorry." Fair enough, I thought. I wasn't entirely surprised. Within half an hour, though, I received a voicemail from Jim.

'"I've been thinking. You know I love you mate, I'd do anything for ya. Give me a buzz when you're back from Vegas and we'll arrange that lunch and do the interview."

'It was the last time I ever heard that famous voice. At least, the authentic version. When I turned on my phone a few days later, after the transatlantic flight home, there was a message from his agent, Terry Baker, telling me that Jim had suffered a massive stroke. He lived for another six and a half years and I visited him on several occasions, but Jim could barely walk or talk. We never did have that lunch at the Lion Inn, although I did attend the Hall of Fame dinner, which was held without him, the following year.

'But that final voicemail was typical of the man – warm and generous. He always had time for people. Not just friends but those who stopped him in the street, just to tell him how great he was. Even though he could genuinely never understand all the fuss being made about a God-given talent which had faded 40 years earlier. Many – including myself – came to love him as a broadcaster on *Saint and Greavsie*, TV-am and as a pundit on ITV Sport. If anything, that second career was a greater source of pride to Jim than his time as a footballer. He claimed he was such a natural as a goalscorer that he didn't really have to think about, or work at, his art. He hated training, scoffed at tactical talk and believed most managers were chancers. But he reckoned broadcasting didn't come so naturally. I'm not so sure. He had such a droll, dry humour and in his stand-up theatre shows, he possessed a sense of timing which seemed as instinctive as those runs into the penalty area decades earlier.

'Jim was also a marvellous newspaper columnist, for many years on *The Sun* and for the final six years before his stroke, on *The People*. I'd heard *The Sun* had made the surprising decision to get rid of Jim. I'd stood in as his ghostwriter on several occasions during an earlier stint at *The Sun* and had always found his gift for an anecdote and for a killer one-liner to be outstanding. At *The People*, we barely had a pot to piddle in but I took a chance and rang up Jim and asked him whether he would like to join us for a weekly column. I made no pretence of the fact that we could only pay him peanuts. He often said he'd have done it for free. I believed him.

'Those weekly calls – we must have enjoyed at least 250 of them – were probably the greatest privilege and pleasure of my career. Rather than straightforward opinion pieces, we'd often find a link between something newsworthy and something from the past, to allow Jim's flair for recounting great tales to flourish. I thought it worked a treat and I know Jim did too.

'I often told Jim that if he hadn't been a footballer, he would have made an excellent journalist, to which he replied that this alternative career would hardly have resulted in him drinking any less.

'One aspect that often entertained me, and hopefully our readers, was Jim's uncanny knack for allowing us a glimpse of the "human" side of some of football's most legendary figures. He told me how he'd once watched Pelé – to me a saintly figure – leap up to floor an Argentinian centre-half with a headbutt during a four-team tournament involving England, sparking a near riot, which had Jim and his spectating team-mates fleeing for safety from their pitchside seats.

'He reckoned Bobby Charlton was the biggest on-pitch moaner in football, with starstruck match officials often allowing him to pretty much referee matches he was playing in. Stanley Matthews apparently ran a sideline in black-market cigarettes, while the great Russian keeper Lev Yashin was always desperate to get his famous hands on "superior" western smokes.

'Then there was his extraordinary recollection of playing in the 1962 World Cup in Chile – of how incredibly small-time the competition was back then and how primitive the England squad's living conditions had been. Apparently, they had arrived at the railway station in the copper-mining town of Rancagua – where they would play in the group stage – and were greeted by the world's worst brass band playing an almost-incomprehensible version of "God Save The Queen", while being attacked by stray chickens. Jim recalled spending the next month billeted in a hut with a corrugated metal roof, and that his team-mate Peter Swan almost died of dysentery there.

'Jim would also tell you that all footballers have always been inveterate cheats – and this was no modern phenomenon brought into the English game by foreign imports. All managers were bullshit artists, pocketing hefty pay-outs for failures. Tactics were a nonsense, football was always "glorified chaos". This was all delivered with a gentle humour, the kind we all enjoyed during Jim's television days.

'Everyone knows that Jim was a truly great footballer and a brilliantly funny man. What often gets lost is an appreciation of his serious side and his ability for supreme empathy.

'When the teenaged Pakistan fast bowler Mohammad Amir was arrested – and later jailed – for his part in the spot-fixing scandal during the 2011 Lord's Test match – I'd lazily assumed that Jim would join most of the world in demanding a lifetime ban for Amir and a throwing away of the key. Not so.

'Instead, Jim spoke of a similar incident in his own early days in professional sport as a rookie first-teamer at Chelsea. He revealed that the club captain, Peter Sillett, had been offered a bribe for the team to "throw" a relatively meaningless end-of-season match. Jim recalled that Sillett had told his fellow players he did not want any part of the match-fixing but still felt he should canvas opinion among the team – especially given that these were the days before the abolition of the maximum wage, meaning that top-flight footballers were by no means wealthy.

'Jim told me that there was not a single player in the Chelsea dressing room who wanted to take the bribe but he told me that if – like the young cricketer Amir – he had been pressured by senior players into doing so, he believes he would probably have. He had huge sympathy with Amir, who had been influenced by experienced players in the Pakistan team. Jim was a lone voice in the media in expressing that opinion and, for my money, he was right.

'When Jim died in September 2021, the tributes were fulsome and genuine but what I felt was missing was much mention of his role as a pioneer in discussing addiction and mental health.

'Many people are aware that he was a recovering alcoholic for more than half of his life but, perhaps because he wasn't evangelical about such issues – as many who have been through such life-changing experiences, quite understandably, are – his immense courage in speaking out about his addiction was underplayed.

'Jim was decades ahead of his time in speaking so honestly and bluntly about subjects which have only very recently lost their stigma in wider public discourse. When he first wrote and spoke about his alcoholism, just a year after his final drink, back in 1979, the impact was huge. Yet, with hindsight, it is almost certainly true that, as a nation, we weren't fully ready for such conversations.

'That year, Jim released an autobiography *This One's On Me* and was also the subject of a TV documentary, *Just For Today*, in which he discussed his descent into addiction and the early stages of his recovery. You can dip into either today and feel genuinely staggered that the man was talking more than 40 years ago. At the time, Jim's words would surely have inspired some fellow addicts. They would have changed lives and they probably saved a few too, but discussing mental health would not begin to lose its taboo status for more than three decades after that.

'Tony Adams, another great footballer so affected by alcoholism, opened his Sporting Chance Clinic in 2000, to support sportspeople with mental and emotional health problems. The clinic has helped many thousands but, until fairly recently, stigma remained, many who needed help would not seek it, and many others in the competitive world of sport would remain ignorant and disdainful. Jim understood, though, always. He had an uncommon empathy for fellow addicts and he would rarely indulge in knee-jerk criticism of others being vilified for crimes and misdemeanours either.

'Shortly after Jim's death, I watched a video clip on the internet from 1981, in which Jim was interviewed by the late, great journalist Ian Wooldridge. There, he discusses his experience of missing the

1966 World Cup Final with honesty, clarity, depth and supreme self-awareness.

'It couldn't have been much further away from the "funny old game" routine he was more famous for. Again, that interview feels a whole generation ahead of its time.

'And while most of our newspaper columns were breezy and nostalgic, those I remember best were the serious ones. Soon after Jim had performed a short theatre tour with Paul Gascoigne, the grimly predictable news was widely reported that Gazza had fallen off the wagon in fairly spectacular style. I wasn't sure whether Jim would want to discuss it, particularly as he had spent a lot of recent time in Gascoigne's company. Yet he immediately dictated – and this was dictation not ghostwriting – a bleak, stark, fearful piece about the nature of alcoholism, his pessimism for Gascoigne and his enduring grief for his dear friend George Best. It was probably the best piece of copy I ever filed and I had virtually nothing to do with it.

'We are now, thank heaven, in an age of increasing enlightenment and openness about mental health. Jimmy Greaves was there in 1979. But as any opposition defender would tell you, he always arrived before you expected him.'

29

Dave Mackay

Team-mate

DAVE MACKAY felt Tottenham Hotspur could win the treble when they bought Jimmy Greaves – 37 years before Sir Alex Ferguson achieved it managing Manchester United.

Jimmy arrived at White Hart Lane for £99,999 from AC Milan in December 1961 with Spurs striving to secure a first European Cup to go with a second successive double of league and FA Cup.

And the player he was to consider the best ever to play for Spurs clearly sensed Jimmy could provide the goal threat to make those dreams come true.

Jimmy and Dave had to settle for just the FA Cup in the end – helping the Lilywhites to a Wembley final success against Burnley with our subject opening the scoring – but the pair combined to ensure Tottenham made a fist of realising their other two aims.

They finished just four points behind Ipswich Town in the First Division and it was generally agreed the championship would have returned to London N17 but for two defeats against the Suffolk side.

And they were a whisker away from the European Cup Final, pipped 4-3 over two pulsating legs by eventual winners Benfica in the semis, with Jimmy having goals disallowed for offside and Dave hitting the bar late on in the second at White Hart Lane.

But hindsight is a wonderful thing, as the saying goes, and Dave's prediction was entirely justified at the time.

He knew first-hand just how much Jimmy could inspire, before the prolific ace stepped foot off his plane from Italy, having played alongside him in a 1-0 win for a Football League side versus a Scottish League team at Highbury in March 1960, and against him when Greaves was en route to 132 goals in 169 games for Chelsea. He also suffered Greaves scoring a hat-trick as he boosted England to a 9-3 victory against his beloved Scotland before almost 100,000 at Wembley in April 1961.

Dave, who passed in 2015, said in his autobiography, 'I had played against Jimmy when he was at Chelsea and when he had played for England, and he never had a bad game. At that time, Jimmy was the best player in the country and if Bill had said to me that he had £100,000 to spend and asked who he should buy, I would have said Jimmy, no doubt.'

The Scot believed Jimmy instantly confirmed his belief when the strike ace debuted for the first team alongside him against Blackpool at White Hart Lane on Saturday, 16 December 1961, Dave lending a direct helping hand.

Jimmy had warmed up with two goals for Spurs in a reserve match at Plymouth the previous week. But he bettered the prelude by one against the mid-table Tangerines, captained by Greaves's England team-mate Jimmy Armfield, to help carry on the knack he had of scoring in every major debut. Dave assisted in Jimmy's opening goal as the striker immediately showed why the Scotland international had so much faith in him.

Dave had netted in Tottenham's previous fixture, a 3-1 home victory against Birmingham City, wearing the number ten shirt, but he passed that one on for Greaves to sport as he reverted to his usual six in place of Tony Marchi.

The cameras picked up Dave as he picked up the ball on the sidelines for a throw-in. The Scot hurled it long into the penalty box to the surprise of Blackpool's defenders who had come short and could only watch the ball float over their heads. Jimmy gave his marker Dave Durie the slip with a couple of deft feints. The ball came to him chest-high. He considered the alternatives in the blink of an eye – to control with his chest to put in a team-mate or go for goal? He decided on the latter, but to succeed he had to carry out a scissor kick. It required timing and technique, and he needed to be airborne. There was the risk of injury if he got the connection wrong. Catching the ball with the toe end of his boot might damage his instep or, perhaps, the Achilles tendon. The connection was, of course, spot on. He'd seen a spot to the left of goalkeeper Tony Waiters, an England international, and found it as he fell to the muddy surface.

The strike was deserving of all this detail as it was historic; the beginning of Jimmy's march to the top of Spurs' list of all-time goalscorers.

Les Allen, whose goal had clinched the title in the April, had done nothing wrong and lined up with Jimmy that wintry afternoon, but Bill Nicholson felt he had brought in a player who could improve the double team. And Allen, who notched a second successive goal double against Blackpool, was the one who largely made way.

Dave said in his autobiography, 'Jimmy was immediately starting a love affair with Tottenham fans that survives to this day.' He added that Jimmy was 'like a man possessed' as he was on his way to firing home 30 goals by the close of the campaign. Dave continued, 'The treble was beginning to look like a serious possibility. Our league form had not been as explosive as the previous season, but we were up there and no other club was running away with it as we had done, and the FA Cup campaign was yet to start.'

Dave and Jimmy partnered up on the way to that emphatic and historic 1963 European Cup Winners' Cup Final win over Atlético Madrid in Rotterdam.

Dave was at his peak and shone in every tie on the path to the decider in the Dutch seaport, even chipping in a couple of goals, while Jimmy netted three.

But the mauling of Madrid at the De Kuip stadium left Dave in bittersweet tears on the sidelines as he missed out through injury, yet he revealed that Jimmy, who hit two goals against the Spaniards, helped to soften the blow.

He said in his autobiography, 'Jimmy Greaves says in his autobiography that he came over to me while the cup was being paraded around the ground during the post-match celebrations and that he tried to comfort me, as I was not feeling part of it.

'He remarks it was the only time he saw me cry. Cry I did, but I was feeling a cocktail of emotions that evening and the occasion had shaken and stirred them. Delirium at our success and disappointment at having not been part of the climax … it remains one of the regrets of my career.'

It was clear there was a mutual admiration society going on between the pair, who played together for seven fruitful years. Greaves, via his friend and agent Terry Baker, said, 'Dave was a lion of a man. In my opinion the best player ever to play for Spurs. He had everything. He was a great friend to us all.'

Dave, who came back from twice breaking his leg to help ensure a second FA Cup Final win against Chelsea in 1967 for him and Jimmy, moved on for an Indian summer with Brian Clough's Derby County the following year, helping Rams to the Second Division title and winning the Football Writers' Association Player of the Year award jointly with Tony Book. It later emerged, through an interview with presenter Brian Moore, that Jimmy, after he had retired as a full-time professional, was offered the opportunity to also move to the Baseball Ground by Clough.

Dave supported Jimmy when his old Spurs team-mate celebrated his 70th birthday at the O2 Arena in London on 20 February 2010; joined, of course by other Tottenham legends such as Cliff Jones, Pat Jennings, Terry Dyson, Terry Medwin, Martin Chivers and Steve Perryman, plus World Cup heroes Geoff Hurst, Martin Peters and George Cohen, on stage.

30

Bobby Moore

Team-mate and 'best pal'

BOBBY MOORE was in two England World Cup squads with Jimmy Greaves, a club-mate and on-the-field rival. He was also described by Jimmy as 'my best pal' in Saint and Greavsie's *Funny Old Games* book.

Bobby, of course, captained the host country to the 1966 World Cup, with Greaves missing the deciding triumph after being injured early in the finals. He was described in 2015 by Pelé as the 'best' defender he ever faced, in a career in which the Brazilian was considered the Player of the 20th Century, having become the only three-time World Cup winner and scoring over 1,000 goals.

But Bobby's rise began alongside England colleague and room-mate Jimmy, on and off the field. Bobby and Jimmy started to develop their friendship from when they were teenagers. It was to last a lifetime, to when Moore tragically passed with bowel cancer aged just 51 on 24 February 1993, four days after Greaves's 53rd birthday.

They both hailed from east London, Jimmy from Manor Park and Bobby from Barking. Bobby played for Barking Boys and Jimmy turned out for Dagenham Boys before the pair were picked up by West Ham United and Chelsea respectively.

Bobby outlined the Jimmy he knew in his 1967 autobiography *My Soccer Story*. He said, 'I have known Jimmy for a long time and he is one of my best friends – except, of course, when we are face to face on the field. I played against him several times when we were younger – although he was being described as the most sensational player in the game when I was still a West Ham reserve.'

Bobby remembered coming up against Jimmy shortly after turning professional with West Ham at the age of 17. He noted the fellow teenager's fast-growing reputation as a first-team prodigy, while he himself was being limited to reserve football at best, due to the form of wing-half John Smith, who was to become one of Jimmy's club-mates at Tottenham.

And suffered when he marked Greaves who scored in an FA Youth Cup win for Chelsea against Moore's Hammers.

Bobby developed a deep appreciation of Jimmy the footballer alongside the friend. He said, 'When he is moving into your penalty area something seems to come over him. It's as though he finds a double-ration of sheer power in the penalty area – and it is almost impossible to take the ball off him. Time is what counts in the area and the great goalscorers always seem to have that second's edge on everyone else.

'Of the eight games I played for England under-23 side one of the most dramatic was at Aberdeen, where we beat Scotland 4-2.

'Jimmy soon showed that Aberdeen crowd why he was worth £99,000 to Spurs (as he scored twice).

Bobby had also impressed in the victory, which saw him and Jimmy secure a place in the England senior squad for the 1962 World Cup in the summer. The defender remembered how Jimmy was able to wipe away the memory of England being 'drubbed' on his first full international appearance as Bobby made his baptism for the senior national side. Bobby said, 'It was an important match for me. It was also in the nature of a grudge match for England. Five of our team – [Jimmy] Armfield, [Ron] Flowers, [Johnny] Haynes, [Bobby] Charlton and Greaves – had been in the England team severely drubbed by Peru in 1959 during a

South American tour. We beat Peru 4-0. Jimmy Greaves scored three of the goals.'

And so to the 1962 World Cup finals. Bobby and Jimmy laid in their beds as the heavy rain beat down and echoed off the corrugated roof of their shared sleeping quarters. The pals from their early footballing days were at the England base in the foothills of the Andes mountains at Coya in Chile.

It was clearly evident to Bobby and Jimmy – and indeed the rest of the England party – that the storms prevalent that time of year were not letting up for them to sleep like babies to aid preparation and increase their chances of global glory.

It was considered the wettest time of the year in the area, as England found out when they kicked off their World Cup finals against Hungary in pouring rain. The match was in the mining town of Rancagua, about 16 miles west of Coya, and ended in a 2-1 defeat for Winterbottom's soggy boys.

Jimmy and Bobby linked up again as they returned to Rancagua to defeat Argentina 3-1 with Our Jim on target before a 0-0 draw with Bulgaria sealed a quarter-final place.

But the pals were on the plane home with the rest of the squad after being unable to stifle Pelé-less eventual winners Brazil as they missed out on a last-four spot.

Bobby remembered how he and Jimmy helped England celebrate the centenary of 'organised football' in the country by defeating the Rest of the World 2-1 in front of 100,000 at Wembley and an estimated total of 250 million watching on across 23 countries in October 1963.

After Denis Law had equalised a Terry Paine opener for England, Jimmy hit the winner. Bobby said, 'The ball bobbed about in their half for a bit. Then it came to Greaves. A quick shot – and with three minutes left we had won.'

Jimmy scored in both games as England beat Scotland and Hungary. The pair then shared a room on tour in Yugoslavia before a

1-1 draw. Bobby said, 'On the morning of the match, Greavsie and I were suddenly woken up by a fantastic bang. The whole room shook.

'"That was like a bomb," said Jimmy. Squadrons of jets roared over the hotel. We got up and looked out the window. There was an army in the street – great tanks and marching soldiers. We didn't know if war had been declared or Yugoslavia had decided to give the game a military send-off. In fact it was a march in honour of President Tito.'

The friendship was why Moore was in an almost perfect position to judge the reaction of Jimmy when our subject missed the opportunity to play alongside his pal as England lifted the World Cup in 1966.

The pair were roomed up again, swapping their more rustic accommodation in South America for the luxury of the four-star Hendon Hall Hotel, a 16th-century Georgian mansion in its own gardens five miles from Wembley, for the duration of the tournament.

Bobby said in *Bobby Moore: The Life and Times of a Sporting Hero* by Jeff Powell, 'Greavsie was sick at being out. He was to be a lot sicker by the end of the tournament.'

Bobby, more than most, knew what it meant for his mate – 'the closest of all his footballing friends', stated Powell – to miss the match of his life, the final. He discovered Jimmy tidily packing his suitcase on the morning of the match.

Bobby said in Powell's book, 'Jimmy was hurt. I don't care what people say about Jimmy, about how he didn't work and didn't care, how his attitude was all wrong. I knew the man and I knew what he was going through. All he wanted was to play in the World Cup Final. He believed he could get the goals to win it for England. He believed he was something special and it broke his heart not to have the chance to prove it.

'That moment began Jimmy's disenchantment with football. I knew that if he'd stayed fit or got his place back the Germans would have been frightened of him. I believe Jimmy Greaves would have won us the cup. But I also knew Alf Ramsey couldn't change the team.

'Geoff had come in and done too well. It was helpful to have someone else in the team who knew me and Martin Peters as players. From the start he had a good understanding with Roger Hunt and their running had opened the way for Bobby Charlton to start scoring vital goals. Alf had been given that bonus out of nothing. He couldn't turn it down now. Not for this match.'

Bobby spoke in Powell's book about Jimmy missing the post-match celebrations at the Royal Garden Hotel in Kensington, 'It was just fabulous. The memories of the Royal Garden are sharper. That was when you realised what you'd done. Only one thing was wrong. No Greavsie.'

Jimmy had reportedly quietly slipped out of Wembley once the final had finished, and, with luggage packed, went on holiday with his family.

It was understood Ramsey was worried about Jimmy and his 'motives'. But Bobby, in Powell's book, said he told his manager during the celebrations, 'Don't take it wrong, Alf. He's not doing anything malicious. It's not a protest. He's not walking out on you. He's not even angry. Just disappointed. He's better off away from all the fuss.'

Bobby revealed how delighted he was to see his old mucker on the eve of the 1970 World Cup. He had remained the England captain and was preparing to lead his country's defence on his return to South America. But Jimmy would not be his room-mate. He had not earned selection after a few months of upheaval.

Jimmy had been axed from Spurs' team, lingered in the reserves, decided to compete in the 1970 World Cup Rally which ran from Wembley to Mexico across two continents, and joined Bobby and Geoff Hurst at West Ham in the March in exchange for Martin Peters.

But Bobby remembered the bizarre circumstances he met up with Jimmy. He had been falsely accused of stealing a bracelet from a jewellery shop at a hotel in Bogotá, Colombia, where England were stopping over on their way to the finals in Mexico after warm-up wins in Colombia and Ecuador.

He was holed up in a British embassy house in Mexico City trying to escape media attention when Jimmy walked in the back entrance to say hello after finishing his rally, having heard about Bobby's situation and reportedly said, 'Come on Mooro, you've got your release. Let's go out for a drink for an hour.' Jimmy was challenged by the 'housekeeper'. And Bobby said, 'Please. Mr Greaves is a great friend of mine and we've played together for many years and there's no one I'd like to see more than him.'

The friends and club-mates were involved in an incident which upset West Ham manager Ron Greenwood.

It occurred the evening before an FA Cup third-round tie against Blackpool at Bloomfield Road on 2 January 1971. There were suggestions the match would be called off due to an iced-up pitch. Moore and Greaves sat in the hotel foyer after dinner with West Ham team-mates Brian Dear and Clyde Best, and club physio Robbie Jenkins. They were joined by members of a TV crew who suggested they were off to the 007 Club run by ex-boxer Brian London in the town. The footballers joined them 'on the spur of the moment'.

The four players were reported to have stayed in the club for 'little more than an hour', returned before one in the morning and got up at 10am.

The night was to 'mushroom into the biggest disciplinary incident Greenwood had to handle' after Hammers lost 4-0.

It was reported that a supporter had got to hear about the visit to London's club and, disappointed with the result, expressed his views to Greenwood in front of West Ham chairman Reg Pratt. That the same fan phoned the newspapers. The ball was rolling. Bobby and

Jimmy, along with Dear, incurred a fortnight's suspension and the docking of a week's wages.

Bobby said to Powell, 'Greavsie and I were nauseated the way Blackpool was blown up out of all proportion.'

Jimmy revealed his reaction to the passing of his old pal along with insights into their fond friendship in a 1993 interview with legendary television presenter Brian Moore published by VisionSports TV in September 2020.

He said, 'We'd been great friends ever since he was a Barking Boy and I was a Dagenham Boy. We had a chat as young men. I think we more or less had the same ambitions and to a degree we fulfilled them.

'I was privileged to be a friend of his. And we had a lot of fun together.

'This one wonderful image which Bob portrayed was absolutely true.

'But there was another side to him. He did have a wicked, if evil, sense of humour. Many a time he's gone along the England line introducing the players by the wrong name. Ray Wilson would be George Cohen. I'd be Roger Hunt. Mooro would wink and go, "This is Roger Hunt." And the dignitaries wouldn't know. Mooro was just straight-faced. He'd do things like that.

'Mooro got me into more trouble than any other in football I've ever known. And I've played with some villains!

'On one 1964 tour, when we went to New York. It'd be about quarter to 12 at night and he said, "Come on, we're going out." "Where we going?" He said, "I want to see Ella Fitzgerald." So I said, "OK mate," because I was his room-mate so he's got to drag me along.

'So Alf Ramsey's put a curfew on the lads going out. We're staying at the Waldorf Astoria in New York. And, of course, down in the lift we go and we get to this little bar where Ella Fitzgerald is. We can't even get in. The place is packed to the gunnels. So we poked our heads around the door just to see Ella Fitzgerald. Just to say we've seen her, really. We're back within an hour. And that wasn't the best thing to do because Alf got to know about it and threatened us.'

31

Gary Newbon

Television colleague

GARY NEWBON reckoned there were 'four influential people' in his 50-year career as a TV sports broadcaster on ITV and Sky. Football managers Brian Clough and Sir Alex Ferguson, along with world champion boxer Chris Eubank, are on the list. And the fourth? Jimmy Greaves.

The impact that Jimmy had on Gary began when he made him laugh; an ability he was to prove to have off as well as on screen.

Gary said, 'I've never known anyone in sport to be as funny as he was. Jimmy was a pioneer in lots of ways. Especially with the banter.' He revealed how Jimmy was grateful to him for encouraging him to display that humour as the goalscoring genius launched a second glittering career which cemented our subject's place in our hearts as a national treasure.

Gary appeared on thousands of programmes over half a century on the small screen, including seven World Cups, three Olympic Games, English top-flight and European Champions League football, world-title boxing bouts, and darts. And he was made an MBE in the 2019 New Year's Honours list for 'services to media, to sport and to charity'.

But, directly pertinent to this book, Gary was assistant and then controller of sport on ATV (West Midlands) and Central TV where he worked with Jimmy for close to 20 years.

Jimmy praised Gary for his help in his second career. Gary said, 'Jimmy credited me with teaching him the ropes. What I can claim is that I nursed him through his early times. I'd been in television 12 years by then and had my chops.

'He was always great as a player with the media but it took a little while for him to settle down. Yet Jim proved a natural and great to work with. The only advantages of being controller of sport was that I could tell if people could do it or not. I could tell whether they would overcome the initial situation.

'I'd seen Jimmy play at Spurs during holidays when I was at boarding school, in the same year as John Motson funnily enough. I never thought I'd be working with Jimmy one day, of course.

'It's funny how you end up working with some of your heroes later in life and they become people not heroes. It was THE Billy Wright – head of sport for ATV [which became Central TV in 1982] – who brought me from Westward TV to Birmingham in December 1971 as assistant head of sport with Trevor East and he gave us complete freedom. As a kid I knew all about Billy Wright. I was 13 when he retired as a player in 1958. So obviously I grew up with him as the England captain. And then, suddenly, there was the GREAT Jimmy Greaves. Billy, who was worth his weight in gold in helping to sell millions of pounds of advertising, was there when we picked him.

'I didn't think of Jim initially. We were looking for an analyst for *Star Soccer* [a weekly highlights show]. So we were toying around with the idea. There were four of us. Billy Wright, me, Trevor East and a bloke called Tony Flanagan, an executive producer. We just couldn't settle on anybody. We were going through all the Midlands people we could use but couldn't really find anybody we wanted to work with who was suitable. Ron Atkinson, for instance, was still in management.

'It was a Tuesday or Wednesday of the week we were opening on the Saturday, the first day of the season. Tony Flanagan was reading *The Sun* and he suddenly said, "What about this bloke Jimmy Greaves?" He'd seen a column Jimmy had done in the paper. I said, "I've just seen a documentary he's done for ATV about his efforts to control his alcoholism. He can talk." So Trevor East said, "I'll ring him." So Trevor rang him and Jimmy said, "No thanks, Trev. I don't fancy it. I live in deepest Essex. Not for me." So we went back to the drawing board. We were still struggling when on Thursday Jimmy rang Trevor East and said to him, "My old lady Irene said I've gotta take this – am I too late?"

'Trevor said to him, "No Jim, but you have to be here tomorrow if you want to join us and appear on the local news programme *ATV Today*, where we have a sports section with Gary, who is going to be your partner on screen to announce your arrival."

'Jimmy arrived on the Friday, which was 15 August 1980. Jimmy, myself and Billy Wright had our picture taken together and he goes on the show. He's very nervous. The Midlands in the next two or three weeks goes potty. "Why have you got a f***ing Cockney on. Why haven't you got a Midlander?" The usual parochial stuff I had to put up with.

'And then, a few weeks in, he started cracking funny lines. One of the Coventry players had a nightmare and he said, "He floats like a bee and stings like a butterfly." Then another one was at a Birmingham v Blackpool game. It was Alan Ainscow of Blackpool, I think. He appeared to take a dive to get a penalty. And Jimmy said it was a dive which reminded him of one by [French oceanographer] Jacques Cousteau. And in another match Manchester City were playing Coventry and Tommy Hutchison on the wing sent the Man City full-back Mal Donachie one way and then another way and then another way, and finally crossed the ball. Jimmy said at half-time, "Gal, you'll have to tell Donachie where he's been." You'd never heard anything like this before.

'I started p***ing myself with laughter. I couldn't believe it. I've got a lot of credit for him being really funny – and I've taken the credit by the way! – but actually I didn't know he was going to be that funny.

'One incident I remember upset [Brian] Clough, actually. I was Clough's favourite interviewer along with Brian Moore. He used to give me all these interviews but he gave me a bit of a volley this occasion. Cloughie didn't like people running on his pitch. And at the start of one match, which we were covering for *Star Soccer*, a guy – 6ft 2in and a Forest fan – came on to the pitch dressed completely as a circus clown with make-up. He went to join the captains for the toss-up. Well, Clough – and dress is quite important for this story – was wearing white plimsolls, white shorts and green top. It was a hot day. Clough marched out and did a citizen's arrest. Frog-marched the bloke off the pitch. We showed the incident to Jimmy live on air. We thought Greavsie would come up with something and he said, "Well, before we go any farther, I think we should explain to the viewers that Cloughie's the one with the shorts." Clough went potty at it.

'The whole Midlands was having a great laugh. Friends I knew were recording it on early VCRs so they could watch reruns in their downtime. We used Jim more and more on Friday nights when we had a sports preview programme. He was deliberately giving me a "hard time". There were lots of laughs.

'Jeff Farmer was a great sports editor for me who went on to be head of sport of ITV and is sadly no longer with us. He used to tell me how people down his golf club used to watch the programme. He'd say, "All they'd talk about on Monday is Jimmy Greaves giving you a hard time." It was all set up, of course. Jimmy knew I didn't care. We worked really well together. All this with Jim was a whole new ball game for us.'

Jimmy's star was on the rise in this new kingdom as he also showed his versatility. He did a fun feature in *Star Soccer* called the 'Greaves Report', in which he took on tennis ace John McEnroe, cricketer Bob Willis, boxer Frank Bruno, squash star Jonah

Barrington, motorbike racer Barry Sheene and wrestler Kendo Nagasaki. He also appeared on *The Saturday Show* with Isla St Clair and Tommy Boyd.

He earned an ITV network appearance at the 1982 World Cup where he was part of a pundits' panel which also included Brian Clough and Jack Charlton, with Brian Moore the presenter.

Gary said, 'They didn't want to use Greaves. Trevor and I had to go down and persuade John Bromley [who served as ITV and London Weekend Television head of sport] that you should. He went with our judgement against other people's desires. And of course they "discovered" Greavsie in the World Cup where he was the star of the show.'

It was rise and rise for Jimmy as he secured other network roles. He became a TV critic on breakfast show *Good Morning Britain* with Nick Owen, who had been a colleague on *Star Soccer* (see the Nick Owen chapter). Jimmy also appeared on ITV's *On The Ball*, a Saturday lunchtime preview show before the afternoon football, hosting it – linking up from Central TV's Birmingham studio – with Ian St John in succession to Brian Moore.

His biggest breakthrough came when ITV launched *Saint and Greavsie*, with Jimmy and Ian, the iconic and still much-loved programme. Gary had a role to play in it. He said, 'It was a brilliant show and wish I could claim it. I had almost nothing to do with it. All I did was go down with Trevor East to persuade John Bromley who again respected our judgement. It was a brilliant idea by a chap called Bob Patience, a nice bloke who helped produce it [with Richard Worth] and was a big mate of Sir Alex Ferguson.'

Gary disclosed a desire by Jimmy which would take him away from covering sport. He said, 'Jim made it clear to the Central bosses he wanted his own chat show. So they gave him a producer called Roy Bottomley and I think quite honestly the show [*The Jimmy Greaves Show*] wasn't very good. The format wasn't very good. Jimmy didn't look at ease with it. He also did a quiz show called

Sporting Triangles. Saint and Greavsie had far more legs than any of them.'

Gary revealed how Jimmy's sense of fun extended to behind the scenes. He said, 'Jimmy used to come in every Friday, Saturday and Sunday. I remember once, my secretary Olivia, who was with me for 30-odd years, pinned up a picture out of *The Sun* or whatever else in the Central TV sports department. It was of one of Jim's daughters who had given birth and he said, "They are not married, you know [referring to the particular daughter and her partner]?" As we all looked at him, he added, "Nor are his grandparents!" Him and Irene had gone through divorce proceedings over his drinking (an alcohol addiction which came to light in the 1970s).

'His sense of humour could also have caused me a lot of grief one time. This was before emails and computers. We were on the top floor of this massive building, which doesn't exist now, the ATV/Central studios.

'I tried to look after the staff. We'd been working on a Saturday night. It was when I would get my secretary to draw a £100 petty cash. I asked Greavsie to go down the Chung Ying to get a Chinese takeaway in bags and bring it back. He did and we laid it across the big desk in the sports department. I'd invite all the technicians, all my staff, the whole lot, to come and eat about nine o'clock.

'At the end of the food we would just sweep it all into these massive wastepaper bins. What we didn't know was that mice, who had come up the canal alongside the building, were managing to come up four floors to where we were and helping themselves to the remains of it.

'So I got a memo, as they called them in those days, from one of the senior management right at the top forbidding me to do this takeaway because of the mice. What I didn't know at the time was Olivia opened it – she did that with the mail unless it was marked really private – and showed it to Greavsie. And Greavsie said, "Don't show it to the gaffer Gary because he'll have to do what the management say. I'll answer it on behalf of the mice!" So he sent this reply, without my knowledge, that read something like, "My lords, what is your game? Jimmy and Gary get the Chinese nosh for the boys and girls who have been flogging their guts out to make you lots of money from adverts, while you are sitting at home, no doubt with your feet up with your family having a bottle or two of wine, and a nice meal. Please stop sending these stupid memos to our leader." And he signed it something like "from the Three Blind Mice". I didn't know about it for two months. I nearly died a death when I found out. The upshot was the management were so shocked that they ignored it and we carried on.

'Another thing, from Jim's early days with us. It was 1980. I said to Greavsie, "The senior management want you to speak at a lunch, and he said, "I don't want to do that, Gal." I said, "I'm asking you, Jim. Listen, I don't ask you much." He said, "Gal, I don't want to do it." I said, "Why Jim?" He said, "It's nothing to do with the drink, Gal. It is because I come in here every week. You pay me good money, really good money, and they don't know who I am. But once they discover who I am they might not want me working for you." I said, "Jim, these people are in the television business. They know exactly who you are. You are doing brilliantly. Everybody loves you. Now would you please speak at this lunch?" He got a bit grumpy. So off he went and did it.

'I wasn't there but I learned he got up to speak surrounded by empty bottles to the real bosses. He said [Gary impersonated Jimmy, who was having a bit of fun], "I know you are wondering whether I still drink but I am a drunk who doesn't drink. I've not had a drink since 1978. Mind you, I've been working for Newbon and Billy Wright now for three months and I've got to tell you confidentially I am the ONLY member of the sport department WITHOUT a drink problem!" I never asked him to do that again! To go anywhere near my bosses ever again! But what a great line. It was like, "What's going on in the sport department?"'

Even after Jimmy's television career was over, Gary recalled how his former colleague still tickled the funny bone as an after-dinner speaker. He said, 'He made a very good living from it with Terry Baker. I took my wife Katie to a Nordoff Robbins event [the HMV Football Extravaganza music therapy charity] organised by Richard Keys and Geoff Shreeves at the Grosvenor House Hotel. It raised around £250,000.

'All the Premier League managers and their wives were there. They wanted to host a Lifetime Achievement Award for Bobby Robson at it. It was before Bobby was ill. He was absolutely fine then. And it was very moving. Jimmy was the guest speaker. I said to him, "Please don't eff and blind, all the wives are here." He said, "Gal, I'll do what I do, if it comes out, it comes out." So I thought, "Oh, no!"

'When he spoke, he put a twist on a supposed conversation with Sir Alex Ferguson, making up something Alex said for comic effect. He joked, "When I got here I bumped into Sir Alex Ferguson – and he spoke to me! I was really chuffed. I say he spoke to me, but I went up to him and said, "'Allo, Alex." And he said, "F**k off, Greavsie." The place just collapsed. I'd like to underline Ferguson would NEVER say that. He's very polite when you meet him.'

Gary revealed it wasn't always sweetness and light between him and Jimmy, although they always patched up any differences. He said, 'We had one or two disagreements. One was a bit of an unfortunate row over a sweater. We were involved with the *Sporting Triangles* quiz show together. There were three teams and I made Jimmy, Andy Gray [Scotland international footballer] and Tessa Sanderson [Olympic javelin champion] captains, with Nick Owen presenting it. Jimmy wanted to present it. And I said, "No." He got really upset about that. The show didn't work very well so I poached Emlyn Hughes from *A Question of Sport*.

'With Emlyn, there was a certain make of sweater he was contracted to wear. I agreed they could be worn as long as there weren't any motifs on it. I said to Jimmy, "You've got to wear this sweater." So he agreed but by the time he'd got home – and I don't know if he'd been wound up or not – he said he wasn't going to wear one. I lost my cool a bit. I shouldn't have done. He eventually agreed to wear one.

'It was unfortunate I had to move him on eventually. I got offered Andy Gray by a mutual friend, David Ismay, a comedian who was Andy's agent because Andy had been one of the captains of *Sporting Triangles* and I'd used Andy when Jimmy wasn't available. He was playing for Everton at the time after leaving Aston Villa. He wanted to join me. But I just didn't have enough money in the budget to stretch to having an extra guy.

'So they said they'd had an offer from BSB [British Sky Broadcasting, which became just Sky]. I said, "Well take it and I'll come back when I'm ready." Famous last statement as it turned out (with Gray developing a high profile at Sky). I stayed faithful to Jimmy.

'At the 1994 World Cup in America, I was the ITV reporter with the Republic of Ireland, which was the only team that had any vague interest for people on our shores because all the home countries, including England, didn't qualify. I was talking to Andy Townsend, who was the Irish and Aston Villa captain – our station covered Villa – in the lift. I was staying at the same hotel as the Irish squad. I said to Andy, "What do you want to do when you pack up?" He said, "I want to work in your sort of line." I said, "Do you fancy doing our *Central Sports Special* programme when you get back?" So he said yes. So I moved Greavsie out to co-commentary at matches – still paid him the same – but he didn't seem to be quite as motivated doing that.

'I decided I wanted to take on Andy full-time. He was then playing at Middlesbrough and was prepared to travel back to the Midlands to work with us. So I met Jimmy at The Bridge Inn at Huntingdon, which is about halfway between his Essex home and the Birmingham studios. It was a hot day. I bought him lunch and explained I wasn't renewing his contract, to which he said to me, "You are sacking me, aren't you?" I said, "I prefer to use the phrase, I'm not renewing your contract." He said, "You're sacking me." So I said "OK, if that's the way you want to put it."

'We had a pleasant lunch and he said to me at the time, and I'll never forget it, "You should have done it a year ago, shouldn't you," which I should have done really, but I said, "Jimmy, I love you as a bloke. We've had fantastic years and it is the hardest decision I have ever had to make, but I'm controller of sport, and I have to look at it from a company point of view and Townsend is making huge progress." Anyway, I thought Jimmy took it really well. I'd deliberately met him halfway. I wanted to do it face to face, not on the phone. I didn't want to do it on the phone.' Gary reported he later read a newspaper interview with Jimmy which he felt contradicted events but the pair made their peace.

Gary said he and Jimmy reunited when Bob Patience passed away in 2013. He said, 'I'd gone down south from the Midlands for the funeral the night before as it was a morning funeral. It was 20-odd miles away. So I contacted Jimmy and asked him if I could have a lift. He said, "Yes." We had a lovely journey and stayed mates. It was a good way to make up.'

Gary worked for Sky when it revived *Saint and Greavsie*. He said, 'Jimmy was really annoyed they dropped it after a few weeks. Anyway, I rang Jimmy to say, "Do you want to come on *Sporting Heroes* [a Sky programme Gary was presenting] and I'll pay you a couple of grand. He said, "No, I'm not doing anything for Sky. They let me down." I said, "Jimmy, it's for me and I'm trying to give you a show to put you on." I don't think he was doing much. But he wouldn't do it and we didn't fall out over it.'

Gary felt Jimmy deserved a knighthood. He said, 'I was lucky enough to get my MBE, although I think I earned it, and I am happy with it. But it's disgraceful this country took until near the end to give Jim something. And it shouldn't have been an MBE. He deserved more in my book. It should have been either a knighthood – I backed a *Daily Mail* newspaper campaign for one, although it shouldn't have come to that – or at the least a CBE, especially when you see the way they are handing them out.'

Gary, a supporter of the Jimmy Greaves Foundation, thought Jimmy would do well as a broadcaster today, 'Jimmy would have been all right now. Broadcasting is a serious business. I think you've got heads of diversity at the BBC with different agendas. You've got political correctness.

'Jimmy would not have fallen foul of political correctness because he wasn't that way inclined. He never cracked jokes about women or whatever. That was never going to be a problem. There was no malice in Jimmy. It was not in his nature. Jimmy was very respectful of people. You've got to be absolutely careful with what you say but his humour was quite harmless.'

Gary insisted Jimmy will always be a treasured broadcasting figure. He said, 'I loved the bloke. He was a fantastic success on ITV. I loved *Saint and Greavsie*. He was a great success in the Midlands, his spiritual TV home. The Midlands loved him to the end in return. I absolutely loved him. He was a Midlands treasure and a national treasure. I didn't and don't know anyone who didn't like Greavsie.'

32

Bill Nicholson

Manager

BILL NICHOLSON knew Jimmy Greaves from when the striker rated England's greatest goalscorer was a schoolboy footballer.

The most successful, lauded and respected manager in Tottenham Hotspur's 140-year history signed Greaves from AC Milan in late 1961.

He said in his autobiography *Glory, Glory* in 1984, 'I remember watching him play for London Schools at White Hart Lane. He had the natural instinct of the born goalscorer which cannot be coached. Everyone knew Greaves would succeed, however, because he had penetration.'

Then the assistant manager, Bill was convinced Spurs needed to sign Jimmy when he witnessed the precocious 17-year-old Essex prodigy's league debut in which he netted for Chelsea against his hosts at White Hart Lane in August 1957.

He said, 'I wanted him from the moment I saw him score his first goal in league football … It had the hallmarks of his game, improvisation and genius.'

He briefly reflected on how Jimmy could have become 'one of our own' in London N17 during the time Spurs' manager was Arthur Rowe, whose push and run team featuring Nicholson had secured back-to-back title triumphs at the start of the decade. Nicholson said, 'Arthur Rowe … anticipated that Greaves would sign as one of his apprentices. Why Greaves chose Chelsea can only be answered by him.'

But Bill was swift to sign Jimmy when the opportunity arose. It was certainly no surprise when Bill, who had replaced Jimmy Anderson in the hot seat, went to Italy and signed him, even though he had guided Spurs to the historic double of First Division and FA Cup the season before, and sparked a decade of treasured memories for the player, his team-mates and fans.

Bill said, 'Whether or not Tottenham could have had Greaves straight from school was not the most vital issue. As the best of his type around, it was important that we signed him eventually even though it required a record fee.'

Nicholson was confident of getting his man when it was clear the player was far from happy in Italy because of a chance meeting and chat in the toilet during an evening at the Café Royal in London's West End months earlier.

Nicholson said, '"Why didn't you join a better club than AC Milan?" I asked. "You should have come to Tottenham." I meant it as light-hearted banter to start a conversation, but he retorted, "I think I will next time." Jimmy was a witty man … and though his reply was typical of him I thought it might have serious undertones. A few weeks later it was obvious he was far from happy with the Italian team and their coach Nereo Rocco. I opened negotiations.'

Bill and Jimmy combined to help secure two FA Cups and a European Cup Winners' Cup for the Lilywhites, before their ways parted and the boss went on to manage Spurs to two League Cups and one UEFA Cup prior while completing 16 years in charge.

Bill, who passed in 2004 – Jimmy spoke at his memorial service – said, 'Greaves had the natural gift of timing. Greaves gave the keeper no chance.

'The accuracy of his shooting was uncanny. His anticipation was first class. It was as though he was willing the ball to come to him. He had fantastically quick reactions. His ratio of success was unmatched.

'He did not like training but, like so many geniuses, he realised that his gift had to be worked at and he would practise scoring like a golfer practises his swing.'

Bill named Jimmy in his all-time best Spurs squad. He said, 'Besides having the telepathic ability to be in the right place when it mattered, he was also a highly accomplished footballer.'

Bill's complete squad was Pat Jennings, Ted Ditchburn, Alf Ramsey, Mike England, Maurice Norman, Dave Mackay, Cyril Knowles, Ron Burgess, John White, Danny Blanchflower, Ossie Ardiles, Jimmy Greaves, Alan Gilzean, Bobby Smith, Cliff Jones, Martin Peters.

33

Nick Owen

Television colleague

NICK OWEN fondly recalled the almost weekly car journeys from London to the Midlands with Jimmy Greaves. With Jimmy at the wheel, they chewed the fat from the Camden studios of TV-am in north London until our subject dropped off his passenger at Nick's Birmingham home.

The broadcaster said, 'We'd have long, long chats. Philosophical chats about the world at large, about football, about anything.'

The pair were working together on *Good Morning Britain* when the legendary TV-am show Nick co-hosted with Anne Diamond pioneered breakfast television in the UK in the early to mid 1980s. Nick said, 'In the early days of breakfast telly when I was working at TV-am down in Camden in north London, I was still living in the Midlands, having worked in the area for ATV which became Central TV, and Jimmy was doing stuff for Central. Jim used to come in on a Friday to TV-am and would quite often run me home.

'I was in on the first day of TV-am, launching their production of breakfast telly on ITV, having worked with ITV Sport.

'After three or four months, our boss Greg Dyke [who became director-general of the BBC and the FA chairman] invited Jimmy to become part of the programme I was presenting with Anne and be a contributor, talking about television. Greg wanted him to appeal to the masses and try and build up the audience, which was quite limited in those days because breakfast television hadn't arrived seriously by then. People hadn't got used to it. So Jimmy said, "Because I don't drink anymore (having had an alchol addiction revealed), I'm watching television all the time. Perhaps I can do a regular spot about what's on telly." Greg said, "That's it. Great." And so Jimmy became a regular contributor to TV-am.'

The duo crossed paths 'many times' in their broadcasting careers from the late 1970s to the late 1990s. Nick said, 'It is remarkable. First of all it happened because we were so versatile. I could do sport as well as current affairs, topical programmes. He was the perfect fit for them and I was doing them. It was fate, but you could understand how it happened. He was really entertaining. When he was on TV-am, we always had a laugh. He was always outrageous. Brilliant to work with. An absolute joy.'

Nick was a schoolboy when he first became aware of Jimmy. He said, 'I first heard his name in my life back in 1958 when I was about ten, first getting into professional football, watching a children's programme which had a little newscast in it. Like a newsround, way before the BBC's *Newsround*. They had these black and white shots up of a young lad scoring FIVE goals against Wolves. Wolves were then the best team in the land. They were the champions. And Jimmy's Chelsea, unbelievably, beat them. It was at Stamford Bridge. And, to repeat, this young lad called Jimmy Greaves had scored five! Absolutely unbelievable. That was the first time I'd heard his name.

'I also noticed that one of the people marking him was the great Billy Wright, who later gave me my first job in telly and became a great friend.

'I grew up and got into football and my local team, Luton Town. I also went to Spurs with my father quite a lot. That's where I first saw Jimmy live. He was just fantastic. I remember him playing in an FA Cup semi-final in 1967 at Hillsborough. I was at Leeds University at the time so it was quite an easy jaunt down to

Hillsborough. I saw him score a goal that day. When that man got the ball there was a hum and a buzz of anticipation. And so I knew him as an absolutely brilliant footballer. He was sensational. When you look at his record as a striker, it's crazy.'

Nick first met Jimmy in the late 1970s when he interviewed our subject, who was promoting his book *This One's On Me*, in which he declared, 'My name is Jimmy Greaves … I am a professional footballer. And I am an alcoholic.'

Nick said, 'By this time I was working in television with ATV in the Midlands. I had all my memories and knowledge of him at the back of my head.

'*This One's On Me* was essentially about his football career and his drink problem, and how he'd come out of it. And he was doing the rounds promoting the book when I was deputed to interview him. I never thought any more about it, that I'd be speaking to him again. It was, as I said, just "Wow, I've met Jimmy Greaves. I've interviewed Jimmy Greaves."'

That interview was an inadvertent tiny step towards launching Jimmy's stellar television career to follow on from a more-than-stellar career as a professional footballer, although Nick played down his role.

Nick said, 'For whatever reason, Jimmy gave me his phone number. So I held on to it and later ITV got the rights to do Saturday night football. Because it was going to be a live programme [*Star Soccer*] on a Saturday, the powers that be felt we needed a pundit on it. There were lots of names talked about, particularly Derek Dougan, who was a big name at Wolves. And others. But none of these people were available and so someone suggested Jimmy Greaves, which I personally felt was a strange decision because it was all about Midlands football. Then it was thought about. Jimmy was beyond geography. A big name. Let's give it a go. And they said, "How do we get in touch with him?" I said, "I've got his phone number!"'

As we know from Gary Newbon, Jimmy initially turned down the offer to join the broadcasters before eventually agreeing to link up with Nick's employers. But there was another obstacle to overcome.

Nick revealed, 'Jimmy said, "I work for *The Sun* on a Saturday." After much discussion with *The Sun*, it was agreed he'd cover a game for the newspaper, which would be the same as our main game, and he would then come into the studios. I would never say I helped launch his television career! They'd have got the number from somewhere else, wouldn't they? It just so happened I was the one who had his number that day. He became very good very quickly. And very amusing and, of course, he was already very knowledgeable. He became a real asset to the programmes he got involved with.'

Nick, who covered the 1980 European Championship and 1982 World Cup, began working with Greaves. He said, 'Jimmy became a very good friend. We were regular studio companions. While the programmes were being put together, with cuts being edited and scripts written, I often went to the bar with him for a drink.

'He would have a Coke, I'd have a lager. I said, "Are you sure you are all right with this, Jim, me having a pint? He said, "Nah, it's fine." We had some wonderful times before we went on air live.

'When I left TV-am, having been asked to go back to ITV Sport, I presented *Midweek Sports Special*, and lots of other bits and pieces. I was working with Jim loads in the studio.

'I did work with Ian St John a lot too, having him on my programmes as an expert. I also had people like Gary Lineker. And Brian Clough, Jack Charlton and Denis Law in particular. They'd come on and be pundits in the middle of *Midweek Sports Special*, covering international matches or whatever. I remember the semi-final of the World Cup in 1990 between England and West Germany and my panel included Gordon Banks, Geoff Hurst and Jimmy.

'Jim was one of the captains when I hosted a quiz show called *Sporting Triangles*. So there was I working with him again. I think I did the occasional contribution for *Saint and Greavsie*. I might be at a ground where the featured game was on and there was a story around it. A player wanted a move or a manager had been sacked. So I'd do a live piece from the pitch. I didn't work particularly with *Saint and Greavsie* because that was a whole different animal, really.

'I got back together with Anne Diamond to do *Good Morning with Anne and Nick* which was on BBC at ten o'clock-ish – and Jim became a regular visitor to that as well. From about 1978, 79, to the mid-to-late 90s. I was working with him in so many different environments.'

What was Jimmy's appeal to viewers, the young, middle-aged and old, men and women? Nick said, 'Jim was an absolute national treasure. As a footballer he transcended whatever team you supported because he was a cheeky chappie and a master goalscorer who could dribble with the ball at pace in the days pitches were not like the carpets they have now and you could be tackled from behind. He'd be a revelation now.

'Yet there'll be generations who only knew him as a television presenter, pundit. In the same way the generation now would be surprised to learn that Gary Lineker used to be a footballer because they see him presenting *Match of the Day* on television all the time.

'A lot of people will remember Jimmy Greaves as a great personality. He had a certain aura about him which made him compulsive listening and viewing. I think everyone could relate to him. The older generation because he was an absolute legend and the younger generation because he was such a nice chap. Perhaps avuncular but with a cheeky smile, a glint in his eye and a great sense of humour. He always had a laugh, such as when he worked with Ian St John on *Saint and Greavsie*. When he spoke he was down to earth. He spoke the same language as his audience. He had the same things he enjoyed on telly as them. He was also popular with the media.

'He was a very, very popular guy. Acceptable, approachable. All those things. Not quite a one-off but there aren't many like that. So much *joie de vivre*, bonhomie and just generally a very, very friendly guy. He seemed to have time for everyone. And he really did have time for everyone.

'Isn't it a shame all these giants of the game, absolute heroes are all gone? As well as Jimmy, for instance, there is his Spurs team-mate Dave Mackay. I got to know Dave when he went to Derby County. What a good bloke. What a "ledge". All of them will always be remembered.'

Nick revealed how much he treasured his personal relationship with Jimmy. He said, 'I'm proud to have called him a friend. As I got to know him, I got to love him. He was always the most modest of people, particularly when you think about his record in football and career in television. An absolute delight.

'One of my favourite lines from him? Talking about his problems with alcohol, I asked him, "When did it all start? Chelsea, AC Milan in Italy, Spurs, West Ham?" He joked, "I definitely had a problem when I was in Italy because I remember one day I went to Pisa and the tower looked absolutely fine to me!"

'He was great delivering the quick one-liners. That one was probably written by someone else, but he delivered it so well. An after-dinner-type line. Classic.'

Nick discovered the 'non-conformist' in his pal. He said, 'He certainly was a footballer who was a bit different. All non-conformists are, of course, aren't they really? He was never going to be your bog-standard footballer. He was always going to stand out. And he was brilliant. He was talking about moving away from Chelsea when he was very, very young because he already had ambitions. He was scoring an immense amount of goals in the lower reaches of the First Division, 30, 40 goals a season. He knew he was an outstanding footballer – not that he'd ever articulate that – and thought Chelsea weren't ever going to win anything because they let in so many goals. He went to Italy for about £140 a week, I think. A staggering sum then.'

Nick even got to know members of Jimmy's family. He said, 'I met other members of the Greaves family over the years. Those who came up to the studios, particularly [Jimmy's wife] Irene. And the boys [Danny and Andy]. A very nice family. Irene was quite reserved, self-effacing. A lovely person. I didn't get to know her that well but thought she was an absolute delight.'

Nick said he kept in touch with Jimmy after his television career finished, 'I did for a while. I met him at the odd event he was speaking at. I remember when I became chairman of Luton Town [in 2008] and he moved to Hertfordshire for a while – to be near one of his kids. And that is obviously not far from Luton in Bedfordshire. I remember saying to him, "Look Jim, I'll give you a shout soon and get you come to a game." He said with a smile, "I'll look forward to that call – WITH DREAD!"

'But in later times the contact did diminish a bit until I got in touch with one of his daughters after he'd had his major stroke. I cherish the memories of being with him during his glory years on telly.'

Nick revealed a double heartache on the day Greaves passed. The presenter for a BBC regional news programme since 1997 at the time of writing said, 'I found out Jimmy had passed when I got a text from a friend saying, "RIP Greavsie".

'He'd been in a terrible state for quite a few years. And his quality of life must have been very limited. It was a very strange day for me because one of my closest friends also died on it. That was John Challis, the actor. Boycie from *Only Fools and Horses*.

'I'd got the text about Jimmy at about seven or eight in the morning and an hour later John's wife Carol rang me and said, "He's gone." And it turned out they'd both died within an hour of each other in the early hours of Sunday morning. Devastating. The next 24 hours was a whirlwind because – as a friend of both – I was interviewed on radio and telly starting on BBC 5 Live on Sunday night and then *BBC Breakfast* the next morning, about five or six local radio stations, then television on Monday evening. So it was a very, very sad 24 hours for me. It remains so now. I think so fondly of John Challis, who I had some lovely times with, and Greavsie.'

34

Steve Perryman
Team-mate

JIMMY GREAVES ruffled the hair of a 17-year-old team-mate who had only debuted 21 days earlier. It is a moment that will live with that player until he breathes his last. Steve Perryman was to appear a record 854 times for Tottenham Hotspur, become the club's most decorated player and captain for 11 seasons, a Footballer of the Year, an England international and, like Jimmy, an MBE. But he was a rookie making just his fifth Spurs appearance when he laid on one of two goals for Jimmy against Newcastle United on 18 October 1969 and helped seal a 2-1 for the hosts in front of over 33,000 at White Hart Lane.

Steve said, 'I'm not blowing my own trumpet here, because all I did was win a tackle on the edge of the box. Jim was hanging around, which was what Jim's game was, and it broke to him and he turned and then he ran at goal.

'I was only watching a bit of film of it the other day. I dispossessed Bobby Moncur to leave the ball running free to Jimmy and Jimmy did his bit. Beat one defender, took it round the goalie and tapped it in. He ran back. Lots of people were congratulating him and I'm thinking, "Where am I?" I'd gone back guarding the halfway line and as Jimmy reached me he ruffled my hair. That moment, with that piece of film, will live with me forever.'

Contrastingly, Steve remembered when Jimmy was not best pleased with his teenage colleague. He said, 'I gave away a goal once at Bradford City in the FA Cup [in January 1970]. One of those banana-skin ties in which we got out of jail and drew 2-2 and went on to beat them 5-0 in the replay. That would have been in my first ten games. The ball came to me and I tried to put it through the player's legs – which is not my game – to Jimmy. My ball was cut out and they broke away and scored their second goal.

'Bill Nicholson spent more time talking to Jimmy about it at half-time than me because he was suggesting that Jimmy was behind the player and therefore he should have been moving to make an angle. And at the end of Bill Nick giving him advice, Jim turned to me and says, "Don't try to nutmeg someone again, I'll get a b*****king! I've been hard done by there. I'm getting done for it and it was your mistake." In a way he was right. Maybe Bill was trying to shield me a little being a young player. It was all in good humour, but there was a serious message there.'

Steve signed for Spurs immediately after cheering Jimmy and the team to victory against Chelsea in the FA Cup Final of May 1967. He said, 'I was already aware of his class and goalscoring genius because I'd have been aware of England games he'd played in, like when he scored the winner for his country against the Rest of the World at Wembley. There were other games in which I saw him score "goalscorers' goals". I'm not sure if I thought that then, but he was a professional goalscorer. A Rolls-Royce of a goalscorer.

'I don't think you could say that Jimmy was an athlete. He was definitely sharp in his brain, sharp in his first few metres with the ball. People say to me what about Jimmy and George Best on today's pitches? I think they floated over the ground, those two, and the rest of us ploughed through the muddy ones we played on.

'So those pitches in our day were actually to Jim and George's advantage. Jim was also like a Rolls-Royce in movement with the ball. A Rolls-Royce able to dart about him, show balance and a bit of cunning. Able to calm things down when everyone else was panicking as defenders tried to defend against him. If you have all that in the same mix, you've got a hell of a goalscorer. The best I have seen close at hand.

'At Jim's funeral, Norman Giller [journalist and author who was a friend of Jimmy's] mentioned him being Messi with bells on. Harry Redknapp said he'd never seen Messi do anything that Jimmy couldn't have done. And that puts it in some kind of context as per today.'

Steve, while part of Spurs' youth set-up, learned from Jimmy while watching him train. He said, 'Us young players started training before the first team and as we'd walk in we'd stop and watch them train. Jimmy would be playing. It'd be 11 v 11. You watched his movement. Maybe if you were a defender you watched how the defenders were trying to deal with him. Or the first team doing a finishing practice. You could write a book on Jimmy Greaves's finishes there and, of course, in matches. He very rarely seemed to smash it in the goal. He passed it.

'I'd be thinking, "Have I got a good enough touch? Am I a good enough long passer? Am I fit enough?" And there was this little genius. The more the pressure was on him with regard to a goalscoring chance the calmer he got. There was no panic in him. He knew. A very, very intelligent guy, because he knew exactly what the defender was trying to do against him. How could you defend against him? Say he was breaking from the halfway line and he's got a recovering defender. He knew that that fellow had to try and get on the line between Jimmy, the ball and the goal. And as soon as the defender did get on that line of recovery Jimmy would just nip inside his line and the defender's gone.

'As much as a good finisher that he was – and he was – it was how he got himself to the finishing position that interested me from a defensive point of view. It taught me that if you are recovering to that player on the break, don't ever get on the line between the ball and the goal because a good player will use it against you. So you stay inside that line, you have to show him a bit of the goal and trust your keeper. So it is like all these things, you can spin it around. From the attacking part to the defending of it. I think more defenders these days should learn about that.

'I don't remember training with Jim. I got in the first team after very few reserve games. You leave school at 15 and you are in the first team at 17. And you are not only in the first team, you are playing alongside Jimmy Greaves! My God, what an entrance that is. You could die a death with it. But I was so naïve that I just assumed that although Jim and other team-mates like Gilly [Alan Gilzean], Mike England and Cyril Knowles had special talents, they were just decent, normal people. And with Jim you'd think he didn't take anything too seriously, that it was part of his make-up. He was there purely for the enjoyment. And his enjoyment came when he scored.

'There might have been some problems behind the scenes I didn't know about. And why should I? I was a young man who wasn't invited around the houses of Jim and the other players for tea and stuff at the time. I was kept at a distance, which was right. But when they dealt with me they were respectful and all that went with it. That continued right through to the very end with Jim.'

Steve appreciated his time playing with 'a gentleman from a nice family' who he considered a national treasure. He said, 'Jimmy entertained crowds and you didn't have to be a Spurs supporter, a Chelsea supporter or any other team's supporter when he was playing. He put bums on seats. And I'd been in a team with him in it. And there were other big names in our side too. But when we played, say, Coventry, wherever, it was like "the gunslinger's in town". People used to turn up to see Jimmy Greaves. What greater accolade could you have than that!

'I think he scored a hat-trick at Fulham one day and with one of them was such a goal that the whole crowd stood up and applauded

Gary Newbon and Billy Wright with Greaves (The Gary Newbon Collection)

Bill Nicholson negotiates signing Greaves for Spurs (A)

Nick Owen (second right) with Greaves, Geoff Hurst, Gordon Banks and Trevor East

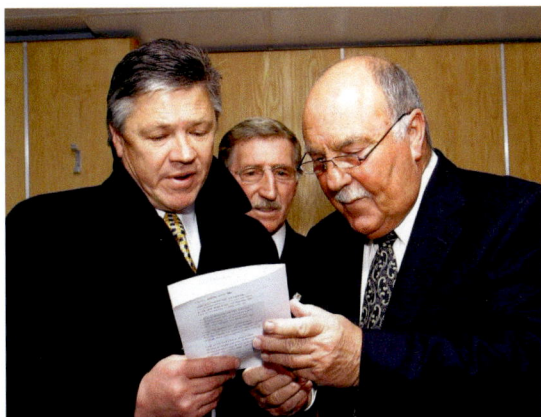

Steve Perryman with Greaves and Cliff Jones looking on (TBC)

Gianni Rivera welcomes Greaves to AC Milan
(Colorsport)

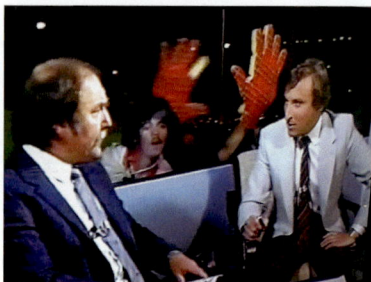

Jim Rosenthal with Greaves (The Jim
Rosenthal Collection)

John Sillett (back row, far right) and Greaves (front row, second left) at Chelsea (DBC)

Harry Redknapp (left) with Greaves, plus West Ham teammates Bryan 'Pop' Robson and Geoff Hurst at our subject's East Ham travel agency business (GI)

Greaves with his Spitting Image puppet (A)

Richard Worth with Saint and Greavsie in New York (The Richard Worth Collection)

Outside Tottenham Hotspur Stadium on 19 September 2021 (MD)

Spurs, Chelsea, management, match officials and the crowd take part in a minute's applause in tribute to Greaves at the Tottenham Hotspur Stadium on 19 September 2021 (A)

Ledley King tribute (MD)

Martin Chivers tribute (MD)

Gary Mabbutt
tribute (MD)

Paul Gascoigne and
Greaves with Freda and
Terry Baker
(TBC)

Theatre guest George Best (DBC)

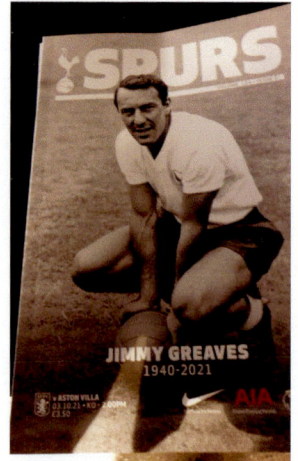
Greaves tribute programme (MD)

Pat Jennings pays his last respects at the funeral of Spurs team-mate Greaves (A)

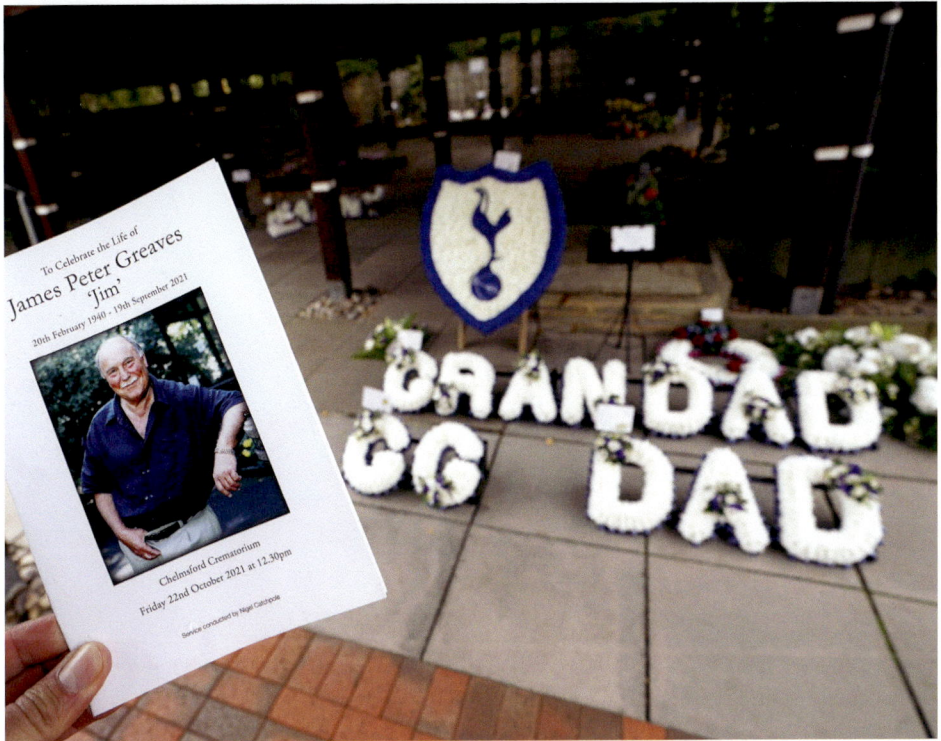

Family flowers and programme at Greaves' funeral (A)

Greaves' famous goal for Spurs against Manchester United in 1965. It was rated by United superstar and Greaves theatre colleague George Best as the best goal he'd ever seen (A)

Greaves celebrates his 70th birthday with (left to right) Bobby Smith, Cliff Jones, Terry Dyson, Peter Bonetti, Martin Chivers and George Cohen (TBC)

The Jimmy Greaves we knew (TBC)

him. Even the Fulham people. That says something about Jimmy's character, and how he conducted himself.

'It was a different game, then, I know, and that sort of thing may not apply today because there's more hatred amongst supporters. But then, it was the product of football that was the most important thing. And Jimmy brought a class to the product.

'He was – and remains – a national treasure in more ways than one because he ended up on the television and in the theatre although of course the number one bit was on the football field. He had a style about him, whatever he was doing.

'You'd have to say it was a one-off style. I'm so happy about being able to play with him. Unfortunately I only had six months with him in the team. OK, I was there for two and a half years at the club while he was there, but it was mainly with me as an apprentice. And you didn't spend too long with the first team if you were. Everybody's favourite player? You're not kidding! Of course he was. It was his character which shone through his name.

'I remember watching him on *The Big Match*, playing against Bobby Moore. They had a great friendship. And they did a little jig arm in arm. Just amazing. That was Jim. Some people would do that stuff and you would think that was them belittling the game but it didn't come across like that with Jim. He was full of respect for the game of football and what it had given him.

'He could handle the banter. I remember once him being involved in something which happened in the dressing room before a match that had such an effect on me. In my memory he was always ready to go to either play or train. He might have come in a bit late, closer to the starting time than normal, this day. Someone said, "Just in time there, Jim? Cut it a bit fine." Or something like it. He said [impersonating Jimmy], "You know, I was up all night, laying in my bed and hearing this creaking. I was thinking, 'What's that bloody noise?' I go downstairs: it's my trophy cabinet!" There's no answer to that!'

Steve vividly recalled the moment he got Jimmy back with his strike partner Alan Gilzean in 2013.

The G-Men had not seen each other for over 30 years. Jimmy had developed his media career while Gilly avoided the spotlight, living quietly on his own in Weston-super-Mare in Somerset.

Steve himself had re-established contact with Gilzean – who had reportedly lost touch with all his old Spurs team-mates – three years earlier when they met in a Bristol hotel where Gilzean was interviewed for a television programme about Scotland's greatest ever team following his induction into the Scottish FA Hall of Fame. And Steve was asked along to comment on Gilly.

Steve said, 'I said [to the reporter], "Are you talking to Gilly?" "Yeah, he's doing a couple of hours before you." I said, "Would you ask him whether he'd mind if I got there a bit early to make sure I see him?" So the answer came straight back, "Gilly said he'd love to see you." We did and it was lovely.

'Jimmy was doing a talk on Guernsey [in 2013] at a hotel of a friend of mine, Dave Nussbaumer, a Spurs supporter. And within a conversation about me going over there for the event, well, it came about. I was more than happy to see Jimmy. I was seeing him quite regularly then. Dave asked me, "You have been in touch with Gilly, haven't you?" I said, "Yes, Dave, I have." So Dave said, "Do you think Gilly would come to Guernsey?" I said, "He would love it and Guernsey is very accessible from Exeter Airport." So I phoned up Gilly and he was up for it. We met at the airport and flew to Guernsey and Gilly met Greavsie.

'They hadn't seen each other for over 30 years. I took a photograph of the occasion. I wish I'd have taken a video of it – you can take a video at a moment's notice these days on your phone – because of the respect these two showed for each other. It was immense. Emotional. There are moments in your life. One of my moments is seeing that happen. These two great people, these two great players showing their love and respect for one another.

Geniuses in tandem, like they were together on the field when Gilly would flick the ball on for Greavsie to get a goal.'

Steve's love and respect for Jimmy was underlined when his old team-mate helped him out a couple of years later, not long before Our Jim suffered his major stroke. He was by this time director of football at Exeter City, close to his Devon home. The Grecians were in financial trouble and Steve contacted Jimmy. Steve said, 'Jim got a crowd of 450 people and was bright, alive, entertaining. One of the nights which kept the club going. God bless him. He'd been there for me right to the end.'

Steve thrived when paired with Jimmy as the latter took to the stage for theatre gigs. He said, 'In later years when I became a name at Tottenham I was used by Jim and his agent Terry Baker in some of Jimmy's shows when they were down in the west country. I just used to love listening to Jimmy.

'If I needed to be there at 5.30pm, I'd be there at 4.30pm just so I could spend time in the dressing room listening to this man. What I've always said, and I think it applies to Essex people in general, is that he had his eyes and ears about him. He proved this when his show came to Exeter. I'm at Exeter City and the lowest in the league. Jimmy would have known our last result, our top goalscorer, where we were in the league. Jimmy Greaves knowing all this about Exeter City. He would also know why Essex cricketers didn't take enough wickets last year and finished third in the table rather than where he wanted them to be – at the top. He was the same with the England team. A very bright man with a wicked sense of humour.

'Martin Chivers told a story about Jimmy saying to Bill Nick who had paid a lot of money for Martin, "I think I ought to tell you Bill, your new goalscorer just told me he can't play on the f****** pitch. Apparently the pitch had sand on it!" Got Martin right in trouble! That was Jim. I just adored being in his company.

'His humour came across when he went on television. The quip. He was proper. He always gave you a nice face, Jim. That's what I liked. I said in my own book that I don't read books but I read faces. And Jim always gave you a good message in his face.

'In those theatre dressing-room moments in his later life, normally the man on the door would come and say, "Jim, there's a fellow at the door and he said he played with you at Chelmsford City." He'd say, "OK. Right – show him in." Sometimes Jim knew the chap and did all the regular stuff. And sometimes he didn't know the chap. But he always, always gave them respect and listened to them and asked them questions about what they are doing now. He was quite amazing. He wasn't the superstar his ability suggested he should be. I'm not saying he should be a superstar in his actions. He shouldn't be. But he was a proper man, Jimmy Greaves. A proper, proper man.

'I was honoured to play in his testimonial [against Feyenoord in 1972]. I think I laid on his goal. Everyone knew Jimmy was going to score! He scored on every debut he ever had and that was his testimonial debut, I think. A nice thing to be part of. Great moments.

'A good man, Jim. I can't speak highly enough of him. I don't really ever want to see my face on telly or make comments or whatever but when it is about proper people, I'm there. I was asked to do it on *BBC Breakfast* and it's not as if it was any effort to do it. It's not as if you've got to prepare your words. It just flows, about Jim.

'It was so sad when his drinking troubles came to light. They talk about comedians when they come off stage; they are almost depressed after being alive on it when a different person takes over. There might have been a bit of that in Jim. I'm not sure if it was because I didn't really know him off the pitch then. Only in later life when all that had finished. And he certainly wasn't like it when I got to know him later. Every moment before the show, after the show, he was a bundle of joy.

'I was particularly proud to be at his funeral, because you needed to show respect to this great man as well as, of course, great footballer. His sister [Marion] read out this great poem and it was called 'The Dash'. Although it isn't about Jim as such, it is about life. It is about when you visit a graveside you read about the year the person was born – and when they died. And that it is not important when you were born or when you die it is how you lived "the dash".

'We all had special thoughts about Jim, a special person. He'd said to me one day, "These theatre things, do you enjoy doing them?" "Yeah Jim, you invite me anytime and I'm there." And he said, "My audiences are not dwindling but the people are dying! They aren't getting fed up with me but they just die." I suppose he made light of such serious matters. I loved him for it. I loved and respected him for a lot more too.'

35

Harry Redknapp

Team-mate

HARRY REDKNAPP warmly recalled 'coats for goalposts' sessions on public land with Jimmy Greaves when the pair were off duty at West Ham United.

Jimmy linked up with Harry – and World Cup heroes Bobby Moore and Geoff Hurst – at the Hammers in 1970 and performed in the top flight of English football, but many of them still enjoyed the pleasures of the grassroots game.

Jimmy might have smashed goal records for fun at the highest level for club and country and Bobby might have captained England to the World Cup. But the pair, with Redknapp and fellow West Ham first-teamers, relished the simple pleasures of a relaxed kick-about with their mates in the close season; an exercise which seems unlikely to be seen today with the multimillionaire superstars largely detached from public view in their downtime.

Redknapp said, 'In the off-season when we hadn't gone back to work, we used to play football on Sunday over Chigwell or Hainault in Essex. We'd put our coats down and play football. Jimmy, Mooro. All of 'em. First-team players playing with our mates. There'd be 16, 18 of us all together. And when we were in Chigwell we'd go for a drink up the Retreat pub afterwards. Maybe sometimes it'd be on a Tuesday or Wednesday night. We loved to go out and play.

'We got a bit more sophisticated. We got the groundsman to open a training ground nearby and we'd jump over there. Play, have a shower, get dressed and all go out for a drink together.

'Jimmy would also go and play for Greaves and Penn Sports Shop on a Sunday morning [in Harlow Essex]. Jim co-owned the shop with Ron Penn who ran the team. He just loved having a game of football, Jim. Liked to go out and play. Jimmy was just Jimmy. One of the boys.'

The ace goalscorer had left Tottenham as a makeweight in a record £200,000 exchange deal which saw Martin Peters, the final part of the West Ham triptych which sealed global glory for Alf Ramsey's hosts four years earlier, move to White Hart Lane.

Harry revealed that the whole move was a shock. He said, 'Martin was a fantastic footballer and him leaving West Ham came out the blue, really. Martin had been left out the team, the FA Cup team at West Ham by Ron Greenwood. Then suddenly was gone to Tottenham and Jimmy came in.'

But Jimmy was welcomed with open arms. Redknapp said, 'Everybody loved Jimmy. He was great mates with Bobby anyway. Mooro and Jimmy were really good buddies. The move was obviously late in his career but he was down to earth even though he had been such an incredible player. A great person. Great guy. One of your own. No airs and graces with Jim. I never met anyone who would have a bad word to say about Jimmy.'

Redknapp reckoned Jimmy remained a goal threat at West Ham, where he continued a habit of scoring debut goals with two in a 5-1 victory over Manchester City at Maine Road on 21 March 1970, while Hurst (with two) and Ronnie Boyce completed the scoring. And he went on to average around one goal in three games while with the Hammers.

Harry said, 'It was late in his career, but he still scored goals. We all knew Jimmy and what he was about. I just remember Jimmy walking past three or four players as though they weren't there.

Time used to stop still when Jimmy got the ball in the penalty box. People would come lunging, jumping, rushing in to get the ball. He'd move one way and an opponent would slide past him the other. Someone else would dive in to block it but he would go past them, walk round the goalie and roll it into an empty net. That was Jim. It was just incredible how his mind worked in the penalty box. You can't give that to someone. A genius. An absolute genius as a footballer. Jimmy was an incredible player. He was one of the greatest I've ever seen.'

Would Harry have put him in the Spurs team he managed for four years from 2008? Or even in any England side had he got the job he was touted for in 2012 in place of Fabio Capello before Roy Hodgson eventually took charge? He said, 'Are you kidding?! I'd have put him in a world XI. Jimmy would be among the best three or four players EVER to play for Tottenham. Who's the best player to play for Spurs? Dave Mackay? Glenn Hoddle? Greavsie would be in the frame.'

Harry compared Jimmy to the modern-day Lionel Messi, the Argentina, Barcelona and Paris Saint-Germain superstar. He said, 'Today Jimmy would definitely be like Lionel Messi. Jimmy ran with the ball as if his laces had tied the ball to his boot before, as I've said, walking round everyone and rolling the ball into the net. That's the way Messi has done it these days.'

Harry remembered Jimmy the schoolboy international and Chelsea player. He saw the 18-year-old score five against a Wolves team including England captain Billy Wright. Harry said, 'I followed his career from when he was a schoolboy. I remember seeing him on the television playing for England Schoolboys. Me and my dad would go to Chelsea and watch Jimmy play. He was fantastic then. A natural.'

Harry attended training sessions at Spurs when Jimmy was in Bill Nicholson's first team. He said, 'Our paths didn't cross at Spurs then, though. I obviously got to know him later but was never around to meet Jim back in the day. I was only a little kid and never signed for Tottenham. I only used to go training at the club. I was 12 or 13 and used to go during the school holidays. I would go to West Ham some days. As a kid I had the chance to go to all the London clubs. Every week I'd get tickets sent from Chelsea, Tottenham, West Ham and Arsenal. I was having a look round to see where I'd finish up. I had the choice of going to Tottenham. All of them, really, and decided to go to West Ham.'

Harry reckoned Jimmy was 'one of the first picks' for England when they went into the 1966 World Cup finals, but he felt that 'circumstances conspired' against the strike legend, who was to become his club-mate when Greaves missed the decider against West Germany.

Redknapp said, 'What it must have done to Jim you couldn't imagine. Jimmy was one of the first picks in the team but got injured and that was it. Geoff came in, scored, kept his place. He got a hat-trick in the final. Nobody will do that again in history. Who can argue with what Alf Ramsey did? You can't, can you?

'Jimmy got that injury against France in the qualifying round. It is just a shame there wasn't substitutes in those days because Jimmy would have come on at some stage anyway. His heart was broken in 1966 when he missed the final.'

Harry followed Jimmy in developing a television career, featuring in *Harry's Heroes* and *I'm a Celebrity...Get Me Out of Here!*, among other shows. He rated the career Jimmy embarked on after getting an alcohol problem under control as 'great'.

Of Jimmy's legacy, Redknapp, who attended his funeral, said, 'You can only remember someone as you remember them. I remember Jim as an absolutely fantastic footballer. And as a person, just a great bloke. I absolutely loved him. He was special.'

36

Jimmy Robertson

Team-mate

THE STANDING joke is that the Scots hate the English. Not so when the 'Sassenach' involved is Jimmy Greaves. Just ask Jimmy Robertson, the number seven to Greaves's number eight as Tottenham Hotspur lifted the 1967 FA Cup.

Robertson, a goalscoring hero as he helped Greaves secure his second winners' medal in the competition, was born north of the border in Cardonald, Glasgow. He said, 'Jimmy was loved in Scotland. You mention Greavsie's name there and they'll tell you how much. Scots are supposed to dislike the English. That's what is said but with Jimmy it was the opposite. I had two brothers and they absolutely adored him.

'All this despite the fact he scored lots of goals against us, especially when he got a hat-trick when England beat us 9-3 at Wembley in 1961.

'Why? I believe his character came through to people in Scotland. They liked him as a player. They knew he was brilliant. And I think they just picked up on his personality, which just shone through whenever he was interviewed. He was the sort of guy that as soon as you met him you liked him.

'I think people also saw the real character that made him so popular when he did those television shows with Ian St John, who was a Scot, of course. Jim was so quick-witted. He was the same on the park when we played together. Everything he did, he did it quickly. Tidily. Effectively. Some people are loved because they have got "it". Whatever "it" is, that's what he had.'

There was certainly a positive Anglo-Scottish alliance at White Hart Lane between Greaves and strike partner Alan Gilzean.

And Robertson played with the dynamic duo for over four years, including the Wembley win over Chelsea.

He said, 'They were deadly together. Gilly would flick the ball on and Greavsie would pounce on it. Certain players you just click with. I believe it is true that good football partnerships are based on each being able to anticipate what the other is going to do. A sixth sense.

'In the 1960s and 70s strike partnerships were a "thing", one playing off the other. They say it is coming back into the game a little bit. We had a dream forward line when Jimmy and Gilly were playing together. Remember we had Cliff Jones in it too. Overall, though, as I said before, you knew with Greavsie in the forward line you'd get goals.'

Robertson explained, though, that Greaves, Gilzean and the rest of Tottenham's front line would have to face up to a few hard men. Especially Greaves, it seems.

He said, 'People would man-mark Jim. I remember against Manchester United, that Nobby Stiles would do that. I think Jim used to wind up Nobby. Talk to him.'

Robertson revealed he was Greavsie's tea boy. He said, 'Jim was a room-mate. Bill Nick put him in with me for away games after I came down from St Mirren in 1964.

'We got on great. I always made his tea in the morning. He always wanted a cup of tea. I became the tea boy. I don't think he had any sugar! Sweet enough? Yeah! He was always good company. Always had a laugh, not just with me, with everybody. He could be serious at times as well, especially when he started smoking his pipe!

'He had no side on him at all, Greavsie. He was as you saw him. That was him. He was a superstar but there was no "I am the big player" or whatever. He was as down to earth as most of us were.'

The pair, who played alongside each other until Robertson joined Arsenal in 1969, might have been room-mates with the club but they only socialised occasionally.

He said, 'We'd mix a lot more on away games, say ones in Europe. He was one of the guys and we had lots of laughs but Jim and I never went out together beyond that. Greavsie lived Brentwood way and I lived in Enfield. So there was a bit of a trek between us.

'I was amazed when we all found out he had a drink problem after not seeing him for years. All the time I knew him, we'd have a drink together but it was never much. Not more than anyone else.'

Robertson smiled when he recalled the Greavsie of the training ground – comparing him to a ballet dancer and telling the tale of the milk float.

He said, 'Jimmy wasn't the best trainer in the world. He just wanted to do enough. It was always a bit of a joke. He was a super athlete; one of those guys who was naturally fit. When he picked up the ball his movement was so athletic. Like a ballet dancer in some ways. But training-wise, say pre-season when it was always hard in the three or four weeks before the start, he would just do what he had to do.

'I can remember we used to do cross-country training at Cheshunt, out into the Hertfordshire countryside, and go on road runs. Eddie Baily, a member of Spurs' push and run team who was then a coach, used to take us and go on a bike because he had bad knees. He'd ride it at the front of us. We had to fall in line and jog. We'd probably do about three or four miles along the lanes. Alan Gilzean and Greavsie would be at the back. There was an electric milk float which would float by. So, we're on this run this day and the milk float goes past and there was Greavsie and Gilly on the back of it! We – the players – saw them but Eddie Baily couldn't. When we got back to the training ground Jimmy and Alan were there. Eddie couldn't figure it out. He'd say, "How did you get back so quickly?!"'

Robertson also remembered practising on the ball court at White Hart Lane with Greaves and their team-mates. He said, 'Our favourite time in training was always on the ball court on a Friday. It was one of the highlights because it wasn't the same as normal training. It was a bit of a relief from it.

'The ball was always in play. The court had little goals – and brick walls. When the ball was played against the wall a player would sometimes be up against it too. If Dave Mackay was playing you'd end up plastered to the wall!

'They had tours of the ground which included the ball court. The guides would bring in the punters but they'd have to open the door very quietly and peak in to see if it was safe to enter – otherwise they might get hurt! Anyway, Greavsie was like all of us. He thought the sessions were good fun and wanted to win.

'He was brilliant. He just played as he always did, playing one-twos. People couldn't get near him. If someone came in to tackle him, he'd just lay it off. You'd never catch him in possession. That was typical Greavsie.'

The biggest moment Robertson shared with Greaves was that 1967 Wembley triumph, sealed with a 2-1 victory over Chelsea, the Scot opening the scoring with a volley from the edge of the box after an Alan Mullery piledriver had rebounded to him. Frank Saul later bagged Tottenham's second.

And Robertson remained grateful to Greaves for the support he gave him on that unforgettable day for the Scot. He said, 'Jimmy had played in several cup finals by then. He never got too wound up about things, or nervous. He treated it as just another game. He was a good influence on me. It turned out all right for me as I managed to score. Was that my number one moment in football? I would like to think I've had quite a few, but, yes, it stands up. It'll always be there in my mind because it was the FA Cup Final.'

Robertson recalled how he, Greaves and the rest of the cup-final squad made a pre-final visit to EMI Studios in Abbey Road, where the Beatles had completed laying down tracks for their classic album *Sgt. Pepper's Lonely Hearts Club Band* ten days earlier. Greaves took lead vocal on the song, 'Strollin".

Robertson said, 'We were asked to make a record. We went into the studio the Monday morning after we'd beaten Nottingham Forest in the semi-final. We had been given the day off.

'We gathered there at ten o'clock and they gave us some champagne. They knew what they were doing and by the time the recording started one or two were "quite happy". We made an EP with Jimmy's version of "Strollin'" on it. There's a picture of us sitting round the microphone with Jimmy singing it; I sung "I Belong To Glasgow" with Dave Mackay and Alan Gilzean. Terry Venables was a good singer and did a very polished version of "Bye Bye Blackbird". There were a few all the team joined in on like "Glory Hallelujah". The idea was that money made from the sale of the record would go into the players' pool. I found it got to somewhere in the top ten and sold something like 25,000 copies. We thought, "Oh, we'll make some money out of this." We got nothing. By the time they put the costs to it and everything else there wasn't anything left!'

Robertson felt for his old room-mate when he learned Greaves had his major stroke. He said, 'I found it very sad. The last time I saw him in the flesh I was at the memorial service for Bill Nicholson at White Hart Lane in 2004. He was fine and made a moving speech which was part of the service.'

Robertson insisted Greaves remains an 'icon' for players and fans alike. He said, 'Even now you get people who probably never saw him play in the flesh who think that. They've seen video film and learned about him. All I can say is that if you are talking about the best goalscorer you've ever seen then Greavsie would be there ahead of everybody else. He could be playing 89 minutes and you wouldn't know he was playing and he'd get a goal in the 90th.

'He had this tremendous knack of, when he had the ball, turning on a sixpence, and going on to score. You look at his goals. You wouldn't believe some of them. He whisked past people and it was in the net. When he was one on one with the keeper you would back Greavsie 99 times out of 100.

'A classic moment was against Manchester United when we beat them 5-1. It came when Greavsie picked the ball up on the halfway line and just started a run. He beat five players and chipped it past the goalkeeper. An iconic goal.'

Robertson believed Greaves has not been 'bigged up' enough when it comes to discussing the world's all-time best goalscorers, in contrast to the likes of Lionel Messi in the modern day.

He said, 'Messi? Well, there has been and are a lot of great goalscorers around. There's this glamour thing. That foreign players do things better. It is an easy headline with somebody coming from Spain, South America. The press can build them up. We are reserved [in the UK] but should shout it out from the rooftops about Greaves. As I said, we still haven't seen anyone better than Greavsie.

'He would be just as good today, or even better. Without question. He would walk into any team you'd care to mention. He'd get more protection from the referees as well as having decent pitches to play on. When you got to mid-season in the 60s, you'd be lucky to find grass on the pitches. You never see a player with mud on their shorts now.'

Robertson accepted Greaves would be the higher earner at Tottenham. He said, 'I remember I'd have discussions with Bill about a new contract. I might say "Greavsie's getting this" or whatever. Bill Nicholson put up a great defence, telling me, "Jim can score 30 goals a season." I could talk all day about him. Everybody had respect for him as a bloke as well as a player. He was a great guy, had a great personality, and was a very special talent. There are some you can compare him with but nobody's got to his level as far as I'm concerned.'

37

Jim Rosenthal

Television colleague

JIM ROSENTHAL worked on the *Oxford Mail* newspaper in his younger days, and could do 110 words a minute in Pitman shorthand. He revealed how that pace slowed but was quick to remember how Jimmy Greaves tested the knowledge he had retained of his roots.

The start of Rosenthal's glittering television broadcasting career, including covering eight World Cups, three Rugby World Cups, two Olympic Games and an estimated 150 Formula One motor races, began with ITV in 1980 when Greaves laid the foundations of his own. And for 12 years his path crossed constantly with the former football superstar.

One time they teamed up for ITV was at the 1986 League Cup Final between Oxford-born Rosenthal's hometown team and Queens Park Rangers at the old Wembley Stadium on 20 April.

Rosenthal, back in Oxford hosting a breakfast show for JACK Radio called *JACK's Wake Up Call*, said, 'We turned up at Wembley and Jim comes up to me and says, "I don't know anything about your team. Can you help me, mate?" This was on the day of the game! I told him, "Well, you've got the old centre-half there, Malcolm Shotton. He'll take 'em out. And there's quite a clever midfield player, Trevor Hebberd, and there's John Aldridge up front." But then again you wouldn't have known that he hadn't known anything. He delivered. He always delivered, despite doing it very much his own way. Week in, week out, it was, "What's he going to do?" And of course every time, in football terms, the ball went into the penalty area and Jim put it in the back of the net. That was Jim.'

Rosenthal grew up idolising Jimmy, thus reflecting the general appeal of our subject beyond tribalism. He revelled in the development of their shared career on programmes such as *The Big Match* and *Saint and Greavsie*. He said, 'Jimmy was my hero as a kid. I remember my dad took me to a game at White Hart Lane. That game when Spurs played Liverpool and won 7-2. Jimmy got four goals that day. And I was on the Tube train and we were talking about it. I said to my dad, "The thing is, Dad, he didn't do much else other than score." And the whole carriage fell about, as he'd got those four against Bill Shankly's Liverpool. It was Jim all over. When you wanted him to score, he was there.

'I remember watching the World Cup in 1966 and how upset I was when he didn't play in the final after getting a nasty injury. I was lucky enough to see England win the World Cup that day, standing behind the goal. But it was still tinged with a little bit of sadness for me because Jimmy wasn't playing. I felt he should have been.

'Then things wind forward and you start working with him. We worked on the 1982 World Cup. He was this end – in the studio – and I was over in Spain with England. But mainly over the years we were together on *The Big Match* and *Saint and Greavsie*.'

They teamed up to cover ITV's first ever live league game in a landmark season which saw the introduction of such matches on television as a regular feature, having been done once in 1960. The chosen fixture was between Tottenham Hotspur and Nottingham Forest at White Hart Lane on Sunday, 2 October 1983.

Rosenthal said, 'Jim was the expert and I was the "hello and welcome" guy. Brian Clough, Forest's manager, was saying, "Nobody is going to interrupt my Sunday lunch, I'm not turning up!" Jimmy, of course, loved all that.

'Jim was a pundit who told it like it was but the central thing was his humour. That humorous ingredient was so important. He was quick. Goodness me, he was quick-witted, Jimmy. Really, really, really good.

'These days punditry is so serious, po-faced. And you think, "Come on, it's an entertainment. You don't have to hammer people." Of course, Jimmy could do it but I can't remember him being cruel to a player. It wasn't in his lexicon, armoury, really.

'Sometimes I'd look across and think, "He's not interested at all." But then I'd ask him a question and he sparkled away. Brilliant. He made people laugh. I think he also made people feel comfy. He entertained and performed in equal measure, with the cast-iron credentials that nobody had ever scored more goals than him in the English top flight. Not a bad CV for any sportsman. And he had the ability to communicate it, to empathise with players because he'd been there and done it. He never said, "Cor I got a great goal there. You should show that." He wasn't interested blowing his own trumpet. He was very unassuming.'

Rosenthal fondly remembered his time on *Saint and Greavsie*, 'The *Saint and Greavsie* partnership was gold dust. It was so new and different. It broke the mould to have these two – both with impeccable credentials, by the way – talking football, with Jimmy being allowed to be himself, a maverick if you like. And within that there was a lot of good stuff journalistically. It all made people watch it. It suited Jimmy. Nobody ever told him what to say or what not to say.

'He drove the Saint crazy because it was absolutely huge commercially. They were getting offered silly sums of money. Jim would say, "Where is it [the gig], Saint?" If it was a bit of a distance, he would say, "I can't be arsed to go up there." Poor old Saint.

'It's like a lot of partnerships. It wasn't as if away from the screen they were going on holidays together. But on Saturday lunchtimes they gelled beautifully and I still think it is just about the greatest sporting partnership on television there's ever been because of the way they were.

'Jim used to rip me to pieces verbally in the programme. I was the whipping boy. Once I went on holiday to Florida and the weather was terrible over there. It can be a bit hit or miss. I told someone on the programme, "It's colder in Florida than England." You couldn't do it now, but they got hold of some icy pictures and showed them, saying, "This is where Jim Rosenthal's gone on holiday," and Greavsie loved it, of course. They weren't pictures of Florida at all. People got very upset. The Florida tourist board certainly did. They were saying, "What are you doing to us, it's not that bad!" Jimmy was involved, of course.

'You took it, in fact I quite enjoyed it. There was no malice in it all. Jimmy and the others were having a laugh at my expense and you could have a laugh at their expense as well. If you didn't have a sense of humour on that show you didn't last very long. Jimmy had that characteristic of not caring and then at the end of it there'd be a little smile. Pretty much at the end of every show he'd say, "Had you lot jumping around."'

Rosenthal reckoned Jimmy supplied 'magic' on television. He said, 'In many ways Greavsie's television days mirror his ones as a footballer in that he was – in the preparation and build-up – occasionally infuriating. He didn't really want to do any rehearsal, or anything. But when the light was on, there was that magic. As a footballer he wasn't a great trainer or listener to tactics. It was quick fag or whatever before he went out. But when the ball came to him in the penalty area he delivered. In some ways in those two careers, his attitude was exactly the same. There were certain things that jump out.

'There was a wonderful producer of *Saint and Greavsie* called Bob Patience. Bob was a really good journalist and responsible for setting the tone of the show.

'At Bob's funeral, we were all going back to Wentworth Golf Club and I got on to Jim and said, "You've got to go." And I added,

"You will say something won't you." He'd say, "Oh, Rosie, I can't be bothered, mate. No one wants to hear from me. Got to get back." I said, "Jim, you've got to do something." He said, "Oh, all right." He went and got up and was absolutely mesmerising. He said, "I've got to say working on *Saint and Greavsie* have been the most enjoyable years of my life. Much more enjoyable than football." People were in tears. That was staggering. In some ways it was, "Can you believe he said that?" But I thought about it and it did make sense.

'I don't think you'll get any football coach who would say, "I improved Jimmy Greaves as a player." He was a natural. He probably had to work a bit more on the telly which probably gave him that bit more satisfaction.'

Rosenthal is full of admiration at the way Jimmy built his television career after an extended problem with alcohol. He said, 'He did a "sit down" with Brian Moore talking about how he had lost five years of his life, if you like, drinking. He really spills how low he was. Nicking drink out of bins. Forgetting great chunks of his existence.

'You've always got to remember he came back from that to become that TV personality, which was phenomenal, really. One time Jim and I were up doing a game near Liverpool. Bloody perishing. The floor manager came up and gave us a couple of coffees and said, "I've put something in there to warm you up." I said, "You haven't put anything in them, have you?" He said, "Just a couple shots of brandy." I just took the cup away from Jim and said, "You don't want that." Jim said, "If he [the floor manager] hadn't have said that I probably would have drunk it and it wouldn't have done me a lot of good." So that was the narrow ledge he was on.

'I had a silly Sunday football team. Jimmy was drinking then. We played his team on Hackney Marshes. He had this packaging company or something. It happened to be a midweek afternoon, with the normal four inches of mud on Hackney Marshes. And there's Jimmy. We said to our team-mate John Motson to "just follow Jimmy wherever he goes and stop him. We'll count you out the game." Jimmy got four goals in the first 16 minutes. We are looking at John saying, "What the f*** is going on here?!" He said, "I'm trying, he's just too good."'

Rosenthal tried to stay in touch – even after Jimmy had a major stroke. He said, 'I kept in touch as much as possible. It was impossible after that stroke. It was obviously a really sad time for him. I spoke to Ian St John about it and he said Jimmy bravely said to him, "I don't want to be around." That's probably how he was for the last few years really.

'I rang the family and Terry Baker, asking, "What about me going to see him? I really want to see him." They all said the same thing, "Don't go. It'll be upsetting." So you stay away.'

Rosenthal tried to sum up his old pal, 'Everybody loved him. What he had was immaculate timing on the pitch and on telly. And he timed his death before a Tottenham-Chelsea game. The reaction he got at it from 60,000 people showed the love that people have for him. If you could go round and find somebody who said "I hate Jimmy Greaves" they would be a rare and very sad character.'

Jimmy, as a dog lover, would have got a kick over freelance Rosenthal covering the world-famous Crufts show in recent years. And he would no doubt have provided an amusing commentary alongside him full of one-line quips. The broadcasting pair back in harness? Rosenthal pondered the scenario, and said, 'My starting to do Crufts coincided with Jimmy's major stroke so it wouldn't have been possible but I'll always remember Jimmy with huge affection.'

38

I Rossoneri
Team-mates

GIANNI RIVERA, hailed as one of the world's greatest players of all time, knew Jimmy Greaves from their time together at AC Milan. Gianni was nonplussed by Jimmy's 'consistent rebellion against the system' at *I Rossoneri*.

The Italian playmaker supreme was quoted in *This One's On Me*, which highlighted Jimmy's addiction to alcohol, saying in broken English, 'Yimmy, why do you do these things? Why you fight [coach Nereo] Rocco all the time? It is surely easier to give in and do as he wants. The money it is good, no?'

Greaves was long gone as Rivera helped guide the San Siro giants to the Serie A title by the end of the season and the European Cup in the following campaign, stepping stones to a glittering career which saw him help *I Rossoneri* to two more domestic championships, five Coppa Italias and another European Cup while playing in four World Cups, before becoming a politician.

Gianni might have had enough influence as a future Member of the European Parliament from 2005 to 2009, but Jimmy's head was not for turning back in 1961 when the Italian forward tried to advise our subject to accept the status quo. Simply put, Jimmy did not want to be there.

He had agreed to an £80,000 move from Chelsea in need of the-then bumper pay packet of an estimated £6,700-a-year salary and £15,000 signing-on fee, with his wife Irene imminently expecting.

Jimmy tried to get out of the move when the maximum wage ceiling of £20 per week back home was smashed shortly afterwards and he provisionally agreed to stay at Stamford Bridge for five times the amount. But it was no dice. He felt AC Milan would take the matter to FIFA which would get him banned from playing should he renege on their arrangement, so he agreed to an improved three-year offer from them.

Four days after the birth of second daughter Mitzi on 4 August 1961, Jimmy flew out to Milan and a reality of life he instantly struggled to tolerate. He felt the writing was on the wall with the club threatening to fine him £50 a day after delaying his scheduled arrival on 17 July as he was awaiting his second daughter's birth.. And it didn't improve for him as he began his spell at the San Siro.

He believed the club was 'run on the lines of an expensive home for delinquent boys'; that he was 'being treated like a naughty schoolboy'; that coach Nereo Rocco 'made my life hell', was 'aggressive and dogmatic', paid him constant 'attention', even 'ordering my meals'. The coach considered drinking beer 'a mortal sin' and sat guard outside Jimmy's room to ensure he didn't go out when the player's brother-in-law Tom visited him. Jimmy, in short, recalled, 'He and I didn't hit it off.'

He also claimed a pre-season training camp was 'so much like a prison camp' with the players 'locked together'. The routine, being unable to join in conversations in Italian and 'childish discipline' were giving him 'a fit of depression' and made him consider doing a 'bunk' after a few days.

Jimmy also got 'a terrific hammer in the press' which he felt portrayed him in 'wild stories' as 'king of the playboys' while he said, 'I wasn't far off being in solitary confinement.' He felt that if he went out, the public would report his every action. Our subject considered his freedom as an individual was challenged in 'an outrageous, petty, laughable world'.

Mind you, despite his off-the-field troubles, Jimmy impressed those he played alongside. Giovanni Trapattoni enjoyed a glittering managerial career influenced by Rocco's tactics. Along with Carlo Ancelotti, Ernst Happel, José Mourinho and Tomislav Ivić, Rocco's name will live on as part of an exclusive club of managers to have won titles in four different countries, collecting a total of ten in Italy, Germany, Portugal and Austria. He is also the only person to manage the same club – Juventus – to European Cup, Cup Winners' Cup and UEFA Cup triumphs. On top, he bossed Inter Milan, Bayern Munich, Benfica, Italy and the Republic of Ireland.

But his time as a defender-cum defensive midfielder behind Jimmy up top sparked the start of a trophy-laden playing career with AC Milan which took in two Serie A titles, the Coppa Italia, two European Cups and the Cup Winners' Cup. And Trapattoni praised Jimmy while pointing out his non-conformist ways in his four-month stay in the capital of Lombardy.

Jimmy was still black and red hot in the goals department at the start of the 1961/62 campaign, scoring an average of almost one per game despite the adoption of the defensive *catenaccio* system pioneered in Italy by Rocco and beginning to be adopted across the country. He netted in a friendly against Brazilian outfit Botafogo on his debut, then on 27 August he hit the mark on his first league outing for *I Rossoneri*, a 3-0 victory at Lanerossi Vicenza. He was building his name for scoring goals on debuts.

Jimmy bagged doubles in two successive home league games, a 4-3 win over Udinese and 3-2 loss versus Sampdoria. And he went on to score nine in almost as many appearances, the most significant against table-topping Inter in the *Derby della Madonnina* in front of 77,500 at the San Siro on 1 October.

Trapattoni revealed his opinions in his autobiography *Non dire Gatto* . He wrote of Jimmy, 'He blew everyone away. How many goals he scored! How many defenders he sent crazy! In October he won the Milan derby for us 3-1. We were without José Altafini and Sandro Salvadore.

'And then no sooner did he arrive than he was gone. As a matter of fact Milan sent him back to Tottenham because he was unmanageable. He tended to drink, as the English do, and then disappear like one of those stray cats. If he could, Rocco would have throttled him. He used to yell out in his Triestino dialect and send us all over Milanello looking for him. But it was no use. You could never find him.'

Rossoneri captain Cesare Maldini, who skippered and managed Italy, also spoke of the Jimmy he knew. Maldini, who passed in April 2016 aged 84, was another Rocco acolyte. He was appointed his mentor's assistant in 1970 before coaching AC Milan to the European Cup Winners' Cup and Coppa Italia in 1973 when Jimmy's *bête noire* was technical director. He then succeeded *El Paròn* as head managerial honcho the following year and was also in charge of Italy's 1996 European Under-21 Championship winners, featuring Gianluigi Buffon, Francesco Totti and Fabio Cannavaro, who all helped their country lift the 2006 World Cup.

But the defender was an experienced leader on the field for 21-year-old Jimmy and lifted what was his fourth Serie A title trophy by the end of the 1961/62 season after securing the first in 1954/55. He partnered Trapattoni in that European Cup triumph the following term.

The father of legendary Italian full-back Paolo and grandfather to modern-day *Rossoneri* midfielder Daniel recalled a dressing-down Jimmy received from Rocco and how he struggled to not burst out laughing.

He said in the Rocco biography *El Paròn* by Gigi Garanzini, 'We were in a hotel on via Napo Torriani. I was in bed, [José] Altafini was rooming with me. It was around 11 o'clock at night. We were having a natter and then come midnight it was lights out.

Not too long afterwards we heard a noise. From the light under the door we could see a shadow passing by.

'We got up, opened the door and there was Greaves all dressed up, ready to go out. He was carrying his shoes and tip-toeing very slowly down the corridor. He looked like the Pink Panther. They caught him in a night club in Piazza Diaz.

'The next morning Rocco sent [*Rossoneri* club secretary] Eugenio Conti to wake him up and bring him to the Assassino where he was having his lunch. As soon as he opened his mouth to say sorry the storm we'd all be waiting hours for finally hit. The only problem we had, I can guarantee, was keeping a straight face.'

Maldini also remembered how Jimmy used to take pride in his Jaguar car when reunited with his old team-mate through the auspices of *The Sun*.

Glenn Hoddle's England were due to take on Maldini's Italy, captained by the boss's son Paolo, in a World Cup qualifier at Wembley in February 1997. Greaves, with writer Martin Samuel, flew out to Italy shortly before the *Azzurri* pipped the hosts, thanks to a goal by Gianluca Zola. Samuel, recalling the time in the *Daily Mail* of 20 September 2021, a day after Greaves's passing, wrote, 'Maldini met us in the centre of Milan and the pair got on swimmingly, although with the same language barrier that was no doubt among the many complications in 1961. "Yimmy", Cesare remembered, didn't much care for training but spent a lot of time polishing his "Yaguar". The players would be working, "Yimmy" would be – he mimed the methodical burnishing of a shiny red bonnet.'

Altafini, a World Cup winner as a player with Brazil, recognised that Jimmy was unhappy and homesick. He said to *The Athletic*, 'Jimmy was a top striker. When he came to Italy he was still young but a great player. At the time he joined I thought to myself, "This guy's *fortissimo*." But Greaves missed England.

'He was a good guy, though. I liked him. It was just a shame he couldn't speak Italian. I remember a game in Venice, Milan-Venezia. We were drawing 1-1. I scored a bicycle kick and the ball looked like it might have come off him. We all ran over to Jimmy and asked him if it did or not and he said it didn't. It was a remarkable show of honesty and sportsmanship.'

39

Ian St John

Television colleague, opponent, aficionado

IAN ST JOHN revealed how he and Jimmy Greaves 'hit it off' working together on the iconic, pioneering *Saint and Greavsie*, the much-loved television programme which won the heart of the nation – football fans to general households – for its irreverent, entertaining and informed style.

The former Liverpool and Scotland striker passed aged 82 in March 2021, just six months before Our Jim.

Ian was interviewed by Max Rushden on talkSPORT in February 2020 with the release of the BT Sport documentary *Greavsie* that month.

The amiable, astute anchor was the foil to the off-the-cuff wit of Jimmy in their football preview programme from 1985 to 1992.

Ian, who hosted a show with Graham Beecroft on talkSPORT in the early 2000s, said, 'We loved doing it, there were no rehearsals or anything and it was just a great time for both of us. We really got on well together as pals. We hit it off as a working pair, and he was very funny – well I thought he was very funny! Jimmy had a very sharp wit and entertained people.

'My part in the duo was to try and keep it to the script, to try and do the football thing in a way that Jimmy could bounce in and out. We'd have fun and laugh and go way off the script. At times Jimmy would wander off script completely, but it was funny. It was my job to keep things running in a straight line, but he was never scripted.

'This was Jimmy Greaves, a man who had scored all these goals and played at the top level, so it was great viewing for the public, and you know he's funny when the cameramen laugh on the show floor. It was great fun to do. It was better than working, I used to say. I had so much respect for him having played against him. And for him getting over his alcohol problems. That was a big thing.'

Ian recalled Jimmy and future US president Donald Trump taking part in the 1992 League Cup draw in New York (see Richard Worth chapter). He said, 'That was so funny, because he [Trump] hadn't a clue who either of us were. To do that with a guy who would go on to be the top man in the world in politics! It was just funny looking back at it.'

The Saint described Jimmy as the country's 'number one goalscorer'. 'He was top of the tree, Jimmy. He was the number one goalscorer in the country, for club and country.'

Ian reckoned Jimmy would have 'scored a ton more goals' on modern pitches, saying the surfaces he and his TV partner played on were 'shocking'.

The Saint, in a *Daily Telegraph* article by Jeremy Wilson, said, 'Jimmy Greaves was a phenomenon. He was the only opponent that [St John's Liverpool manager] Bill Shankly paid any attention to in team talks. That includes Law, Best and Charlton. Bill would say, "You must hold him up, don't dive in at him, go double on him." Yet Jimmy would still just pick the ball up and run past people like Messi does. He never thrashed them in from 30 yards. Incredible close control. Wonderful balance. Amazing body swerves. So elusive and composed.'

Ian reportedly showed 'annoyance' that Jimmy 'has never received so much as an MBE' in the interview conducted before he was eventually awarded one.

He said, 'How crazy is that? He gave wonderful enjoyment to football fans and was then on the television for years giving entertainment and fun to people. He had two careers. I'm not knocking other players but Jimmy was operating on a different planet to most of them.'

40

John Sillett

Team-mate

JOHN SILLETT became more known by the wider public when, as a seemingly larger-than-life character, he understandably celebrated Coventry City's lone major triumph in extravagant fashion. Winning the 1987 FA Cup at Wembley before 96,000 in the stadium and a global television audience of millions can turn you into a household name, particularly if you are an extrovert who has plotted a David toppling a Goliath.

Jimmy Greaves, a lifelong pal and former Chelsea team-mate, was a television broadcaster who had played a part on that day.

The unfancied Sky Blues had come from behind twice to defeat favourites Tottenham Hotspur, 3-2. A diving header from Keith Houchen and a Gary Mabbutt own goal did for the Lilywhites who had led 2-1 through Clive Allen, son of Greaves's Spurs team-mate Les, and Mabbutt, with Dave Bennett making it 1-1.

On the victory lap, Sillett, given the nickname 'Snoz', because of the size of his nose, by his old mate, gestured as if he was supping from the cup and said to *The Guardian* before the two sides met again in a third-round tie in January 2002, 'That was for Jimmy Greaves. We used to play together at Chelsea and when I spotted him in the television gantry I shouted up, "I'm going to have a few of these tonight, Greavsie."

'He may have been a former Tottenham player but the truth is that he helped me plot their downfall. He's a bright tactician, Greavsie, and the night before we talked about how I should approach the game.

'I don't think anyone was rooting for Coventry more than him, but I felt a bit sorry for him, I must admit. All the Coventry fans were giving him grief because he had tipped us to lose in every round. What they hadn't realised was that he was just obeying my instructions. I had told him he was the worst tipster in the world. I remember saying: "For God's sake, don't you dare have us down to win." And would you know it? It worked.'

It was the first time in six finals that Spurs had not managed to seal the world's oldest and most famous knockout trophy. It tore up the script, which had Glenn Hoddle, a Tottenham legend, to challenge the status of Greaves at White Hart Lane, making a glorious exit after a 12-year association with the club, having first signed as an apprentice.

The ties that bound Jimmy and John stretched back three decades to their time together at Stamford Bridge. It was poignant the pair should leave us within just over a month of each other, especially when you factor in that John, who passed on 30 November 2021, was able to recall his relationship with Jimmy when his old friend died on 19 September.

Sillett first saw Greaves representing London Schoolboys and was more impressed with his strike partner David Cliss. But the defender's brother Peter, who played alongside our Jim with John for Chelsea, told his sibling Greaves was the one who impressed him with his sharpness, lightning speed, composure and finishing. And John eventually conceded he had a 'touch of genius' about him.

'I had wonderful moments with Jimmy. Our jobs were to clean and look after the snooker room.

'Jimmy had the worst car I have ever seen. It was shocking. The door fell off one day when we were in it.

'Other teams tried to kick him off the park but they couldn't touch him. You used to hear them say, "Get Greaves!" He would say, "Snoz, come and rescue me." 'Jimmy was quiet, he wasn't the mouthy type.

'Jimmy was such a great fellow, such a charming, lovely man. He was a great character with it, we got on great together. He got me to organise a birthday party for him and also a going-away party when he went to Italy. He gave me a lovely cigarette lighter. I've still got that. I'm looking at it now on the shelf. Special moments.'

John remembered Jimmy scoring on his league debut for Chelsea against Spurs at the Lane on 24 August 1957.

John, whose brother Peter and Jimmy's future Spurs team-mate Les Allen were in the Blues' line-up, said to BT Sport, 'He must have gone past four players. Such great body movement. He sent them one way, sent them the other way, got through and just tucked it on the net. And he looked round as if it to say, "That's how I do it."'

He appeared in an advertisement for the beef drink, with the tag line 'Dynamic footballer Jimmy Greaves trains and scores on Bovril'.

After Jimmy had missed chances in a 5-0 reverse against Blackpool, John referred to the deal with the company, which produced a drink that could be consumed by melting beef stock cubes into hot water when jokingly saying, 'Bovril has made you a laughing stock'.

Sillett, it is understood, combined with Greaves to turn luncheon vouchers into 'black market' currency and helped him cope in professional football.

41

Richard Worth
Television colleague

RICHARD WORTH was with Jimmy Greaves at the 'coal face' of *Saint and Greavsie* throughout its magnificent seven-year run on ITV. To Richard, the show's producer and editor with the late Bob Patience, the image conjured of miners, armed with pick axes, putting in blood, sweat and tears to dig out the black rock with energy content at such a spot, would seem a world away from Jimmy's approach to the programme. But Richard always had a sense of danger, which, of course, is something very much inherent working in the shrinking industry. Nothing comparable to collapsing mine shafts, mind; more the unpredictable nature of the show caused by our subject's off-the-cuff remarks and sense of humour. He said, 'I suppose it was dangerous. There were always "moments". It was live and you never knew what Jimmy was going to say.'

Richard resided in retirement on the West Sussex coast at Bosham, the place where legend has it that King Canute attempted to hold back the waves from the English Channel. He lapped up the opportunity to discuss Jimmy and the 'pioneering' programme, which grew so popular it remains in the memory of many households to this day.

But it was clear he recognised resisting the waves of Jimmy's wit and charm would have been counterproductive as they were qualities he felt gave the popular ITV show its 'magic'.

Richard said, 'When you get people who aren't trained broadcasters it gets you on the edge of your seat. Think of a show like BBC's *Have I Got News for You* which is recorded and edited so they can take out any mistakes, any legally questionable stuff. Yes, they do hours and hours of live TV on Sky now but in the *Saint and Greavsie* days the technology was more basic.

'Jimmy might not have had any innate broadcasting skills but he was just one of those people who was lucky enough in life to be good at stuff. His humour came through the screen instantly.

'You've probably heard from so many people that he wasn't the greatest trainer as a footballer but was just a genius and, in a way, his broadcasting career was similar.

'He was this clever guy who came up with funny stuff. And you didn't want to pre-script it. That leaves you open. Today you would probably never get away with it. There'd be 15 lawyers in there going "you can't do that, can't say that". Jim wasn't racist by any means but it appears whatever you say these days somebody is going to object to it. Back then you just hoped for the best.

'I can't remember any specific cases of Jimmy putting his foot in his mouth, although there were one or two occasions so and so at a certain club, or a certain player or whatever objected to what Jimmy said. That was bound to happen.

'There's a lot of malice in the game these days I suppose, but there was never any side, any malice, to anything from Jimmy. It was always him trying to lean on his experience. People he knew well for stories and stuff like that. There was never "I'm going to stick a knife in somebody" because he didn't like them very much. He would never do that. Ever.'

On his working relationship with Jimmy, Richard said, 'We had worked together on by-products like World Cups and stuff – which was before *Saint and Greavsie* established itself – but my primary relationship with him was through the show from start to finish, really. I was there when Saint and Jimmy got teamed up and when it went off-air. I was his producer and editor with another guy who is sadly not with us any more, Bob Patience.

'Bob did a lot of work outside the TV realm with roadshows and books, as well as being producer and editor of the show with me. So we kind of shared that responsibility a little bit for those years.'

Richard took up the story of how he came to be working with Jimmy, 'Well, I was already working at ITV on the South Bank in London when the relationship between Ian and Jimmy was growing. It started off, Ian was presenting *On The Ball* and Jimmy was doing insert pieces on the line.

'It worked so well that the next thing was that it was thought it would make its own "stand alone" show. So Jimmy arrived at the South Bank in the mid-80s and that went on to the early 90s when it stopped.

'He was already very good at broadcasting, having worked in television in the Midlands. All you knew was somewhere these bits of genius would suddenly appear. There was no rhyme or reason to it. He was just bloody good at it.

'It wasn't really straight man–funny man. Ian and Jimmy just had different styles. But they locked together quite nicely. Jimmy was that sort of guy who could find humour in all sorts of things and express it in such a good way that was infectious.

'Ian was smart. He knew he had a good team around him of people putting the show together. Good directors. He didn't really have too many strong opinions, he just said, "Right, tell me what we are doing and I'll get on with it and do it." He didn't extend himself into areas that weren't necessary for him to do. He would let the security blanket around him do its job.

'That was good because these days everybody seems to be a diva. I can say it about both Ian and Jimmy that neither of them had an issue like that. There was none of that, "You know who I am don't you? I'm important." They just got on well doing something they enjoyed doing.

'The funny thing was, that Ian always wore an earpiece so he could hear the countdowns like "you've got ten seconds before we are off air" and know when to shut Jimmy up! Jimmy didn't wear one for most of the time. He was oblivious. It wasn't so much he wouldn't do it. Everybody thought the lead guy, the anchor of the show [St John], obviously needed to hear what the director's saying, what the PA is saying, what's going on. Jimmy didn't need to know all that. He was just the permanent studio guest. A free spirit. That was Jimmy. So one guy knew when they had to shut up, the other guy had no clue. It worked. Of course it did. It always did.

'He did put an earpiece on for the last couple of years and we could have put it in right at the start. But it is also a very difficult technique and you see a lot of ex-professionals these days who turn up on Sky or whatever and one or two are wearing an earpiece and one or two are not. If you can hear in your head all the team people going "camera three, you've got 40 seconds on this, then we are going to go", do you need all that in your head while you are trying to think of something funny to say? You don't really. The anchor has to have all that noise in his head, but not everybody does.

'These days, the amount of content out there is just enormous. Every game seems to be televised one way or the other. Every news conference covered, recorded on tape or telephone or something. There's pictures of some things everywhere.

'The mid-to-late 1980s was just the start of the technological boom, as I suggested earlier. Stuff became more readily available. But there wasn't much then. You were relying on what games were covered in midweek for *Saint and Greavsie*. You'd show the goals again. You'd need a couple of good stories to reflect whatever the big games were. To get crews out on the road was new. The Jim Rosenthals and the Martin Tylers going out doing stories for us. You had your bits of content but how do you make sure the show is different? Jimmy had the kind of character that made it different.

'It meant my idea of writing a script was, "Got pieces on story A, story B, goals A, goals B. In between, Saint and Jim chat for a minute and a half." And that's all you had to write. Of course, you would rehearse and you'd say like, "Right, let's talk Coventry," and Jim would say, "Yeah, my old mate Snoz [John Sillett] is up there. I'll say some stuff about him. I've got it. Don't worry." You were sort of reliant on that.

'Ian would travel down from Liverpool on a Friday because he still lived up in the Wirral. And he'd arrive Friday lunchtime early afternoon, sit with us, be forensic and say, "What we doing, what's going on?" We were still pulling everything together. "Have we got this, have we got that live interview tomorrow?" Jimmy didn't ever come until Saturday morning. He didn't need to as he was, as I said, a guest in a certain way.

'I would quite often when I was doing the show ring Jimmy on a Friday, out of courtesy really, and say, "Right Jim, here's what we got. We've got this. A story with this guy." Jim would go, "Oh, that's all right. I'll just see it all tomorrow." I'd say, "But Jim you might want to think about it, a few stories might come into your head." He'd say, "That's all right, Richard, I'm fine." He didn't really seem to want to know, generally!

'It was like, "You don't need to tell me what's going on. I'll figure it out in the morning." He did, I believe, lean on [journalist and book collaborator] Norman Giller quite a lot though, saying, "OK, I'll give Norman a ring and he'll give me a few one-liners or little points." Which he did, I'm sure, on a regular basis. So that was a bit of preparation he did.

'But if you said to Jimmy, "We've got this great story with the x, y or z person you used to play with 25 years ago, why don't we jump in the car on Tuesday, go to his house, film a little interview?" He would say, "No, I'm all right, mate, I don't want to do that." He just didn't usually want to get involved in the content of the show. He did now and again, where he'd say, "I'd love to do that." But it was very rare he would say, "What can I do this week? What story can I go and do?" His general attitude was, "Turn up on a Saturday, do what I do and go home at lunchtime. That's fine."'

Saint and Greavsie remains in the nation's affections. Richard said, 'It is amazing how beloved *Saint and Greavsie* is, really. It was fun doing it. We had no clue that we were doing anything that was out of the ordinary. Sadly, Jimmy Greaves and Ian St John both died within months of each other in 2021 and it all came back with people saying, "Wasn't that a great show", "brilliant", "clever". And I think, "Well, oh, we must have been doing something right." Obviously in those days it was quite a pioneering show in a way. Nobody had ever tried to be anything other than very serious in TV sport. It's the way they did it. *Saint and Greavsie* was a trendsetter for a lot of stuff. It grew out of Jimmy's personality. If he hadn't have had that personality you wouldn't have had that show. What was the show's X factor? Well, I suppose it was the irreverence you were expecting.'

Richard recalled how he accompanied Jimmy and Ian for a 1992 'special' to New York and a now legendary meeting with future US president Donald Trump, when he was a high-profile businessman in the Big Apple.

Richard said, 'It was right before the draw for the preliminary round for the 1994 World Cup [with the finals being staged in the United States]. So the idea was we go to it at Madison Square Garden. Do the whole show from over there. It also happened to be the week where we would do the draw for the Rumbelows [League] Cup, which ITV had the rights to at the time. That whole week was bizarre. We just thought we'd figure out how we would do it when we got there. It just so happened we stumbled across Donald Trump at either Trump Tower or Trump Plaza. We said, "Well let's do it with him if he would agree." And he did.

'It was just luck. Not pre-planned. In the end, we'd have found somebody. Pelé or somebody. FIFA had people in town to make things look nice. Years later it looked brilliant that we thought of that but it was just pure luck. It came out of the draw Leeds v Manchester United. And United manager Alex Ferguson went potty! He said, "This is a gimmick. The whole thing. What's all that?!" Probably more because they'd drawn Leeds!

'Jimmy got on with Donald Trump fine. Literally, we all walked into his office, set up the cameras, did the thing, walked out half an hour later. That was it. It was all right. You said, "Donald sit here. Jimmy you draw the away teams, Donald the home." That was it. Game over.

'I don't think Donald Trump really knew who the people were. For him, I think it was "my opportunity to be on telly somewhere".

'I've been very pleasant about Jimmy, but he could be an awkward customer. And I say that with reservation because who knows how anyone is going to behave if they've been an alcoholic. When I knew and worked with him he was a recovering alcoholic.

'He never touched a drop of drink all the time I worked with him at all. I never saw him do it. I guess he had given up and was absolutely strict with himself at that time. But what that does to your personality and body I don't know. I can imagine it'd make you a bit grumpy.

'So often it was hard to get him started on a Saturday morning. He would always have a row brewing with the car park guy at London Weekend Television's studios at the South Bank. He would drive over from wherever he was in Essex and when he got there, Jimmy would come up to the car park bloke and say, "Hello, I'm Jimmy Greaves and there's a car park spot for me." Car park bloke would go, "Haven't got you on the list, mate." Jimmy would go, "It's Saturday morning, there's nobody in here!"

'And Jim would go to us, "Why is this?" He would quite literally say, next week, if my car park space is not ready, I'm off. I'm going to turn the car round and go home.

'It became a thing. We had to literally phone the guy who would actually be on duty on the car park on Saturday morning to be sure he wouldn't be difficult and would let Jim in. So that was a bit awkward.

'If he came in with a bit of a grump, I'd have a technique of dealing with it. I'd go, "Hello Jim, how you doin'?" He'd reply, "I'm all right, mate." That didn't mean he was OK. He'd add, "I'll be all right in a minute. I just need a cup of tea." I said, "OK." So we'd sit in the canteen to talk through the content of the show. We had techniques to warm him up. You'd have to be off point, not talk about the show. Wind him up with a couple of jokes and a few quiz questions. So you'd go, "Three Everton players in the 1970s whose surnames begin with K." He'd go, "Hang on a minute, hang on … right, let's start with Kendall." Then he'd be fine.

'There was always in the background, "I'm not feeling that well." And us going, "What are we going to do?" It happened on the 1990 Christmas show. Jim said, "Oh, Richard, I've got a terrible cold. I just can't do it." I said, "Bloody hell, Jim – it's our Christmas show. It is going to be awkward isn't it." And in the end, I can't remember if it was me or somebody else said, "Why don't we just do it with a puppet?"

'That was great but we didn't think it would be as easy as it sounded. We had to start doing it on the Friday and have it done by Saturday. There was an existing puppet of Jim – made by the people who produce [TV satire] *Spitting Image*. I knew [commentator] Peter Brackley, who is now sadly not with us. I knew him very well because we were from the same neck of the woods in Sussex and had worked together a lot. I knew he could do a Greavsie voice. So I said, "OK, Peter, is there any chance you can come into London tomorrow and do a Greavsie voice with a puppet?" He said, "Blimey!" We said, "Don't worry, we'll look after you." So that's what happened.

'The guys from *Spitting Image* gave us the puppet. Peter came in to do the voice and we rehearsed the show as if it was Jimmy himself really sitting there. There was no genius from Jimmy Greaves on this occasion but genius from Peter Brackley. Peter responded to everything in a way you couldn't imagine.

'Jim had got sick the day before. We had been hoping, like with any long-running show, if one of the presenters had got sick, that they got better. They would be fine and phone up on the Saturday morning and say, "I'm on my way." I remember that a few times with Jim after he said he wasn't well. But on the occasion of the Christmas show it never, of course, turned itself round. We had to have that solution.'

Richard remembered how the end of *Saint and Greavsie* in 1992 came as a surprise, 'A headline in *The Sun* told us that the show was being ditched. But that was just a failure in good communication by the powers that be at ITV at the time. It wasn't unexpected. Nobody had been talking about new set design, or budgets for the show, etc. anyway.

'The final show of the Euros 1992 in from Sweden had Ian and Jimmy cycling off into the distance singing, "This could be the last time, this could be the last time [based on the Rolling Stones record]", as you may have seen.

'The background, of course, was that Sky/BSkyB had acquired the rights to the newly formed Premier League – despite an ITV bid – and this left a show like *Saint and Greavsie* without access to the best rights for football in Britain, and it left not very much to make a show with.

'All good things come to an end, and there were different positive outlets for all of us in future years – but it was an abrupt end for a good group of people who had had a lot of fun together.'

Overall, Richard remembered how well he and Jimmy got on, 'We had a lovely relationship. I never fell out with him the whole time. But all of us are guilty of getting out of the bed the wrong side and we needed those techniques to get him moving.

'And how lucky are any of us to be working with someone who had got this inbuilt comedy genius? You know it is going to be fine. He's going to come up with something that none of us had anticipated. He'll just laugh and smile his way through the show. It was never a problem. That was a skill. A real skill. Not everybody can do it when you've got TV lights shining at you, time deadlines and everything else.

'It was like when everybody said he was a genius as a footballer because he wouldn't have to think about what he was going to do. It would just come so naturally to him. He just had confidence. You think, "I'm OK, I can do anything." He'd been successful as a schoolboy footballer from early years, always found things came easily to him.

'I didn't really keep in touch with him. There was no way to do it. I think Jim was happy being at home with his family. He wasn't looking to "keep all my old relationships going".

'When Bob Patience died in 2013, Jim came to his funeral, along with Sir Alex Ferguson. And Jim was brilliant. He got up and spoke. He was full of life, which was really nice. It was probably the last time I saw him. A couple of years after that he did have his devastating stroke.'

Was Jimmy a national treasure? Worth said, 'Well obviously there's a lot of people when you mention Jimmy Greaves they'd say, "Who?" But in the football realm, absolutely, because of what he's done on the pitch and off it will survive the test of time. Not everybody can say that when they stop. But for two different reasons [his football and TV careers], he created a lot of great memories for people.

'He certainly created a memory my daughter Sarah will never forget. I was also the producer of the athletics for ITV and one weekend I was supposed to go to the Brussels meeting in Belgium in late August and the next day get back to London and do the *Saint and Greavsie* show on Saturday lunchtime. Brussels to London?

Not that difficult. Straightforward enough to do it but my wife was pregnant, due to have a baby. So as I opened the door to leave the house to Brussels on the Friday, she said, "Richard, don't go, don't go." So I didn't. The next morning I was in the hospital with her and my daughter in Brighton. Obviously, I couldn't do the show. I rang to explain that I wasn't in Brussels or coming in for *Saint and Greavsie* because of the baby and that they would have to fix it.

'Fix it they did. The show started, Ian and Jim were there, Jim said to the viewers, "We've got this that and the other … and no producer today because his wife's had a baby. A little girl.

'In those days, there was no texting, WhatsApp, nothing. Just telephones. If you thought about it you'd ring somebody. So there was half my family saying, "We've just heard on the TV your baby's been born." That wouldn't happen these days. You'd be filming it live and send as it happened, more or less!

'That was Jimmy. Again, totally unscripted. And of course for my daughter, now in her 30s, it is a little moment of pride that she could have a little connection with Jimmy Greaves.'

42

Tributes

Aficionados

OSVALDO ARDILES (ex-Spurs player and World Cup winner) tweeted, 'Great player, great man. Very funny. Humble. Jimmy epitomises what Spurs is: "To dare is to do". When you come to meet the great goalscorer in heaven it matters not if you win or lose but how you played the game.'

ARTHUR BLACKLEY (Chelsea colleague of Jimmy, writing in the *Isle of Thanet News*), 'I was an inside-forward just like Greavsie and David Cliss. I was in the youth side and got into the reserves but never quite made the grade. I remember one game in the youth side with Greavsie and he scored seven goals. He was called into manager Ted Drake's office. Drake used to play for Arsenal and once scored seven goals many years ago. Drake said to him, "Congratulations, enjoy the moment son, it only happens once in a lifetime," – and the next week Jimmy scored eight!' *Special thanks to Ray Duffy for finding and sharing this article.*

DANNY BLANCHFLOWER (the late double-winning Spurs captain and godfather to Greaves's son Danny after his future team-mate scored his first league goal for Chelsea against him and his side at White Hart Lane aged 17), 'It was the greatest show I have ever seen from a young player on his league debut. The boy is a natural. He is the greatest youngster I have ever played against.'

FRANK BRUNO (ex-world boxing champion) tweeted, 'We [Bruno and Greaves] spent loads of times together. A brilliant footballer, scoring with every team he played for, a real character. You could sit in a room two hours and he would just speak and make me really laugh constantly.'

MARK BULLINGHAM (FA chief executive), 'When it comes to considering our greatest players of all time, Jimmy has to be up there.'

JAMIE CARRAGHER (pundit and ex-Liverpool player), 'Jimmy Greaves. The best goalscorer we have seen and also part of the best football show we have ever seen.'

CHELSEA, 'Those who witnessed Greaves effortlessly breeze through a defence with the ball at his feet, before passing it beyond the goalkeeper and into the back of the net, universally acclaim him as the finest goalscorer to play for Chelsea FC. They normally go further too, and describe the east Londoner as the best finisher English football has ever seen.'

MARTIN CHIVERS (Spurs team-mate, on Sky Sports), 'You'd have to look at Messi, how he jinks in and out. Jimmy was like that. They'd fly out at him, but he'd tap the ball in the net. He was a cheeky chappie, one that always put me into trouble, all pranks and jokes. But on the field he was deadly.'

TONY COTTEE (ex-West Ham and England player) tweeted, 'There have been many great goalscorers over the years but none have been as good as him.'

JEREMY CROSS (*Daily Star* chief sports writer), 'The word "legend" could have been invented for Jimmy Greaves ... a prodigy, pioneer, a true great of football, later in life appeared capable of charming the birds from the trees.'

PETER CROUCH (ex-Spurs player, on BT Sport), 'In this day and age of stats you go back to Jimmy's goals-to games ratio. It is ridiculous.'

RIO FERDINAND (ex-West Ham and England player, on BT Sport), 'To me as a kid, the first autobiography I ever read was Jimmy Greaves. He has a phenomenal standing in the game. I know him really from *Saint and Greavsie*. I didn't know how good a player he was until you see the records and the amount of goals he scored and you think, "Wow this fellow in any era would have been a superstar."'

ANDY FRYD (Brentwood Town team-mate, to the *Essex Chronicle*), 'It was a Tuesday night [meeting Jimmy] as we trained on Tuesdays and Thursdays unless there was a game. I was the second person into the dressing room. The first person sitting in there was Jimmy Greaves. We had been warned that someone of note was coming to play for the club. Nobody even dreamt that this was going to happen to us. I looked at him and I was absolutely stunned. I couldn't believe it. He was sitting there banging these two old muddy boots together.'

NORMAN GILLER (journalist, who wrote a tribute on Jimmy Greaves for the Sports' Journalists' Association, book collaborator and friend posted on social media on the day of our subject's passing, 'The world has lost a great human being with the passing of Jimmy Greaves today. My thoughts are with his wife Irene, sons Danny and Andy, daughters Lynn and Mitzi and their legion of grand

and great grandchildren. I have spoken to Irene and she thanks everybody for their kind condolences. They were together for the little matter of 63 years, with just a slight hiccup along the way. It is a release for Jimmy and all of us who have been worried sick by his quality of life since his savage stroke in 2015. Only a battler like Jimmy could have held on this long. Naturally, only Jimmy could have chosen today of all days to depart, as his two favourite old clubs Tottenham and Chelsea prepare to square off at the new Lane. We have lost a great human being and The King of goalscorers. I have lost a dear mate of more than 64 years. He was a cracker. See you one day mate. Rest easy.'

GEOFFREY GREEN (the late *Times* journalist describing the manner of Jimmy's scoring), 'It was like someone closing the door of a Rolls-Royce.'

COLIN HART (journalist in *The Sun* and West Ham fan), 'I shall never forget the first time I set eyes on Jimmy. It was Easter Monday, 1957. I had just got home from Cyprus having finished my two years of National Service in the RAF. West Ham were away and my old man persuaded me to go with him to see the England v Ireland youth international at Leyton Orient's ground. We paid one penny for the programme and joined the couple of thousand on the Brisbane Road terraces as the teams lined up.

'Soon after kick-off, the England number eight with the brush crew-cut and baggy shorts received the ball on the edge of the Irish penalty area. In a flash, he dribbled past three green-shirted defenders and slotted the ball into the corner of the net. My old man and I looked at each other and he said, "Who the bloody hell is that?" I think he said bloody. A quick glance at the programme told us it was J. Greaves (Chelsea).

MARK IRWIN (journalist in *The Sun*), 'I was privileged to work with Jimmy at the very beginning of my journalistic career when I ghosted his column for *Shoot!* He was one of the funniest people I have ever met, with absolutely no trace of ego and a withering disdain for the stardom his career warranted. Our Thursday morning chats were the highlight of my week.'

LEDLEY KING (Spurs ambassador and ex-captain) tweeted, 'RIP Legend.'

PAUL JIGGINS (journalist at *The Sun* who passed in March 2022), 'Jimmy Greaves will go down in history as English football's greatest ever goalscorer. But for those born too late to see him play in the flesh, he will be remembered more for his work in another sort of box – the television that is ... Greavsie was a success on the small screen because he was unpretentious and genuine – and viewers in their armchairs across the nation loved him for it.'

BORIS JOHNSON (prime minister on the day Jimmy Greaves died), tweeted, 'He will be remembered as a goalscoring legend and one of the greats of English football.'

ROY KEANE (pundit and ex-Manchester United and Republic of Ireland player, in the *Daily Mail*), '*Saint and Greavsie* was a huge programme for me growing up.'

DENIS LAW (in his autobiography *The King*), 'Greaves was a different player compared to me and other forwards. He was the best pure striker, the best goalscorer, I have ever seen. When he had the ball in front of goal there was always absolute panic among the opposing defence. There weren't that many chances he fluffed. I was an old-fashioned inside-forward, doing work all over the pitch, which included scoring goals. Greaves, though, was an out-and-out poacher. I didn't want Greaves playing for the opposing team at any time, that's how good he was.'

DANIEL LEVY (Spurs chairman), 'Jimmy remains our club's highest ever goalscorer with 266 goals, helping the club to two FA Cups, two Charity Shields and a European Cup Winners' Cup in an illustrious career with us. Incredibly, his record of 366 top-flight goals in Europe – for Tottenham, Chelsea, AC Milan and West Ham United – was only surpassed recently by Cristiano Ronaldo, showing that his contribution to football over the years is only matched by the very best in the game. Not only did Jimmy lead the line in the great Tottenham teams of the 1960s, he was also one of the national team's greatest ever players. He still holds the record for the number of hat-tricks scored by an England player and is his country's fourth highest goalscorer of all time, with 44 goals in just 57 caps.'

GARY LINEKER (*Match of the Day* presenter and ex-Spurs and England player) tweeted, 'Quite possibly the greatest striker this country has ever produced. A truly magnificent footballer who was at home both in the box and on the box. A charismatic, knowledgeable, witty and warm man. A giant of the sport.'

GARY MABBUTT (ex-Spurs player, in the *Daily Telegraph*), 'Goalscoring is the hardest thing in football. He made it look easy.'

JOHN McGOVERN (twice European Cup-winning captain for Nottingham Forest under Brian Clough), 'I remember [with Derby] beating Spurs 5-0. It was some result. When the final whistle went I ran to the touchline. There was typically six inches of mud at the Baseball Ground. And I shook hands with Jimmy Greaves. He was my idol. I kept a scrapbook of him and Denis Law. I was still keeping them. My hands were covered in mud. I sat in the bath with my right arm up so I never got the mud wiped off my hands.

When I got home my mum clouted me behind the ear and said, "Get that washed.""

KEVIN MITCHELL (journalist in *The Guardian*), 'There are some heroes you illogically hope will never die, certainly in the imagination. Muhammad Ali was one. George Best another (despite his best efforts) and Jimmy Greaves too. Even Tottenham fans who never saw him play in the flesh so treasured his deeds it seemed he belonged solely to them.'

JOSÉ MOURINHO (ex-Spurs manager), 'A true legend.'

JOHN MOYNIHAN (the late journalist, summing up the way Jimmy scored), 'Devastating nonchalance.'

ALAN MULLERY (Spurs team-mate, on Sky Sports), 'He was a wonderful, wonderful footballer, the best goalscorer to ever play.'

JEFF POWELL (journalist in the *Daily Mail*), 'The man was a precision instrument with heart of a gold.'

DAVID PLEAT (ex-Spurs manager, in the *Daily Mail*), 'Personally, I recall the excitement of playing for Exeter against the great Tottenham in the League Cup at White Hart Lane in 1968. We had the temerity to take the lead at 2-1. Maybe we were congratulating ourselves, but Jimmy had other ideas. Before long he had scored a magnificent hat-trick.'

THE PREMIER LEAGUE, 'Jimmy Greaves, not just Tottenham's record goalscorer but the finest marksman this country has ever seen.'

BARNEY RONAY (journalist for *The Guardian*), 'The former England manager Terry Venables described playing against a

15-year-old Greaves for the first time with Dagenham Boys. Venables was so captivated he followed Greaves home secretly on the bus, "just staring at him, in the hope of getting some clues about how to become that good".

WAYNE ROONEY (England record goalscorer), tweeted, 'One of the greatest.'

MARTIN SAMUEL (journalist in the *Daily Mail*), 'At the 1994 World Cup when Diego Maradona failed a drugs test and was banned in disgrace, the easy commentary was the rotten cheat, Hand of God, pile-on. Instead Jimmy [as a broadcaster] filed a counter-intuitively sympathetic piece focusing on the fearful kickings Maradona received at the peak of his career, and how injury set him on a path where addictive painkilling drugs, and other medication, became part of his life. It was brave, it was true and, today, the rest of the world has caught up. Jimmy's insights into some of football's most tragic heroes – George Best, Brian Clough, Paul Gascoigne – was always clear-eyed and perceptive. He was so much more than the class clown.'

ALAN SHEARER (pundit and ex-Newcastle United and England striker) tweeted, 'Legend. Goals, Goals, Goals. A remarkable goalscorer.'

GRAEME SOUNESS (ex-Spurs, Liverpool and Scotland player, in the *Daily Mail*), 'If you are judging a striker on goalscoring he is the best ever. I played with [Ian] Rush and [Robbie] Fowler, they were great players. But he was even above them.'

GARETH SOUTHGATE (England manager), 'Jimmy Greaves was someone who was admired by all who love football, regardless of club allegiances. I was privileged to be able to meet Jimmy's family

... at Tottenham Hotspur as the club marked his 80th birthday. Jimmy certainly deserves inclusion in any list of England's best players, given his status as one of our greatest goalscorers and his part in our 1966 World Cup success. His place in our history will never be forgotten.'

CHRIS SUTTON (pundit and ex-Chelsea and England player) tweeted, 'Jimmy Greaves was a genius.'

TOTTENHAM HOTSPUR, 'Not just Tottenham Hotspur's record goalscorer but the finest marksman this country has ever seen. Football will not see his like again.'

WEST HAM UNITED, 'A great friend of Hammers legend Bobby Moore, Jimmy became a popular figure in his time at Upton Park – proof of how his standing in the game and likeable personality transcended the rivalry between the London clubs he played for.'

MIKE WALTERS (journalist in the *Daily Mirror* and *Daily Express*), 'Jimmy Greaves was England's crown jewel who was left standing at the gates of glory when football finally came home ... It will forever remain a stain on the game, and the archaic honours system that he was never knighted. Somewhere at home this correspondent is the portly sandwich filling in a photo with Greaves and Paul Gascoigne, two of English football's all-time greats, taken before their stand-up show at Bournemouth ten years ago. Gazza was a hoot but dear old Jimmy brought the house down. Dusting down his joke book, he revealed his TV work had dried up after a short-lived alliance with Sky. "They didn't let me go, I left them," he said. "It was f***ing freezing putting up those satellite dishes in winter."'

RICHARD WILLIAMS (journalist for *The Guardian*), 'The purest finisher England has ever produced, Greaves functioned with deadly economy.'

IAN WRIGHT (Ex-West Ham, Arsenal and England player) tweeted, 'The first footballer's name I ever heard from my teacher. "No Ian! Finish like Jimmy Greaves!" May he rest in peace.'

PART THREE:
THE PEOPLE

Treasuring Their Treasure

43

The fan club

Memories and thoughts

DON AMOTT, 'I own Mickleover FC. We play in the Northern Premier League. We have erected a board in honour of Jimmy. Look at our Facebook page, please.'

LEE BATRICK, 'I started supporting Spurs in 1967 when I watched the Spurs v Chelsea FA Cup Final. Although Jimmy never scored on the day, I was mesmerised by his skill and quick thinking. My affection for Jimmy grew when he had the strength of character to overcome his illness of being an alcoholic and went on to a legendary TV career. I was lucky enough to meet him at a book signing and although it was only a quick handshake and hello, for a youngster to meet his sporting hero was just fantastic. The memory still lives with me. Like Jimmy, my life, probably like all of us, has taken lots of twists and turns but he showed in his humour that he could always bounce back and keep smiling. Jimmy was my reason to begin my love affair with football but he also taught me much more.'

TONY BENHAM, 'It's coming up to the seventh anniversary of losing my old dad Peter who schooled with Jim at Southwood Lane School in Dagenham. Dad never stopped speaking of Jim his entire life. He was his hero. Me and Dad caught up with Jim when him and Saint were travelling with the *Saint and Greavsie* show at the Thameside Theatre, Grays. At the end of the show when Jim asked for questions, Dad popped his hand up. He hadn't seen Jim since school. And when Dad said who he was, Jim remembered like a shot. Outside in the foyer after, Dad got his book – which I now have and treasure – signed by Jim. They laughed and joked. I was very sad to see Jim go downhill. My old dad had MSA (multiple system atrophy) and it took him down painfully slow for four years.'

DAVE BOWEY, 'As a footballer he meant everything to me.'

GARY BROWNJOHN, 'My late father Roy said he was the best player he ever saw and that's good enough for me. This is for my father.'

NINIAN CASSIDY, 'I got a Spurs trial when Jimmy was still playing for the club. The great Graeme Souness and I attended an evening match against Chelsea. Tommy Doc was manager and Souness and Cassidy had arena passes (posh for sitting on a bench near the dugouts). As we were going to our bench, we had to walk passed the dressing rooms. I went first and Mr S. followed. As he got to the away team dressing room door he stopped and called me back and told me to listen to the final message from Tommy Doc to his players. Some colourful language was used, but his main point of view was to stop Greaves and do it any way you like but don't give a penalty away! Greaves was kicked to bits but managed to do his magic and score two beautiful goals. And the irony of it all was the Doc walking on to the pitch at full time and shaking Jimmy's hand.'

TOM CLARK, 'Thanks for the memories.'

JOHN COCKRAM, 'Having grown up watching Jim on *Saint and Greavsie*, I finally had the privilege of meeting not only a childhood hero but a football icon. He was genuinely the most down to earth, genuine and approachable legend I have met.'

KEVIN CROMWELL, 'Bill Nicholson had introduced Father Christmases at the local infant school, St Pauls in Park Lane. I remember fondly as different Spurs players came dressed up in white beards etc. When Jimmy's turn came, he started giggling and we all guessed it was Mr Greaves. Pat Jennings was the biggest giveaway as his big hands and deep Irish accent gave him away straight away. I just wish I had kept all the toys.'

GRAHAM CUMMING, 'I've supported Chelsea for years and love my stats. So I enjoy studying Jimmy Greaves's goal stats, when he was with the Blues especially.'

DR DARRELL DeSOUZA, 'When I first arrived in the UK from Kenya as a nine-year-old, London was a large, bewildering and strange place for me. Becoming completely obsessed with football was my way of finding my feet and settling into a new way of life. I also needed to choose my football club; 1967/68 and it was all Manchester United. I wanted to support a London team, so I could go and watch the games. Spurs were FA Cup holders. I didn't really have my London bearings, so, although living in west London, I saw the mercurial Jimmy Greaves play for Tottenham – and that was it. Wearing the famous cockerel on his shirt, his elegance, elan and sheer prowess in front of goal exuded class through and through – and it just clicked. Jimmy and Spurs played with that ease of style that meant I was going to be a Jimmy Greaves and therefore a Spurs fan for life. I had the pleasure of seeing Jimmy and Stevie Perryman at the Beck Theatre in Hayes. Jimmy was absolutely hilarious and I treasure the Spurs shirt he signed for me that day and which I wore for the one and only time at White Hart Lane in the 2021/22 season for the tribute game [vs Chelsea] on the day he passed. I did tell him when he signed my shirt that he was the reason I became a Spurs fan and he laughed and apologised!'

SEAN DONOVAN, 'My brother is always talking about Jimmy Greaves. I was too young to see him live but from what I've seen on video film you could tell how special he was as a goalscorer.'

BRIAN EDWARDS, 'First time I met Jim was when he moved back from Italy in 1961 and moved into Harold Hill, Romford. My family lived literally about 100 yards from him. He used to buy his paper/fags etc. in my mum's newsagent shop and she got me his autograph. I then got him to sign a photo at Harold Wood Hospital Fete later in that year, as I was doing country dancing there with my school, Mead Juniors. One of my abiding memories was his goal in the FA Cup Final vs Burnley after three minutes – I was 12 then and converted to a Jimmy Greaves and Tottenham fan there and then. About ten or 12 years went by and I grew up to be a pretty good goalscorer in local semi-pro football. I went to play for Brentwood Town FC. In the mid-1970s Jimmy got signed by Dave Emerick (Brentwood manager) and I had the unique honour of playing with him. He had converted into a midfield "schemer" by then.

'Only a year or so later when I lived in Cranham, I regularly bumped into him in the off-licence in Front Lane, Cranham, on a Saturday in the early evening after football. This I believe was when he was still drinking a lot, but it never showed. In the early part of the 2000s I was in my 50s, my footballing days long gone. Out of the blue I bumped into Jim again at The Warren, a nice golf course near Danbury, where myself and my work chums used to play, as did he with a few of his pals, and I saw him over there quite often in the years to come. The greatest natural goalscorer and one hell of a nice bloke.'

NICK EDWARDS, 'The supreme talent and legendary presence of Jimmy Greaves is so intricately interwoven with my early memories as a Spurs fan that separating him from my love of the club is akin to separating love of family from the house you grew up in. There was hardly any football on television in the early 1960s and my input from the beautiful game was minimal because the three wonderful women who nurtured me were not followers of the sport. Yet some inherent connection at soul level meant I always knew Spurs were my team and that Jimmy was my favourite player, even though I can't consciously recall ever having seen him kick a ball at that tender age.

'On 6 April 1968, I got to see Spurs in the flesh for the first time, having badgered my mum into taking me to White Hart Lane. The whole experience was unforgettable, of course, and seeing Jimmy score twice in a 6-1 win against Southampton was the icing on the cake. I saw him play a few more times over the next couple of seasons, including the rather sad memory of his last ever start for the club on a wintry night at Selhurst Park, as we were knocked out of the FA Cup by Crystal Palace in January 1970. As a south Londoner from Dulwich, I was especially gutted and found a suitable excuse not to go to school the next morning.

'Nonetheless, it still came as a shock when the news broke of his transfer to West Ham a month or so later, even if that move did herald a new era of success for Spurs with the arrival of Martin Peters. It's never easy to see such a hero depart stage right, though.'

TASHA ENNIS, 'I met Jimmy in a very strange yet funny way. It had been common knowledge that the legend himself had moved to our tiny village in Acton. Everyone of course wanted to meet him and others would say they spotted him in the local shop. Well, my experience was somewhat funny, it was a cold wet muddy morning in winter.

'Myself and my best friend Jo Clark were doing our daily power walk across our local aerodrome. A dog came bounding up to us both and started to jump up, covering us in mud. "Get down you stupid dog and go away," is what we were saying as we were getting more and more covered in muddy paws.

'Then far away in the distance I heard a man shouting to get the dog. As he got nearer, he looked scruffy in a dark green long coat and baseball cap. He was just a normal man walking his dog. No way are we getting your dog, we thought, but he continued shouting at us to grab his dog. I will give you what for as you get closer as your bloody dog has made us filthy, I thought.

'As he got nearer I looked at Jo and said, "It's Jimmy Greaves." Well he came and couldn't thank us enough for rescuing his dog Lester. "Sorry about the mud, girls," he said. And us both being so two-faced, said, "That's OK, no problem. We like dogs." From that day on we would meet Jimmy most mornings as he walked Lester, who was always up to mischief and I can't remember how many times we rescued him. I remember one morning seeing Jimmy with a cut and bloody nose; Lester had been up to his normal tricks and it turned out while trying to get him Jimmy had fallen over a fence!

'We were so fortunate to end up getting to know Jimmy. He was full of humour and chat and he ended up calling us Jimmy's Angels for the times we would rescue Lester.

'He was a real character. A kind and very caring man who did not once big himself up. He just wanted to be "Jimmy". He adored his wife Irene and his dog Lester.

'The day he moved back to Chelmsford way, we were there to wave him off. Our morning power walks were not the same without seeing him. He would often tell us about his charity comedy nights at golf clubs, his wife and children; oh, and, of course, the latest antics of Lester. We miss the legend and, of course, Lester the dog as if it wasn't for him we would never have met Jimmy.'

RODNEY FEWTREE, 'I have tears in my eyes just thinking about him. Jimmy, you will live forever for the thousands of us who appreciate a top footballer and goalscorer.'

MARK FRIEDLANDER, 'Jimmy Greaves provided magic moments every time I stood on the East Stand terrace at White Hart Lane.'

MARY AND TONY GIBBONS, 'We first got to meet Jimmy at his 65th birthday celebrations. Tony as a partner to a massive Spurs fan became my chauffeur and photographer on numerous occasions we saw him afterwards. Meeting Jimmy was a great pleasure for both of us, as he just radiated warmth with his honesty and humour. He never took himself seriously, was intelligent and articulate.'

COLIN GRAINGER, 'I was listening to Jimmy playing for England on the radio outside my nan's house in north Woolwich. It made me first a fan of his – and then secondly a Spurs fan. My mother Lily took me to my first game. Unbelievably it was the 1962 European Cup semi-final when we were robbed. I was lucky enough to meet Jimmy a few times over the years. His greatest goal for me? So many memorable ones, but the dribble against Leicester in 1968 stands out. Just magical.'

PAT GUSHLOW, 'For me, Jimmy Greaves will always be the player who sparked my interest in football. I read a newspaper report of a match between England and Wales (having never been the slightest bit interested in football before), Jimmy had scored, and the reporter spoke of him in glowing terms, and from that moment on I was hooked, and followed his career avidly. To me he will always be the greatest player ever. I'm not sure if I've told this one – Jim and Irene went to see the Beatles once in 1964, I think it was. John Lennon found out he was in the theatre and he made him stand up and take a bow.'

PAUL HADRILL, 'I remember Jimmy from the very start of his football life. Being a ballboy at the time, I met him so many times.

He always had time for us lads even in his last match at the Bridge before going to Italy. He found out we were told to protect him at full time with our corner flags. He popped his head in our dressing room and said, "Look after yourselves, boys. They are expecting a pitch invasion so I'll sort myself out." Anyway, when we were changing after he popped in to ask if we were OK. That's the man he was.'

ROY HALES, 'Nobody since has come close to being in the same class as this brilliant player.'

DAVE HARLEY, 'Jimmy Greaves was special even back in 1961 – I probably saw him at White Hart Lane back then with my uncle Mac. Too young to remember any specific details, though.'

PETER HARLEY, 'I was ten years old when I first saw Jimmy play at Plainmoor, Torquay, in the FA Cup in 1965. I was sitting on the grass next to the pitch with many other youngsters absolutely amazed at his skill. The game ended in an exciting 3-3 draw and Spurs easily won the replay. Although supporting Torquay United then, I immediately became a Spurs fan and now 57 years later I still am.'

TONY HARRIS, 'While waiting to get Jimmy Greaves's autobiography signed by the man himself, I realised it would be nice to have a photo with my hero. Upon trying to take the photo, the flash didn't work on the camera. The queue was quite long and I was being ushered off stage when Mr Greaves called me back saying, "It didn't work." He made sure this time it did! I think that says a lot about his down-to-earth character and humility.'

ELVIE HILL, 'I'd like to say how much Jimmy influenced my life. I was only 11 years old when I chose Jimmy as my favourite all-time footballing hero. Having three brothers, I became a lover of football and my chosen team became Spurs. This was because I loved the excitement of following Jimmy. Throughout my teenage years, I made my way to virtually every home game at White Hart Lane (living in Bromley it wasn't easy). Watching Jimmy was magic and you just knew when he got the ball he would dazzle every Spurs fan in the stadium. I carried on admiring him as a footballer and a TV broadcaster but mainly for the humble man he was. My greatest memory of Jimmy was meeting him at a book signing and having a little chat. My big regret was not having a selfie with him. He was the greatest ever in my eyes and always will be.'

JOHN HOLMES, 'I started attending matches at the Lane in 1965 as a 12-year-old with my brother, who is 13 months older. Although the team was packed with great players, to football-mad lads like the two of us, Greavsie was instantly our hero, and has remained so ever since. He never had any airs and graces, and was happy to chat with the fans and sign autographs. I remember one time outside the Bell and Hare pub after a match, he was signing for a group of us when his wife urged him to hurry up, as they needed to get home. His reply was, "Be with you in a moment love, when I've finished here." A world-class footballer and world-class bloke.'

BARRY HOOD, 'In Bradford it was raining. I said to my dad, "What this?" "The FA Cup Final, son." "Who will win?" "Burnley, son." "Who they playing?" "Tottenham Hotspur, son." I sat down and thought, "They sound posh." They walk out of the tunnel in their white and navy and in three minutes we were one up from my hero of all time, Jimmy Greaves.'

TIM HUBBARD, 'I met Jimmy in Florida, February 1993. I was on my honeymoon and my (now ex) wife was getting annoyed with me because she thought I wasn't listening to her, but I said I was distracted because I could hear a familiar voice, believing it to be Jimmy. It was! Him and his wife were in the booth behind us in a restaurant. Maybe they heard our conversation – something along the lines of me just not being able to forget about football for once – when he came over to say hello. Saying I was starstruck is an understatement. I have never forgotten how he went out of his way to be so friendly. He pulled my leg a bit about my team – Grimsby – but I can forgive him that. I was so privileged to meet not only a great footballer but a great man too. One in a million.'

PAUL HUGHES, 'My dad passed away not long before Jimmy. A lifelong Spurs fan and like a giddy 14-year-old when he met Jim. He always said he was England's finest.'

MATT KAVANAGH, 'I first saw Jimmy play at least 55 years ago. Hands on hips standing at the halfway line chatting to the guys marking him as if they were mates while Tottenham were defending for all their worth, then he received the ball and, with a burst of effortless speed, was clear on goal with all the time in the world to stroke the ball into the net so easily. He made the art of scoring so easy. He was my first hero, a real all-time great with the common touch who showed us all the highs and lows in life and never hid away from us. I still have a signed shirt framed in Tottenham blue. That will never be sold in my lifetime.'

LARAINE KEMPSTER, 'Even now, it doesn't seem right to speak about our Jim in the past tense. I have sent Irene a few cards, like I used to do to Jim, just to let her know that she is still being thought of and to send her kind wishes. I have lots of specific memories of Jim from the pitch. I was so incredibly privileged to be old enough to have seen him play, and his shows and bits in between. I gave him my silver, "my last Rolo", as a gift for his 70th at the O2. I was happy to remind Jim regularly by card on his birthday, at Christmas or just randomly, that he was in our thoughts and not forgotten, although he was very ill and out of the spotlight. I used to worry sometimes I was being a nuisance or the family thought I was some silly old fool but you could say, absolutely decades after retirement, it showed what an impact someone like him had on a person's life from an early age. You can see the warmth when people either write or talk about him. One of the lasting legacies was the fact that the "Jimmy G Knighthood" page was active.'

SYLVIA KETTRIDGE, 'We saw him when we had a few days at Butlin's. He was there entertaining us with his stories. I am not a football fan, but he was such a lovely person, talking about his life and treating everyone so nice and made it seem as if we were all having a chat in a pub.'

JOHN KING, 'I am now 72 and have followed Spurs nearly all my life. The reason I started following Tottenham was mainly because of one player, the great Jimmy Greaves. He was the player that lit up a game. A goalscorer extraordinaire. The player that got the crowd buzzing. He was the most talented player I have ever seen. There have been some great players over the years: Pelé, Maradona, George Best, and recently Messi and Ronaldo and of course Harry Kane. But no one in my mind can touch the mercurial wizard that was Jimmy Greaves. I had the pleasure of watching him and met him four times. The last time was in 2010 at Croydon Town Hall with Paul Gascoigne, a night I will never forget. He was also a brilliant commentator on the TV, especially in *Saint and Greavsie* which everyone used to love to watch as he was such a great talker and comedian and made everyone's weekend.'

CHRIS LEE, 'Jimmy Greaves touched my life watching him on the rare appearances on telly in the 1960s. I never saw him play live being a Rochdale fan as we never drew Chelsea, Spurs or West

Ham in the cup. His later appearances on TV never did justice to his greatness. His humbleness belies his greatness. In over 60 years of watching football I've never seen a better goalscorer. I hope that you might find a spot in the book to include this on behalf of the millions of lower-division fans who never got the opportunity to see the great man play live.'

JONATHAN LEWIS, 'ATV signed Jimmy (brave decision at the time) in 1978 and I loved his banter with Gary Newbon and Bob Hall.'

SHARON LOUISE, 'Above my children and grandchildren, Jimmy Greaves's autograph is the most precious thing I have.'

JOSEPH LYONS, 'I have had the pleasure to have watched live Pelé, Maradona, George Best, Denis Law, and many more. Jimmy Greaves was without doubt the greatest goalscorer Spurs or England have had. His records speak for themselves.'

MART MATTHEWS, 'Thoughts on Jimmy Greaves? Let's come at this from a different angle. Do I love Jimmy Greaves? You bet I do. Did he ruin two Christmas Days in a row for a young lad? Guilty as charged.

'For some reason best known to myself, I was an avid Pompey fan from the age of eight and on Christmas Day of 1957 the only present I wanted was a Portsmouth win at Stamford Bridge. Needless to say they got beat by the very rare score of 7-4 and I was forced to sit up and take notice of a teenage sensation called Jimmy Greaves, who had helped himself to four of those seven. So that was one Christmas Day ruined, although Pompey did balance things up by beating Chelsea 3-0 at Fratton Park on Boxing Day.

'My dad, as a Blackburn Rovers man from way back in the mists of time, made it his business to convert me to the blue-and-white-halved religion and after much soul-searching on my part, he succeeded. So when Christmas Day came around again in 1958, I was a fanatical Rover and looked forward to a home win over Chelsea to get into the festive mood. When the news came from Ewood, however, it was not good, with Chelsea winning 3-0 and that annoying man was on the scoresheet again.

'Almost a year later, on 7 November 1959, I was at Stamford Bridge to see Rovers play Chelsea again. I didn't actually see anything at all because London was enveloped in one of those Sherlock Holmes "pea soupers" it was renowned for then. In those days it strained your eyes to see much at Stamford Bridge anyway at the best of times. You were so far from the action without the fog adding to it. Nobody in the ground knew who had scored but they didn't stop the game for trivialities like that in those days. Rovers lost 3-0 and I was sure it would say 'Greaves 3' in the paper the next day but it didn't and for once he let me off lightly.

'I kept meticulous books on the fortunes of Blackburn Rovers with Sellotape and scissors to the fore but my mate, a Chelsea fan, was a bit less serious, and hitting puberty slightly earlier than yours truly, he found a picture of Jimmy Greaves from the paper that had an image of a girl in a bikini at the back of it. So he put the girl in his Chelsea book and wrote underneath, "On the other side of this picture is one of Jimmy Greaves." Sacrilege!

'Suddenly my football life was transformed as Rovers charged to the top of the league in late 1963 and I was there when they won 8-2 at Upton Park on Boxing Day morning. Come 11 January they faced Spurs at White Hart Lane, of blessed memory, and looked like going in at the interval ahead 1-0. I was standing behind the goal as half-time approached and saw the ball fed up to Jimmy just inside the box with his back to goal. I was relaxed because he was tightly marked when suddenly the net bulged just over my head. I was in shock! How could he do that? He had turned and hit it in one instinctive movement.

'In the second half, he grabbed two more and Spurs won 4-1. One of them was unforgettable; a bullet header with his body suspended in the air like a jackknife, which was in the paper next morning. Over 40 years later, I was at one of Jimmy's evening entertainments and stood up to tell him how much I admired him as a player, bringing up his hat-trick in that game all those years ago. When I got to his header he denied that it could have been him that was responsible for it, saying that he was absolutely useless with his head! He was just being modest because I've seen him score some great goals with his head for both Spurs and England.

'Allan Clarke, Robbie Fowler and a few others had some of the natural magic that Jimmy had in front of goal but he was the king of the goalscorers, that one against Manchester United at White Hart Lane being my favourite. Each time you see it you can't believe he can score but he does.

'It isn't only the fact that he was a lovely bloke as well as a great player, although that always helps. He was also a writer who provided an excellent critique of the modern game in his book *The Heart of the Game*.

'He came from a time when a platform was something you stood on to catch the train to an away game and it sure as hell wasn't digital! Happy days brought to life by men like Jimmy Greaves and Bobby Moore, with whom he did that wonderful little dance all those years ago at White Hart Lane that reflected perfectly everything about what was once a beautiful game.'

RUTH McCLUSKEY, 'Jimmy was my hero both as an incredible footballer and as someone willing to readily engage with his fans. It was a privilege to absolutely idolise such a decent, down-to-earth, yet extraordinary human being. I just loved him!'

MIKE McNAMARA, 'Greaves v the Rest of the World 23 October 1963. Many say that this game – albeit a "friendly" – was possibly the best game that Jimmy Greaves played for England. But, friendly or not, he was up against 11 players generally accepted to be among the best on the planet (with egos to match); and from the first moment that he received the ball from Terry Paine's throw-in and promptly ghosted between Schnellinger and Masopust, he seemed determined to force them to live up to their reputations.

'He proceeded to score a goal which – had it counted – would undoubtedly been regarded as one of the best of his career. Receiving a ball from Charlton in the centre circle he turned, leaving Di Stéfano – yes, Di Stéfano – on the floor and tore past Popluhár, riding the attempted trip, before playing a one-two with Bobby Smith, slipping between two defenders before rounding Šoškić (who had replaced Lev Yashin) and slipping the ball home from the acutest of angles. A goal for the ages, except that the referee had already blown for Popluhár's attempted foul.

'His lay-off for Terry Paine's goal and even his own, classically poached, winner after Šoškić had spilled Charlton's ferocious shot, seem scant compensation for the premature whistle that denied a wonderful addition to the list of his best goals.

'But, I suppose the abiding memory of that game will be of a precocious genius carving his way through the best players in the world and proving that he was one of them.'

WENDY MOSELEY, 'Such a lovely man. God bless, our Greavsie'

NICKI OLIVER, 'I met him at a book signing in Borders, Wood Green. He spent ages talking to me and my sister-in-law. Such a warm man.'

DERRICK ORMISTON, 'A true legend of our game, I met him in the Spurs shop when he was signing copies of his book *This One's On Me*. I was gobsmacked to be standing so close to this truly great footballer, a real genius. I managed to blurt out that I wish he was still playing for Spurs, and he said, "Oh so do I, boy, so do I." I walked away almost in tears.'

MARK PARTRIDGE, 'My dad told me all about Jimmy Greaves when I was a youngster and allowed me, as a five-year-old, to go to my first game, Walsall v Tottenham in the FA Cup third round. The only goal scored by Jimmy. Then later in life we're together on a Saturday watching *Saint and Greavsie*.'

GEORGE PAVLIDES, 'Sunday, 19 May 1968. I am pretty sure that nobody can rattle off the top of their head who Spurs played that day? Well, the answer is Anorthosis Famagusta, at the GSE stadium in Famagusta, Cyprus.

'Spurs came to Cyprus on a post-season tour in 1968. I was already excited from a few weeks earlier when I learnt they were coming over, and was hoping Dad would be able to take me and my brothers to one or two of the four scheduled games so we could see our beloved team, our family having moved to Cyprus from London a few years earlier.

'I was only really expecting Dad to take us to the two matches in Nicosia against APOEL and the Cyprus national side, so we were ecstatic on the Sunday morning when he told me, my two brothers and my cousin that he had a treat for us. After hastily grabbing our swimming gear, we piled into the Vauxhall Victor, DJ 797, and drove down to Famagusta to spend the day at the beach, and later on we would go and watch the match against Anorthosis in the afternoon.

'After we'd had an early lunch, Dad relaxed in the shade and us kids went for a stroll along the beach. Suddenly my eyes almost popped out of their sockets. Surely that wasn't Pat Jennings and Joe Kinnear on the beach smearing themselves with suntan lotion? It couldn't be! These guys were playing a match in a few hours. Yet there they were, larger than life. My heart racing, I told my brothers to keep an eye on them and dashed back to my dad as if my swimming trunks were on fire and asked him for a few coppers so I could buy a little notebook to get their autographs.

'Breathless, I ran back, and then walked up to Pat and Joe and asked them to sign my little notebook and they politely obliged, and they also apologised for getting some of the pages oily from the suntan lotion. Apologised?! That was sacred oil now, worth a million trillion a drop!

'Right! There had to be more of the lads. The hunt was on. Apart from Cyril Knowles and Alan Mullery who didn't come on the tour because they were away on England duty, all the rest of the team had come over. They just HAD to be here! We left no speck of sand unturned, wandering down the whole Famagusta beachfront and in and out of every cafe and restaurant there. And it paid off. One by one we were finding everybody. Jimmy Robertson, Tony Want, Phil Beal, Terry Venables, Dave Mackay, Mike England, Cliff Jones, Alan Gilzean. We were trying to take it all in.

'We were slowly making our way back to Dad, pleased as punch, but also very frustrated because there was one autograph we didn't get. We hadn't managed to see HIM. "God" was nowhere to be seen. Until suddenly my brother gave me a tug on my t-shirt and pointed excitedly up at one of the restaurants we'd passed on our way down. There he was! Feet up and enjoying his beloved pint! JIMMY! JIMMY GREAVES! The best centre-forward that ever lived or will ever live. I swear I could see the halo around him!

'I walked up the steps to the restaurant and asked him if he could sign my little notebook, and with a huge smile he obliged. You couldn't help getting the feeling that this was really a genuinely nice man in front of you. He had that aura. I asked him if he was playing in the afternoon and he said he was. "Do you think you'll score?" I said, immediately kicking myself for asking such a daft question! Did "God" himself think he was gonna score? Couldn't I have thought of anything else to say for heaven's sake? "Yeah," he smiled. "I'll score one for you." Jimmy Greaves was going to score one for me. Well, actually he didn't. He lied. He actually didn't score one – he scored two!

'Well, the day on the beach didn't have any ill effects on the team who strolled to a 5-0 win a few hours later. The perfect day. Those images of the lads on the beach will be embedded in my memory forever as long as I live.

'Three days later, it was another 7-1 stroll over AEL in Limassol, but it was a big ask for my dad to take us to Limassol midweek. But I did get to see the remaining two games against the Cyprus national side and APOEL, both 3-0 victories. Jimmy got injured in the match against AEL unfortunately and had to go back home, so we didn't see him in those last two games.

'But there was an added bonus. The Monday after the Anorthosis game was the day of our annual class excursion, and coincidentally it had already been planned that we would be going to Famagusta. As luck would have it, we bumped into most of the lads on the beach again, and even had a kick-about with some of the younger squad members, Peter Collins, Jimmy Pearce and John Pratt. And a stat regarding John Pratt – the match against the Cyprus national team was the first time he played for the first team.

'Sadly, the notebook with all the autographs got lost in the 1974 troubles in Cyprus. Out of all the things that we lost, that little notebook had, as anyone can imagine, untold sentimental value, especially Jimmy's autograph. When he came to Spurs, he was the reason I became more hooked on Spurs than I already was at the time, and all us kids aspired to be him.

'There have been many stars in football over the years, but Jimmy is out there on his own. The world of football was blessed by his presence, and at Spurs we were doubly blessed. He was a one-of-a-kind genius, coupled with being a great personality and human being. We will never see the likes of him again. Thank you for being who you were, Jimmy.'

NOBBY PENNYTOY, 'Jimmy Greaves signed his autobiography *Greavsie* for me back in 2003 at Waterston's in Nottingham.'

GEORGE PHILLIPS, 'In the summer of 1959, I'm nine years old. Like millions of other kids I'm on the street in London with my mates, kicking a ball around. We all are also avid roller skaters. For some reason, an older kid suggests that the "gang" should go on an adventure and skate to Chelsea's ground. Says he knows the way. Somehow we get there, and the big blue gates that seem 100ft tall are shut. But there is a gap under them just big enough for a few skinny kids to crawl under. Had to do it, didn't we? We find our way up the steps and there is the pitch. Green and lush (we are at the Shed end, by the way). Amazingly, there are some players running around the pitch. The older kid whispers, "That's Jimmy Greaves. He's the best player, he's so fast." I scarcely have an idea who Jimmy Greaves is at this moment in time, but I can see that he's fast.

'In August, I find out that a lot of the gang are going to see Chelsea play. I beg Mum to let me go and so on 22 August 1959 I attended my first professional match, and watched as Jimmy scored a hat-trick and I duly became a lifetime member of the Jimmy Greaves Worshippers Club. I have lived in Dallas, Texas, for 30 years. Jimmy Melia, who is godfather to my daughter, invited me over in 1993 to coach youth players. I once asked him about playing against Jimmy, what were his main thoughts on him as a player. He replied, "Greatest goalscorer, two good feet, could pass, and he was so fast." I thought back to that older kid all those years ago. He was right then, wasn't he?'

PAUL PHOENIX, 'I'm a Manchester City fan. I was a kid when I first discovered Jimmy Greaves. First time I saw him, I just knew I'd witnessed greatness, even as a nipper. Even with the great Colin Bell and others in the brilliant City team at the time, Jimmy Greaves was my first football hero. He will always be my favourite

English footballer. The hardest thing to do in football is score goals. Greavsie made it look ridiculously easy.'

WAYNE PORTER, 'A legend as a player. What a duo he formed with the Saint. Unbelievably funny.'

RICHARD PRIDEAUX, 'Alas, I was never fortunate enough to meet the great Jimmy Greaves. I have a fond memory of when I went to watch a match at Anfield where Spurs were playing Liverpool. We were in the paddock section of the ground and I was about knee high to a grasshopper. Kindly, all the burly Liverpool supporters surrounding us saw how small I was and formed a protective shield around us saying, "There you are, you should be able to see the game better now." However, they hadn't realised I was a Spurs supporter and despite several warnings from my dad to keep quiet and not give the game away I found the urge too much. Jimmy was taking the throw-in barely five yards away from me. Grabbing my dad's arm and jumping up and down I shouted, "Dad, Dad, look, look, there's Jimmy Greaves. Come on Jim, run rings round 'em." You could see the colour drain out of my dad's face when he heard this as scores of aforementioned fans turned round in unison and said, "Who's he supporting?" He needn't have worried because they thought it was hilarious and carried on shielding us. Well done, Liverpool fans.'

KEVIN ROGERS, 'I met Jimmy once, back in the 1970s. My mate Mark and I had gone to Wimbledon dogs, it was during Jimmy's, and my, drinking days. I was coming back with two pints in my hand and there he was. I managed to burble, "All right, Jimmy?" He replied, "All right, son." Desperate to lengthen the encounter, I asked if he had any tips. He said, "Trap four in the next." Then like a will-o'-the-wisp, a fox in the box he was gone.

'I told Mark that not only had I seen Jimmy Greaves but had spoken to him and he had given me a tip for the next race. He called me a liar, until I swore on the bones of Iggy Pop that it was true. We emptied our pockets into the hands of the grateful bookie.

'It was a long walk back to north London that night, but where is it written that a genius must be a good dog tipper? I offer this challenge to the young: ask Cristiano or Lionel who they fancy in the 8.47. I dare you.'

IAN ROWLAND, 'I heard once he got back in the changing room after playing a blinder and told the kit man not to bother washing his kit, just save it for next week as it was unmarked. Nobody could get near him.'

BOB SELF, 'I was a Tottenham fan from a very young age as my grandad from Brightlingsea, Essex was a season ticket holder and travelled to Northumberland Park via Colchester and Liverpool Street (quite a trek) for every home game and used to tell me about every match. Hence my footballing loyalties were with Spurs very early. I was lucky enough to go with him for my first live match on 30 January 1965 when we played Ipswich in the FA Cup and, after a 5-0 win, three from Jimmy and a brace from Gilly, I was totally hooked. All five goals scored by the famous G-Men. I went to quite a few games after this in my younger years but, as soon as I left school, got a job and had my own money, well that was it, every home game, most away games, trips to Europe. This was my life. I saw Jimmy score some of the most amazing goals. I have still not seen a finer goalscorer than Our Jim. He was prolific and a legend for our great club. Still is the greatest player I've ever seen.'

ADE SHAW, 'Jimmy Greaves was and is my favourite ever Spurs player. Blessed with outrageous skills and with acceleration over the first five metres and a coolness in front of goal rarely seen. He could pass the ball into the net, hit wonderful volleys and bicycle kicks, not to mention slaloming his way through a packed penalty area before dummying the opposition keeper. The way the crowd would react as he picked up the ball and headed towards the opponents' goal was something I've never experienced with any other player. He was simply the best and like another wonderful striker we currently have, "one of our own".'

SONNY SHULA, 'I live in Milan and have watched the video of his first goal for Milan. His team chose him to take the penalty. The goalkeeper moved full stretch to his right but just couldn't reach Jimmy's effort. Jimmy's coolness and accuracy were the keys to his goals.'

HOWARD SILVERSTONE, 'I was eight when my dad said he would take me to my first game. He was an Arsenal fan, but knew how much I idolised Jimmy, so he got tickets for us to see Spurs v Burnley. It was 1968. I still remember the excitement of walking up the steps to our seat. And then, when the players ran out, I was out of control. Spurs won 5-0 and Jimmy scored twice. Seeing how much I enjoyed it, my dad took me to a bunch more games before Jimmy left for West Ham. I have lived in America since 1985, but still have every programme from every game I went to. I cried when I heard Jimmy died. I cried when I watched the Spurs legends on the pitch to honour Jimmy at the first game after he died. I'm an Arsenal fan, just like my dad was, but I have fond memories of my youth at White Hart Lane and being able to say I saw Jimmy Greaves play. I have a signed photo of Jimmy hanging proudly in my office. I feel so lucky.'

ROB SPROSTON, 'I travelled the country as an agent with Jim doing the after-dinners on his own and with his great mate the Saint, two great characters. Loved them to bits.'

TONY STERN, 'Jimmy has always been my footballing hero and I was lucky enough to meet him many years ago at a Bobby Smith testimonial, I think at Enfield FC. The referee was the father of my best mate at school. We were in his changing room at half-time when the door opened and in walked Jimmy to say, "It's f**king freezing out there ref, don't make half-time too long." Jimmy then realised that I was sitting behind the door when it was opened and he put his arm around me and said sorry for his language. I managed to get Jimmy's autograph after the game on literally everything I had with me.'

PAUL THORNE, 'Jeannie Dunsby and myself wrote to the prime minister, The Queen and the FA bigwigs to get "Sir" Jim the recognition of a knighthood. Alas, we did not succeed but it got things going and, being a member of the Jimmy Greaves [online] group, I'm proud to have tried. He was my idol. I've been a Leeds United fan for 59 years but Jimmy was my hero. An icon. The supreme king of kings as a goalscorer. I based my own game on Sir Jim. I was an old-fashioned centre-forward in the 1970s and watching him made me improve my goals ratio. I admired him from afar and wished he played for Leeds. We would have swept the board by a mile with Jim leading the line. An absolute genius. He'll never be forgotten.'

CHRISTINE TOBIN, 'All my family loved Jimmy Greaves.'

IAN VICKERS, 'In October 1968, I was sat with my dad in the Paxton Road End and can remember so well Jimmy dancing around six Leicester City defenders before rolling the ball past a young Peter Shilton.'

JOHN VINCENT, 'He was very kind to 17 boys at our children's home in Messing, Essex, in 1964 when he opened our new games room. He spent the whole day with us. Happy days for me.'

JOHN WAKELING, 'I saw Jim and Bobby Moore do an entwined jig in the West Ham penalty area many years ago.'

HARRY WALTON, 'I first saw Jimmy Greaves when I was working as a ten-year-old copy boy on an evening newspaper. Part of my Saturday job was to take all the news and sports stories as they arrived in the wire room and distribute them to be dealt with by the correct sub-editors. I also did the same with news and sports photographs from all over the world, watching them slowly appear from the machines. One such photo was of Jimmy Greaves surging forward for Tottenham that afternoon flanked by Alan Gilzean and other players. The photograph was captioned, "The Charge of the Spurs Brigade". I have been a lifelong Spurs fan and I have never forgotten that striking photograph of Jimmy Greaves in action.'

GLEN WARD, 'In class of his own and darned funny.'

ALAN WARR, 'Jimmy is a hero and a legend to Swindon Town fans. He stood up for the fans of my hometown club after we were harshly treated and demoted for financial irregularities.'

MARK WATSON, 'I got a call one Saturday morning back in the mid-1970s from a mate asking me to play for his works football team at Polygram in Chadwell Heath. They were short of a couple of players. I had done this before and they always shoved me up front and I would end up having the odd ruck with the opposition keeper. This game was on a pitch in Upminster. It was a cold, windy day and raining. I was finally being played in what I considered to be my best position, left-back. During the game a bloke was stood watching with his dog. He started advising me on my positioning and told me the right time to push up when the other side was on the attack to catch them offside. This happened a couple of times. He also told me to drop off and move back. Every time it was the correct decision and every time I gave him the thumbs up. One attack, he told me to move up and then changed his mind and told me to drop, then to move up again! I shouted "make your f**king

338

mind up" and we both started laughing. I then realised it, Jimmy Greaves, my greatest football hero ever. So I can say that I was once coached by the greatest ever English goalscorer of all time.'

COLIN WATTERS, 'My dad, Frank, was born in Mullingar in the Irish Midlands in 1939 and spent his early 20s working in north London. While he did play soccer for Hendon and Enfield, he didn't follow any one team in particular, but had a soft spot for Sheffield United, as some of his relatives played for them. That all changed when, while out on a night out with a few mates, he spotted Jimmy Greaves, Dave Mackay and Danny Blanchflower. He only recognised Jimmy and told his mates that he was going to buy him a pint. He walked up to him, said hello and asked Jimmy if he could buy him a pint. Jimmy looked at him and said, "No." Dad didn't know where to look or what to do. As Dad walked away from the lads, tail firmly between his legs, Jimmy called out, "Wouldn't it be a better story, if I bought you a pint?" And so Dad and his two friends sat down for pints with three of the greatest players to ever wear the Lilywhite jersey and, by God, he hasn't shut up about it since. He's now 82 and that moment set off a chain reaction that has seen nearly every member of our family follow Spurs ever since. I'm currently chairman of the Mullingar Spurs Supporters' Group with over 100 supporters in the area and travel over to a few games a season, usually with 15 or 20 in tow and all because Jimmy Greaves bought my dad a pint.'

MARC WHITMORE, 'A striker who brought joy to anyone who ever saw him play.'
STUART WILLOUGHBY, 'Jimmy's shows were great. I went to one in Croydon. His stories were hilarious.'

GARY WRIGHT, 'When Jimmy turned out for Spurs reserves against Arsenal there were over 20,000 fans there to watch.'

MICK WRIGHT, 'I remember a free kick against Liverpool. Jimmy passed the ball into the bottom corner. Liverpool claimed they were not ready. Ian St John went mad and chased the ref. Great memories of the great man.'

Appendices

Appendix 1: Poem

'Jimmy Greaves'
By Kevin Rogers

I have stopped all Auden's clocks.
He is dead!
I explained that the morning rain was;
The tears of a million old men
mourning his passing and their distant youth.

I have often heard it said,
our universe is no more than
A gargantuan insane Steely Dan forever ejaculating nothingness
into an endless void.
This is not my faith.
The Lord is a master choreographer,
Celestial Helpman.
Could brute chance orchestrate such a devout farewell?
Spurs v Chelsea
On the sacred Sabbath day.
All tickets sold; before the Earth was younger than yesterday.

I shall send a vial of my fresh tears.
Petition that it is sprinkled in Elysian penalty box.
Park Lane End.
His kingdom eternal.

* Written on Sunday, 19 September 2022, the day Jimmy Greaves passed away.

Appendix 2: Extras

* Jimmy Greaves would have been saddened by the passing of jockey Lester Piggott aged 86 on Sunday, 29 May 2022. Jimmy wrote about his admiration for another individual who was a great national favourite in humorous terms in the *Saint and Greavsie's Funny Old Games* book, 'One of my great heroes was Lester, who always had a huge following in England when he rode at Longchamp. His army of fans, who had come out on charter flights, celebrated heavily when he won the Prix de l'Arc de Triomphe on Alleged in 1977. One of his followers was poured on the flight for the homeward journey, and he was halfway across the Channel when he became sober enough to remember that he had driven out to Paris.'

* He also wrote in the book of his ownership of racehorses, 'I have owned various bits and pieces of syndicate racehorses over the years, a hoof, a fetlock, a nostril but never an entire horse. But I was never mug enough to put too much money on them.'

* Greaves had a quip for George Best in the same publication. The *Belfast Telegraph* reported on the day of Jimmy's passing how he had 'told broadcaster Jackie Fullerton he had never seen a better player than George Best when discussing who was the greatest footballer of all-time'. Jimmy, who shared a theatre stage with Best, joked in the book, 'George Best, the greatest British footballer of all time, once went through an entire game, in which, to win a bet, he played the ball only with his left foot.'

* Jimmy loved his cricket, writing in the *Funny Old Games* book, 'I wanted to be Godfrey Evans [legendary Kent and England wicketkeeper] when I was a kid. That was in the day when you could play cricket and football, and there were great all-rounders like Denis Compton, Willie Watson and Arthur Milton.'

* On golf, he wrote in it, 'One of my most memorable moments was when I played a round with Seve Ballesteros in Spain.'

* Writing about rugby in the tome, he said, 'I have not seen anything in any sport to match the drama and excitement of Jonny Wilkinson's last-minute drop goal that clinched the World Cup for England in 2003. The sight of a good three-quarter movement, with dummies, acceleration, side-stepping and slick passing, can be as exciting as anything you see in sport.'

* Peter Cook picked up on the Dagenham connection Jimmy shared with the Spurs-supporting satirist, writer and comedian's usual comedy partner Dudley Moore when they teamed up as 'Pete and Jim' to replace 'Pete and Dud' for a day.

    They were filming a light-hearted prelude to a serious documentary by producer Berny Stringle called *Just For Today*, featuring Greaves and George Best, which was screened on ATV in February 1980. The alcoholism theme of it was discussed, but Cook, tongue in cheek, picked up on an insignificant sidebar issue: Greaves's association with Dagenham. He said, 'I know you were born in Dagenham or came from Dagenham. I know this because Dudley is a Dagenham lad and that's a problem in itself, coming from Dagenham.'

* There was also a Jimmy one-liner in an article by Norman Giller posted on the Sports Journalists' Association website on 7 May 2015. Giller quoted Greaves saying, 'It's a fact that I went to Oxford and I got a blue. And if some prat had not jogged my elbow, I would have got the pink and black as well.'

Appendix 3: Statistics

Goals
- League total: 357 in 516 in the English top flight (1957 to 1970)
- Chelsea: 124 (1957 to 1961)
- AC Milan: 9 (1961)
- Tottenham Hotspur: 220 (1961 to 1970)
- West Ham United: 13 (1970/71)
- FA Cup total: 35
- League Cup total: 7
- European competition: 13
- England total: 44 in 57
- Total overall: 465
- England under-23s total: 13 in 12
- Inter-League: 6
- Charity Shield: 2 (for Spurs)
- England v Young England: 2
- England v Football League: 1
- Rest of Europe XI: 2
- Leading English top-flight scorer for a record six seasons: Chelsea 32 (1958/59) and 41 (1960/61); Spurs 37 (1962/63), 35 (1963/64), 29 (1964/65), 27 (1968/69)
- Goals-to-league-games ratio: 0.69
- Leading club scorer: 12 times in 14 campaigns
- Total tally of senior goals: 491
- Scored most of his league goals against Nottingham Forest: 24
- Scored on all his senior debuts: Chelsea at Spurs on 23 August 1957; England under-23s at home to Bulgaria on 25 September 1957; England at Peru on 17 May 1959; AC Milan at home to Botafogo on 7 June 1961; Spurs at home to Blackpool on 16 December 1961; West Ham at Manchester City on 21 March 1970
- Aged 21, youngest player to score 100 league goals in English football
- Aged 23, youngest player with Dixie Dean to score 200 league goals
- Scored 25 English league hat-tricks
- Scored a record six hat-tricks for England

* Based on figures compiled in *Greavsie: The Autobiography* (Time Warner, 2003)

Appendix 4: The Last Word

'I have been a professional footballer, a TV presenter and a newspaper columnist. I was once a hopeless alcoholic but no longer drink. I was a successful businessman, then an unsuccessful businessman. I am a devoted and loving family man. I have travelled the world. I've been places and seen things. You have read my story and you will have formed an opinion about me. But I'm just "some sort of man".'

Jimmy Greaves in *Greavsie: The Autobiography*

Acknowledgements

FIRST, I feel I have to thank Terry Baker, Jimmy Greaves's friend and agent, for coming up with the idea for this book and asking me to write it, while also supplying the foreword and being a willing interviewee for his chapter. It has been the biggest privilege and most enjoyable experience of my professional life.

Jimmy has, since the moment I clapped eyes on him while standing on the East Stand terrace in front of the Shelf at White Hart Lane with my dad and mates, been my football hero. I was in wonderland during the project's process as it brought me in touch with his wonderful family who supplied me with fundamental and moving thoughts and memories of their patriarch. So thank you Irene, Lynn, Mitzi, Danny, Andy, Marion and Des. Jimmy's oldest friend Dave Emerick and close pal Brian Doherty were other prime sources who also helped me get closer to the very essence of the man who was a national treasure.

There were those from his public life who enriched the story by giving me their time, so thank you (in alphabetical order) Matt Barlow, Phil Beal, Barry Davies, Terry Dyson, Mike England, John Fennelly (who also helped in supplying contacts), Jeff Foulser, Barry Fry (with invaluable assistance from Phil Adlam and Joe Dent at Peterborough United), Ron Harris, Glenn Hoddle, Sir Geoff Hurst, Pat Jennings, Cliff Jones, Dave Kidd, Gary Newbon, Nick Owen, Steve Perryman, Harry Redknapp, Jimmy Robertson, Jim Rosenthal and Richard Worth. I am grateful to Spurs for their assistance in getting the Harry Kane chapter together (special thanks to Jon

Rayner), and Chelsea for the information on Frank Blunstone and John Sillett. Ditto to The Athletic regarding the chapter *I Rossoneri*. Bobby Moore's autobiography and Jeff Powell's biography on the England World Cup-winning captain were invaluable sources for the chapter on Jimmy's 'best pal'. TalkSPORT Radio's interview with the late Ian St John and Bill Nicholson's autobiography were equally useful. Also, thanks to the Ford Motor Company publicity folk who promoted Jimmy's participation in the 1970 World Cup Rally and the *Tottenham Hotspur Opus* for helping me put the chapter on the late Tony Fall together. Thank you to Spurs chairman Daniel Levy for his tribute. And many of Jimmy's other friends, colleagues and aficionados, from Norman Giller to Gareth Southgate and everyone else who lauded Our Jim's public life.

I appreciate Jimmy's fans for their heartfelt comments and memories. I also doff my beanie to mentor Kevin Brennan and the Pitch Publishing team of Paul, Jane, Graham, Duncan, Gareth, Dean, Andrea, Alex and co. Also, thanks to Christine, Sean, Kate, Keith, Darren, Kelly, Daniel, Charlie, Sandra, Mark, Tony, Dave, Sue, Tilly, Kev, Pauline, Marc, Nick, Jan, Debbie, Jon, Sadie, Mac, Caroline, Tim, Gail, Glen, Lynn, Jean, Chris, Mark B., Christine, Ade, Maur, Aaron, Ron, Tony U., Sue, Peggy, Dave H., Marc, Louise, Jill, Paul R., Mick, Marg, Clive, Andrea, Joan, Graham C., Pen, Dave M., Imaani, Paul S., Eliza, Paul H., Sally, Tim, Lucy, Terry, Linda, Nigel, Kerrie, Rosemary, Matthew, Benny, Loughton five-a-siders, the rest of the Bexhill Mob, the Beatles, Sandy Denny, the Bevis Frond and anyone else who has helped me directly and indirectly complete the job and inadvertently not been listed.

Image credits

The Greaves Family Collection, Terry Baker, Des Benning, Dave Emerick, Paul Doherty, Barry Davies, Jeff Foulser, Jim Rosenthal, Richard Worth, Tottenham Hotspur FC, The Sun, Associated News, Joe Dent and Peterborough United, Nobby Pennytoy, Mike Donovan, Alamy, Getty and Colorsport. (By the way, thank you Robert Rathbone for your superb picture of Greaves' Spurs teammate Dave Mackay and family in the authorised 2021 publication Football's Braveheart).

Bibliography

Books

A Funny Thing Happened On My Way To Spurs: My Autobiography (Jimmy Greaves as told to Clive Taylor; Nicholas Kaye, 1962)

Alan Mullery: The Autobiography (Alan Mullery with Tony Norman; Headline, 2006)

Bobby Moore: My Soccer Story (Bobby Moore; Stanley Paul, 1967)

Bobby Moore: The Life and Times of a Sporting Hero (Jeff Powell; Robson Books, 2002)

Cliff Jones: It's a Wonderful Life: My Story (Cliff Jones with Ivan Ponting; Vision Sports, 2016)

Dave Mackay: Football's Braveheart: The Authorised Biography (Mike Donovan; Pitch Publishing, 2021)

Geoff Hurst: 1966 And All That: My Autobiography (Geoff Hurst with Michael Hart; Mainstream, 1997)

Glory Glory: My Life With Spurs (Bill Nicholson; Macmillan, 1983)

Glory, Glory Lane: The Extraordinary History of Tottenham Hotspur's Famous Home for 118 Years (Mike Donovan; Pitch Publishing, 2017)

Greavsie: The Autobiography (Jimmy Greaves with Les Scott; Time Warner, 2003)

My World of Soccer (Jimmy Greaves; Stanley Paul, 1966)

Nereo Rocco: La Leggenda del paron (Gigi Garanzini; Baldini & Castoldi, 1999)

Nereo Rocco: La Leggenda del paron continua (Gigi Garanzini; Mondador, 2012)

Non dire Gatto (Giovanni Trapattoni; Rizzoli, 2015)

Pat Jennings: An Autobiography (Pat Jennings with Reg Drury; Panther, 1984)

Saint and Greavsie's Funny Old Games (Jimmy Greaves, Ian St John and Norman Giller; Little Brown Book Group, 2008)

Spurs' Greatest Games (Mike Donovan; Pitch Publishing, 2012)

Spurs' Unsung Hero of the Glory, Glory Years: My Autobiography (Terry Dyson with Mike Donovan; Pitch Publishing, 2015)

The Heart of the Game (Jimmy Greaves; Time Warner, 2005)

The King of White Hart Lane: The Authorised Biography of Alan Gilzean (Mike Donovan; Pitch Publishing, 2018)

The King: My Autobiography (Denis Law with Bob Harris; Bantam, 2004)

The Real Mackay: The Dave Mackay Story (Dave Mackay with Martin Knight; Mainstream, 2004)

The Tottenham Hotspur Opus (Tottenham Hotspur FC, 2007)

This One's On Me (Jimmy Greaves and Norman Giller; Coronet, 1980)

Tottenham Hotspur Player by Player (Ivan Ponting; Guinness, 1993)

Tottenham Hotspur The Complete Record (Bob Goodwin; Derby Books, 2011)

Newspapers and magazines

The Sun
Sunday People
Daily Mirror
The Scotsman
Daily Telegraph
The Guardian
The Independent
Daily Mail
Daily Star
The Times
Backpass

Media

Chelsea
AC Milan
Tottenham Hotspur
West Ham United
The FA

The PFA
Sports Journalists'
Sunset and Vine TV production
ATV/Central TV
TV-am
LWT
ITV
talkSPORT Radio
YouTube
BBC
Wikipedia
11v11.com
Social media, including Facebook and Twitter
Various recommended websites
Podcasts including the *Spurs Show* (hosted by Mike Leigh and
Phil Cornwell) and Steve Perryman